Women, Mothers, Subjects

New Explorations of The Maternal

Edited by

Maura Sheehy

Routledge
Taylor & Francis Group
LONDON AND NEW YORK

First published 2014
by Routledge
2 Park Square, Milton Park, Abingdon, Oxon, OX14 4RN, UK

and by Routledge
711 Third Avenue, New York, NY 10017, USA

Routledge is an imprint of the Taylor & Francis Group, an informa business

British Library Cataloguing in Publication Data
A catalogue record for this book is available from the British Library

ISBN13: 978-0-415-63483-0

Typeset in Garamond
by Taylor & Francis Books

Publisher's Note
The publisher accepts responsibility for any inconsistencies that may have arisen during the conversion of this book from journal articles to book chapters, namely the possible inclusion of journal terminology.

Contents

Citation Information

The following chapters were originally published in *Studies in Gender and Sexuality*, various volumes and issues. When citing this material, please use the original page numbering for each article, as follows:

Chapter 2
Giving Body to Thought: Entwinements Between Women
Velleda C. Ceccoli
Studies in Gender and Sexuality, volume 1, issue 3 (2000) pp. 325-336

Chapter 3
Mothers, Monsters, Mentors
Adrienne Harris
Studies in Gender and Sexuality, volume 3, issue 3 (2002) pp. 281-295

Chapter 4
Lost in a Fog, or "How Difficult Is This MOMMY Stuff, Anyway?"
Maura Sheehy
Studies in Gender and Sexuality, volume 12 (2011) pp. 4-7

Chapter 5
Oi Mother, Keep Ye' Hair On! Impossible Transformations of Maternal Subjectivity
Lisa Baraitser
Studies in Gender and Sexuality, volume 7, issue 3 (2006) pp. 217-238

Chapter 6
What Exactly Is *the Transformation of Motherhood? Commentary on Lisa Baraitser's Paper*
Daphne de Marneffe
Studies in Gender and Sexuality, volume 7, issue 3 (2006) pp. 239-248

Chapter 7
Reply to Commentaries
Lisa Baraitser
Studies in Gender and Sexuality, volume 7, issue 3 (2006) pp. 249-257

Chapter 8
Mum's the Word: Intersubjectivity, Alterity, and the Maternal Subject
Lisa Baraitser
Studies in Gender and Sexuality, volume 9 (2008) pp. 86-110

Chapter 9
Maternal Silence
Miri Rozmarin
Studies in Gender and Sexuality, volume 13 (2012) pp. 4-14

Chapter 10
I'm in the Milk and the Milk Is in Me: Writing from the Night Kitchen
Donna Bassin
Studies in Gender and Sexuality, volume 3, issue 3 (2002) pp. 297-308

Chapter 11
Mother-Writing and the Narrative of Maternal Subjectivity
Suzanne Juhasz
Studies in Gender and Sexuality, volume 4, issue 4 (2003) pp. 395-425

Chapter 12
"It Ain't Fittin'": Cinematic and Fantasmatic Contours of Mammy in Gone with the Wind *and Beyond*
Maria St. John
Studies in Gender and Sexuality, volume 2, issue 2 (2001) pp. 129-162

Chapter 13
What About the Baby? The New Cult of Domesticity and Media Images of Pregnancy
Katie Gentile
Studies in Gender and Sexuality, volume 12 (2011) pp. 38-58

Chapter 14
What About the Episiotomy? A Response to Katie Gentile's Article, "What About the Baby?"
Lynne Zeavin
Studies in Gender and Sexuality, volume 12 (2011) pp. 59-64

Chapter 15
Social Trauma and Models of Ideological Analysis: Commentary on Article by Katie Gentile
Lynne Layton
Studies in Gender and Sexuality, volume 12 (2011) pp. 65-71

Chapter 16
Reply to Commentaries: "What About the Baby? The New Cult of Domesticity and Media Images of Pregnancy"
Katie Gentile
Studies in Gender and Sexuality, volume 12 (2011) pp. 72-77

Please direct any queries you may have about the citations to
clsuk.permissions@cengage.com

Introduction: Writing of Mothers

By Maura Sheehy

This volume, a collection of essays published in the journal *Studies in Gender and Sexuality* over the last 13 years, is a plunge into the many registers of the expanding new field of study known as The Maternal—intrapsychic, theoretical, clinical, philosophical, intersubjective, social and political—in which ideas about motherhood, maternal subjectivity, and women's lives percolate and work upon us. Here, emerging as if from having contrast dye applied to the everyday, we find an expanse of unexamined, unconscious beliefs about mothers and mothering, maternal experience and subjectivity that have only just begun to be heard from and about. Foundational discourses such as patriarchal constructions of "natural" womanhood catch us all up in a moebius loop of feminine aggrandizement and devaluation that makes us question the possibility that a woman can be a thinking, desiring, enunciating mother-as-subject and a "good" mother, focused enough on nurturing, sacrificing enough to allow her child or children's subjectivity to flourish. And then, just as this new territory might be explored or these voices heard, so often the maternal experience is then doubly obscured and dismissed as part of the nondescript and untextured plain of householdery—just laundry, meal-making, mess-cleaning and child-rearing here folks, nothing to see.

Despite the many gains of feminism, this binary maternal subjectivity versus good motherhood has endured, and has resulted in a terrible poverty of language and concept with which to speak or theorize about real lived experiences of motherhood. Thanks now to the work of artists, analysts, academics, writers, mothers and others who are reformulating and exploring territories of the maternal, we are moving beyond projects geared towards gleaning new trinkets of wisdom to enhance our knowledge of babies, child-rearing, or how to be a better, more development-nurturing mother, and beyond projects that reinforce the binary. We are finding new conceptions of The Maternal that embrace the multiplicities and motion, the erotics and play, the intersubjective interplays and unfoldings of self that are at work, and gaining a deeper understanding of the forces that prevent their being known.

These essays open up a meta-view on The Maternal and reveal how many antiquated and limited conceptions of the maternal are cooked into the frameworks of our thinking about women, children, human development, subject/object relations, and constructions of race and gender that we all carry within us. They open up a fascinating roadmap to the kinds of unpacking that needs to be done—from theoretical investigations into maternal subjectivity and its relation to intersubjective phenomena, to peeling back newly complex layers of maternal transferences in the consulting room and beyond, to critiques of popular culture and media, where discourses of the maternal are framed and reified and then internalized by all of us. As the omnipresence of maternal discourses is revealed, we see clearly the limitations of the language and theory we have for it and how much work is to be done.

Power, of course, figures into how we talk to ourselves in our culture about women who become mothers—I speak of "women who become mothers" to remind us that discourses of women and mothers and the misogyny that structures them are never unentwined. The roots of our ideas about the maternal slink always back to discourse and ideology as much as they do to experience, memory, loss, longing and desire, and so always back again to power. The way that a woman who becomes a mother's subjectivity is imagined, described, threatened, threatening, experienced, denied, maintained, performed, or embodied, is riven with the accepted constructions of women, gender, sexuality, and self and other that we all "know to be true" but have not tended to question. When we talk about how women talk to themselves, and how the world talks to them about themselves, we must think about the enormous, never-ending interest in regulating women that is saturated into our global culture and its economies. This work, then, is a feminist project.

So, here, for example, is a question: "What happens to a woman when she becomes a mother?" Asked by Lisa Baraitser in her essay 'Mum's the Word: Intersubjectivity, Alterity, and the Maternal Subject,' the question's simplicity, even its apparent obviousness, belies the fact that no answer is to be found for it in anywhere in the psychoanalytic canon—nor even any sustained engagement with it. Yes, Winnicott (1949) cracked open the door into the maternal psyche, allowing room for maternal hate and ambivalence (in just the right amount, of course), and then infant research, attachment theory, and theories of intersubjectivity kicked the door wider with ideas about mutual regulation, mentalization, and recognition (Beebe and Lachmann, 2005; Fonagy, 2001; Stern, 1998; Benjamin, 1988, 1998). But the main intended beneficiary of the expanded territory was the child and her developmental and emotional needs, to which the explorers promptly returned. Second-wave feminism tried to take the door to female subjectivity off its patriarchal hinges altogether, but ultimately the goal wasn't to liberate *mothers* as much as to liberate women from motherhood. The thrust was a move to decouple the relation of woman/mother as a given, rather than to enunciate maternal subjectivity. It has taken another 30 years to be able to think of The Maternal as a potent subject of study, and of maternal subjectivity as anything but an oxymoron.

Questions like these have simply not been asked until now: How does a woman understand her experience of herself as a mother *and* how it relates, or doesn't, to her other, more ongoing, experiences of herself? How does she bring these various subject positions into relationship? How does the ongoing bump-up against the infant/child influence or even structure her subjectivity? And – hold on – what even goes on between a mother and her kids *for her*? And what is the toll on a mother of her sudden insertion into the Discourse of the Maternal—all the eons of sedimented thoughts about, and expectations of, what a mother is and should be? What is the effect of all of this on her continued development?

Mostly, the psychological concepts we have that relate to the specifically maternal amount to a "description of mothering," says Baraitser. If they even address the *woman's* experience at all. [One might say the same for fathers—and should—but here we will take up the Maternal.] Essentially what are on offer are more endless iterations of "what makes a good mommy or a bad mommy?" As Suzanne Juhasz says in 'Mother-Writing and the Narrative of Maternal Subjectivity,' "Representation of maternal subjectivity is of great importance, for not only has it been culturally denied in Western history, but even now, despite frequent references to its existence, there is no fully-developed theory of maternal subjectivity in psychoanalytic discourse."

Infant research and attachment theory have atomized the maternal–infant relationship into ever more micro moments of communication across the terra incognita of self/other space, trying to illuminate the path to optimal child development (Beebe and Lachmann, 2005; Fonagy and Target, 1997). Therapists—metaphorical mothers—hungrily extrapolate the gleanings to the consulting room, (Kraemer, 1996). Indeed, the relationship between mother and child has been a primordial loam, technically and theoretically, for psychoanalysis. Yet all this without an accompanying body of study about the woman's—mother's—experience of it? It's odd to consider.

Why wouldn't we psychoanalysts want to understand—plunder, even—this affective and psychic landscape, for all the interpersonal, intersubjective, intrapsychic work that gets done here, for the insights into the terrains of pleasure, desire, power, paradox, terror, ambivalence, liminality, hybridity? Why wouldn't philosophy want to access the themes and variations on selfhood and subjectivity that play out in a woman's experience of motherhood? Amidst fear and confusion, loss and gain, formlessness and structure, embodiment of the most visceral and emotional sort, women have a profound experience that begins inside their very bodies and challenges the concept of the unitary self to the core, all whilst they inhabit a culture which regulates maternal thinking from every quarter—religious, political, physical, emotional, and cultural. Why is all this left on the table? How could this rich text not be taken up and read more closely?

As the writers in this volume ponder these questions they are drawn again and again back to the reality of the never-fully-answered questions about the framing of female identity and subjectivity itself, and the forces that work against its easy emergence. Waves and decades of feminists have worked to break up gender fixities (Dimen, 2003; Harris, 2008) so that women could enunciate a place of selfhood apart from their construction as the messy, abjected other to the Unitary Male Subject posited by Western patriarchy. And now, argues Baraitser in 'Oi Mother, Keep Ye' Hair On!: Impossible Transformations of Maternal Subjectivity,' much of the otherness once assigned to the feminine—the affective, physical, relational, and care-related, the chaotic, and irrational—is sloughed off onto the Maternal. The trip from woman to mother is often portrayed as a "transformation" from a now supposedly clean, crisp, organized, unitary pre-maternal (a double of the male subject she was once the "other" to) while the maternal is depicted as a place of formlessness, anxiety and disequilibrium similar to the Kristeva (1982) abject.

The maternal is constructed and reified as that symbolic place where boundaries between self and other, subject and object, break down into the horror of our originary submersion in the womb's boundarylessness, amidst the fluids and meconium and blood and vernix. Rarely (the work of Bracha Ettinger, 2006, is a notable exception) have the many possibilities for play and fluidities of time and space and identity within maternal subjectivity been explored or exploited.

The maternal was doubly marked as the regressive when, as a movement, generally, second-wave feminism was framed as a daughter's struggle, and relationships to the maternal were fraught by the task of having to break with past constructions of the feminine ideal and lived realities of women's lives. In this context, the coming into adult womanhood was often framed as a break from one's mother, philosophically as well as emotionally and psychologically, and symbolically as a break from the messy otherness of the feminine. As art historian Andrea Liss (2009) has written, "the mother, however, remained a silent outcast for many feminists who strategically needed to distance themselves from all that was culturally coded as passive, weak, and irrational."

The essays here present some of the most extensive work to date to reformulate concepts of the maternal. Possibly the most powerful pivot that needed to be made is the shift from viewing and theorizing the maternal from the point-of-view of the daughter and of the child to that of the mother. (Baraitser, 2009; Parker, 2005; Kraemer, 1996; Liss, 2009; De Marneffe, 2004) The shift to recognition and exploration of maternal subjectivity has opened up a view into the maternal experience and how maternal desire exerts both destabilizing and structuring forces upon identity and functioning. We find new templates for complex new experiences of selfhood and relationship that play with temporality and our understanding of self/other relations, and we find in all these a route out of the stifling, musty, still air that permeates so many of the prevalent notions about motherhood in our culture.

So there is the question of what maternal subjectivity *is* and how it forms, and many of the writers here have a crack at it and debate it—something we need much more of. They address the challenges that come with claiming maternal subjectivity—the *how* a woman synthesizes her different subject positions and her different (and often conflictual) desires and roles and the stereotypes that abound about her. Not to mention how she reconciles her own experience with that of her mother, grandmothers, aunts, and previous generations of women all of whom surely had very different options and experiences, and hugely different language (if any at all) with which to frame and share them.

Miri Rozmarin, in her paper 'Maternal Silence', for instance, traces back to De Beauvoir (1989) the notion that for a woman to claim a real, rather than illusory, subjectivity, she must very carefully divide and police her mother self and her non-mother self, lest the mother part engulf the whole. Our very culture buys into and reinforces this notion, trivializing it into cat fights and "mommy wars" and debates about working versus stay-at-home motherhood, refusing to think about the possibility of the subject positions of a woman who is a mother as existing in a more inter-subjective or complexly interwoven relationship, rather than in a death match for supremacy. The political culture in the US participates by denying practical supports such as universal day care or extended family leave rights or affordable health care, all of which could help women and families achieve a smoother day-to-day integration of work achievement and parenting.

But at base there is, perhaps, Comparative Literature Professor Susan Suleiman's (1985) classic formulation that, according to psychoanalytic theory, "Mothers don't write, they are written." Our culture has written and written the mother. She is the studied, the represented, the eternal object who gives birth to a subject and is then returned again to objecthood. Written in the declarative mood: a mother this, a mother that, a mother must or should, does or doesn't, is or isn't, feels, thinks, wants. With a bit of Foucault's Panopticon (1995) thrown in: everyone is watching her, evaluating, judging. The writing of mothers again underlines Kristeva's (1977, 1982) argument (also De Beauvoir's) that, once the baby is born, mother is rendered abject and voiceless and ceases to have a presence. Subjectivity passes over her to the offspring. So many of the writers in this volume speak of silences, the unspoken, and the untheorized, and of the power of words—written or unwritten—to help orient women, whether mothers or not, in the work of claiming subjectivity. For Bassin and Juhasz in different ways the written word and the writing process help structure maternal identity and subjectivity from disparate bits. For Rozmarin there is a need for words to describe the quality of a silence that can be generative and witnessing.

In 'Mothers, Monsters, Mentors', an exploration of women's creative difficulties and their relationship to mothers, mentors, and envy, Adrienne Harris finds a shame-soaked misogyny strangling women's creative voices. "A misogyny that is internal, external, relational, social and intrapsychic, real and imaginary," and which leads to "the gloomy difficulties women have with self-love, self-esteem, and the cache of disgust and shame that adheres to many women's experience of femininity." I think this same misogyny and shame adhere to many women's experiences of and discourses around the maternal. I have often encountered my own shame when trying to integrate my maternal and professional lives, and the shaming attitudes of others in response to work around maternal subjectivity and women's struggles to claim it, and I find maternal shame endlessly experienced by my patients. "My mother did it, why can't I?" is an oft-heard retort by mothers in my practice when I take their misery or struggle to orient themselves amidst their many parts and feelings seriously. As they collude with the culture's maternal ideal (reinforced endlessly by the psychological field) that "a good mother" is a happy, busy, unconflicted mother, they split off great hunks of their own feelings, for fear they will harm their child's mental health with their "selfishness".

Harris, Ceccoli and Bassin frame women's wrestle to find and claim subjectivity—in relation to mothers, men, and culture—largely as a daughter's struggle, but Ceccoli elaborates on the crucial role to be played by a mother freed from shame around her own sexuality and subjectivity, and able to engage with her daughter in a developmental dance of ambivalence around separation and merger, identification and repudiation, agency and desire. Freud, Ceccoli laments, "occluded the role of maternal desire and its influence in the shaping of female sexuality," and she echoes and builds upon work by Benjamin (1988, 1998), Kristeva (1977) and Parker (2005), in trying to address this issue. In clinical work with female patients, Ceccoli finds an "unspoken and unsymbolized [feminine and feminine sexuality] that reverberates through generations of mothers and daughters," and "speaks symptomatically through the body" until she and her patients can find language for the many complex feelings and exchanges that must ensue between mother and daughter around about their bodies, hate, envy, desire, and everything else in the process of healthy development. Ceccoli, in her role as the symbolic mother, shows clearly the challenges involved in staying present with the shifting affects and forces in the room with her and her patients as she tries to stay aware of and hold onto her own subjectivity and desire while engaging with her patients' complex and challenging identifications and disidentifications with her as they both work towards "finding those silenced words". For Ceccoli argues that the words and language must be found—the maternal claiming of subjectivity alone is not enough.

The road to claiming subjectivity requires aggression, of course. But Harris tells us "Women too rarely make clear distinctions between agency and destructiveness, excitement and damage to others, competition and a feeling of or wish to murder." And who could blame a woman who becomes a mother for such confusion when, for instance, psychoanalyst Helene Deutsch (1945), defined "the masochistic-feminine willingness to sacrifice" as the secret to good motherhood. This belief has formed a cornerstone to the core beliefs about mothers and motherhood that we all share. That, as Deutsch puts it, "all the aggression and sexual sensuality in the woman's personality are suppressed and diverted by this central emotional expression of motherliness." So when a woman has a baby it is assumed she no longer has ambition or agency or murderous energies, but of course she does, but we fear they'll harm the baby somehow, either because a mother will put her energies/wants/desires first and leave the baby, quit the roles, or never have the baby in the first place. Or she'll be an awful mother. Somehow. And here we are, talking of her in the third person and she's boxed right in. Despite Sara Ruddick's (1989) great efforts to reframe the concept of maternal work as an ethic of care with activist social value and goals—women who were mothers were engaged in a crucial and activist engagement with the formation of psyches and societies—the conflation of the maternal ethic of care for others and the masochistic self-sacrifice of "natural" womanhood endured. Somehow the idea that a woman who is a mother could care for others, sacrifice, *and* pursue and achieve full expression of self and subjectivity has never quite taken hold.

These essays, by opening the window, and doors, to maternal subjectivity, let in new, fresh air—the maternal perspective—and the thinking begins to shift. We begin to see a new framework for conceptualizing the relationship between mothering and subjectivity and between ethics and care and sacrifice. There is not loss of self, but finding, a finding that is a connecting with, reconnecting with, and a recognition of, self, other, self-by-other, self-in-other, and all the vice versas. The endless binary—it's you or me, kid—is undone, as the claiming of subjectivity is interwoven with maternal desire that does not have to divide choices cleanly between mother's subjectivity and child's needs. There is desire that can be mutually satisfying, mutually reinforcing, or perhaps there's simply room enough for both in a woman's life. One *can* desire, love, and sacrifice, work, be sexual, think, etc, *and* manage the ruptures and repairs, internal and intersubjective, that ensue. Which is not to elide the significant challenges (Kraemer, 1996) inherent in this complexity, but to suggest they be explored more fully. Not a message one hears often in our culture.

Roland Barthes (1975) once wrote that a writer is "someone who plays with the body of his mother" a perfect encapsulation of the de-subjectification of mothers—we are born and then *we* become the subjects—which Suleiman (1985) beautifully resignified with the question, "what if the writer is a mother?" This is the impulse driving the exciting new approaches to the maternal in this volume. At last, perhaps, postcolonial studies comes to the maternal? The mother—the voice from the periphery, the abject, or perhaps the silenced center, speaks? *As* a mother? Our archaic maternal thinking bears a striking resemblance to Edward Said's (1979) concept of Orientalism - the system of thought and writing that constructs the East as an Other who in turn supports our desired construction of the West as an unquestioned given. Regarded through the lens of orientalist theory, the maternal turns out to be raced too. As Maria St. John argues here in '"It Ain't Fittin": Cinematic and Fantasmatic Contours of Mammy in *Gone with the Wind* and Beyond', the Mammy figure serves the cultural construction of whiteness. Obscuring our envy and fear of otherness, the image of the all-nurturing Black mammy allows whiteness to operate as a given, indeed, to "escape the perils of representation altogether..." With maternality thus rendered "an invisible, impregnable, naturalized source of power...we stave off our envy by repeatedly exposing this fantasied mammy to the public gaze; we force her to absorb the hateful impulses of the dominant cultural psyche and to respond with a smile and a pancake."

And thanks to the essays by Katie Gentile, Lynne Zeavin, and Lynne Layton, the supermarket aisle magazine rack will never be a place of boredom—or light reading—again. In their masterful deconstructions of mass media depictions of mothers and pregnancy they show how The Maternal is employed on multiple levels. To manipulate our fears of vulnerability, loss, and post-9/11 anxieties about the possibility of a future, to construct and reinforce ideologies of progress, modernity, and time itself. Through changes in the ways pregnancy, the female body, and gender roles are depicted in the lives of celebrities and supermodels, not only women but all of us receive a constant stream of images and words about how to think about mothers, and these ways of thinking then make their way into our lives and affect how we think about ourselves and the world in which we are embedded. The Fredric Jameson-esque (1991) cognitive mapping these essays provide is an invaluable guide to how our unconscious desires, needs, and fears make it into the social via the unexpected route of Maternal discourse and through the pages of magazines and the regulation of women's bodies to serve political and historical ends.

One wonders about how the new drive to represent and theorize maternal subjectivity might have an impact on the issues raised by Harris, St. John, Ceccoli, Gentile, and the others mentioned above. As mothers become subjects, new dimensions and textures of the relating process between mother and child are illuminated. Thanks to the back-breaking, discourse-busting, path-clearing work of previous waves of feminist thinkers, a re-engagement with the maternal has been ignited by a post-second-wave feminist generation that feels able to, and eager to, push for a further integration of their maternal experience into their subjectivity and demand more visibility for their maternal selves. Rather than motherhood exerting destabilizing effects on women's lives, or needing to be feared or abjected, hidden or triumphed over, we can see here maternal desire working to open up these unanswered questions about who we are and how we work as women. So perhaps the question becomes, again, anew: what does it mean to be a woman? But this time without the maternal split off, hidden, or ignored in the process.

The import of this volume is not just for the philosopher practitioner, then. These inquiries have profound implications for women in the trenches of motherhood. We see how our understanding of the needs of infants and children proliferates by the minute, and fairly instantly slides from the lab and clinic down the cultural esophagus into parenting magazines and consulting rooms, for use in the real-time lives of women and parents. However, the tools for deconstructing the maternal experience that a mother has to make sense of or respond to *her* daily life and feelings is like a museum of artifacts—bits of stereotype and patriarchal good/bad prohibition disguised as wisdom and mixed with myth and guilt—with no curator on duty to contextualize them.

The essays in this book comprise a working manual that should have been written long ago. As it unfolds, new formulations of the maternal can help mothers navigate these million mes, not-mes, others, mothers, culture, and shame that press in from without, well up from within, and talk to mothers about their every move and thought while denying them a route or a language with which to situate themselves within this vast and unrepresentable totality.

But what might this *look* like in real life terms? It's always fascinating to me that theoretical work and maternal work can be so unaware of each other. Recently I was browsing artworks for sale on the online shop Etsy, and I was drawn to the vivid colors and shapes of a painting by Ashley Adair, titled "Laundry Line No. 10". I scrolled down to read the artist's statement, and found a woman's voice.

> Now that I have a little one, art making has changed. I'm trying to sink into this season and make art from the place of motherhood rather than fighting with it for time and space to create. Baby Kentucky is only 9 mo. old and I'm still in the midst of figuring out what this means. I've started working on several projects simultaneously, doing a little bit on each every day. I'm thinking about getting comfortable in my skin as a woman, a mother, and a wife. I'm pondering the way domestic chores, child care, career, art-making, cultural perceptions, and gender roles shape my dailyness.

Here is a maternal subject enacting the creation of maternal subjectivity by bringing the parts of herself together into a "grammar", as Juhasz terms it, that finds in the interconnectedness of her parts not breakdown, but structure. This is not regression, not a ceding of the territory of subjectivity, not a renouncing of the need for a Room of One's Own. The assumption is that her maternal experience is an ongoing act of creativity: Her subjectivity *is* her project, not just a theoretical construct or something that someone else can say she's got or not got. There is a faith, not a fear, that sounds most clearly here. A faith that her embeddedness in the constantly negotiated experience of loss and gain can contain both her *and* her child, somehow, despite the challenges that will ensue, with neither being cancelled out.

There is an embrace of tension here that reminds me of Juhasz's concept of maternal desire as "a tonal register" that is "an aggregate of wanting to have and wanting to be". There is a notable absence of fear that echoes Donna Bassin's examination of her anxious writing process, in her essay, "I'm in the Milk and the Milk is in Me: Writing from the Night Kitchen". Bassin finds a complex imagined relationship with her mother that touches on a similar fear-into-desire to "move from the comfort of the already known—the already theorized—to the exciting anguish of the unfamiliar." There is a fear-into-desire that bridges the gulf between the parts of a woman's subjectivity that are so often depicted as unbridgeable—where there is pleasure in the process though the process is neither easy nor ever really complete. We can hear an echo of Rozmarin's attempt to create "an alchemy of sorts" that "would enable a way to integrate or even synthesize the movement from Otherness to subjectivity into some productive holism."

The words here are important: "alchemy of sorts", "some productive holism", "thinking" and "pondering" and "figuring out." This is *process*. The relationship of the maternal to time itself has shifted, from the jerky lurch between parts of the self and conflicting desires that the word "multiplicity" tried to elevate and honor, but always seemed inadequate to me, though I couldn't quite place why. Process and unfinishedness, exploring and unfolding, are also d ifferent from the fixedness of former constructions of "transformation" into mother, that seemed to leave so much behind or to retrospectively recast the former self into something far more cleanly-constructed than it was. Time here is unfolding, momentary and ongoing. There are shifting affects and textures and ways of being with self and other that don't squash or foreclose agency but become a new kind of agency. And don't foreclose separateness, either, because here relatedness is not synonymous with continuous togetherness or formlessness or becoming lost in the other. As De Marneffe (2004) writes, she "experiences her desire to relate to her child as her own desire".

Perhaps it was important for this artist mother to write this description of her project as a part of the construction of her maternal subjectivity. "Writing from a maternal perspective," says Juhasz, "can form connections between subject positions, including those which have been split off or denied because of culturally induced ambivalence, to establish a subjectivity that is multiple rather than split...." And beyond, mother-writing, she says, "can be understood as a gesture toward recognition....for the mother/writer". Surely, differences in class, race, and circumstances of dailyness (double-shifts of hourly wage work versus being an artist) exert many different nuances of pressure on a woman who becomes a mother, just as perhaps they often don't, which is why we desperately need more research, more voices and more words for what is happening, or we won't know how the lines of connection and difference and cross-pollination can be drawn.

As a mother, I've wanted to find a way to make sense of the co-existence of so many disparate and contradictory-seeming parts of my experience, from the pleasure of *being* the mother of the family, bent over the timeless task, to the fear of (and/or pleasure in) being drowned or sucked dry from demands and giving (giving milk, giving time, giving over) and so much more in an endless complexity that I've rarely read or heard described. I've felt a need for concepts to validate and explain to me the feelings I've had, the desires I've had, so that I could more comfortably settle in to them and know myself as a mother. In the absence of a more robust and articulated vision of forms of maternal experience, doubt and shame can creep in, and one is more susceptible to discourse. New ideas, new language, new forms, like those explored in these essays, can disperse into the air and shift discourse as we breathe the new thoughts into our minds and muscles.

So that we may form a new Habitus, French philosopher Pierre Bordieu's (1977) term for "the way society becomes deposited in persons in the form of lasting dispositions, or trained capacities and structured propensities to think, feel and act in determinant ways, which then guide them". I—we—can only frame our own experiences in the terms we are given and the myriad distorted and impoverished binaries "mother" or "woman" are what underlie in part the intense anxieties that often surface in motherhood. As the critic Carolyn Heilbrun (1988) wrote, "What matters is that lives do not serve as models; only stories do that. And it is a hard thing to make up stories to live by. We can only retell and live by the stories we have read or heard. We live our lives through texts. They may be read, or chanted, or experienced electronically, or come to us, like the murmurings of our mothers, telling us what conventions demand. Whatever their form or medium, these stories have formed us all; they are what we must use to make new fictions, new narratives."

As the thinking in these essays disperses, on hopes that the stories we tell about maternal dynamics can offer a broader and more elastic view that includes tension, conflict, ambivalence, and ambition, but in which time and relationship are not keyed so much to the transformative or fear of foreclosure but can also embrace generativity and connectivity, interpenetratedness, and the unfolding and undulating contours of inextricableness that exist alongside possibilities for separateness and difference and for the changing meanings of motherhood to a woman (or any caretaker's life) as that life unfolds. We can hope that with this fuller grammar will one day be available "off-the-shelf" to those who become mothers rather than needing to be invented and constructed DIY anew by each woman alone.

Virginia Woolf, in *A Room of One's Own*, (1929) declared that the story of women needed to be written and that to do so would require new language and form. Writing it would "light a torch in that vast chamber where nobody has yet been. It is all half lights and profound shadows like those serpentine caves where one goes with a candle peering up and down, not knowing where one is stepping."

In this volume, Rozmarin calls for a "cultural and theoretical space in which maternal subjectivity can be thought in its unique relations with the Other". I hope this volume begins to construct such a space. It is a labor that continues the work of feminism: to dig a way under, around, and through discourse and ideology and interpellation, to create new paradigms and languages, and new arrangements of power and perspective, that make room for women's experience and desire to exist and *to be represented in language* in the fullest way possible.

REFERENCES

Baraitser, L. (2009). *Maternal Encounters: An Ethic of Interruption*. New York: Routledge.

Barthes, R. (1975). *The Pleasure of the Text*. Translated by Richard Miller. New York: Hill and Wang.

Bordieu, P. (1977). *Outline of a Theory of Practice*. Cambridge: Cambridge University Press.

Beebe, B. and Lachmann, F. (2005). *Infant Research and Adult Treatment: Co-constructing Interactions*. Hillsdale, NJ: Analytic Press.

Benjamin, J. (1988). *The Bonds of Love: Psychoanalysis, feminism, and the problem of domination*. New York: Pantheon.

Benjamin, J. (1998). *Shadow of the Other: Intersubjectivity and Gender in Psychoanalysis*. New York: Routledge.

Ettinger, B. (2006). *The Matrixial Borderspace*. Minneapolis, MN: University of Minnesota Press.

De Beauvoir, S. (1989). *The Second Sex*. Transl. and Ed. H. M. Parshley. New York: Vintage Books.

De Marneffe, D. (2004). *Maternal Desire: On children, love and the inner life*. New York: Little Brown.

Deutsch, H. (1945). *The Psychology of Women: A Psychoanalytic Interpretation, Vol. 2: Motherhood*. New York: Grune & Stratton.

Dimen, M. (2003). *Sexuality, Intimacy, Power*. New York: Routledge.

Fonagy, P. (2001). *Attachment Theory and Psychoanalysis*. New York: Other Press.

Fonagy, P., and Target, M. (1997). Attachment and reflective function: Their role in self-organization. *Development and Psychopathology*, 9, 679–700.

Foucault, M. (1995). *Discipline and Punish: The Birth of the Prison*. New York: Vintage Books.

Harris, A. (2008). *Gender as Soft Assembly*. New York: Routledge.

Heilbrun, C. (1988). *Writing A Woman's Life*. New York: Norton.

Jameson, F. (1991). *Postmodernism, or the Cultural Logic of Late Capitalism*. Post-Contemporary Interventions. Durham, NC: Duke University Press.

Kraemer, S. B. (1996). Betwixt the dark and the daylight of maternal subjectivity: Meditations on the threshold. *Psychoanalytic Dialogue*, 6: 765-791.

Kristeva, J. (1982). *Powers of Horror: An Essay on Abjection*. Transl. Leon S. Roudiez. New York: Columbia University Press.

Kristeva, J. (1977). Stabat Mater. Translated from French by León S. Roudiez. *In:* Moi, T., ed. *The Kristeva Reader*. Oxford: Basil Blackwell, 1986, 160–86.

Liss, A. (2009). *Feminist Art and The Maternal*. Minneapolis, MN: University of Minnesota Press.

Parker, R. (2005). *Torn in Two: The experience of maternal ambivalence.* London: Virago Press.

Ruddick, S. (1989). *Maternal Thinking: Towards a Politics of Peace.* Boston: Beacon Press.

Said, E. (1979). *Orientalism*. New York: Vintage.

Stern, Daniel N. (1998). *The Motherhood Constellation*. London:

Suleiman, S. R. (1985). Writing and Motherhood. *In:* Davey, M., ed. *Mother Reader: Essential Writings on Motherhood.* New York: Seven Stories Press, 113–137.

Winnicott, D.W. (1949). Hate in the Counter-Transference. *International Journal of Psycho-Analysis*, 30: 69–74.

Woolf, V. (1929). *A Room of One's Own*. Harcourt Brace Jovanovich, Inc.

Part I: Mothers in the Consulting Room

Giving Body to Thought

Entwinements Between Women

Velleda C. Ceccoli, Ph.D.

This essay explores the entanglements concerning sexuality and femininity that take place in the treatment relationship between female analysts and female patients. Focusing on the female analyst's contribution by way of her embodied gender and its symbolic functions, it advocates that women seek something specific to their sexual identities from other women and that, as women analysts, we can provide a gendered container for our patients' concrete and symbolic identity needs. This idea is developed within the context of post-Lacanian views of femininity and sexuality.

"I think she needs to work with a woman," a colleague tells me of a referral she is making. "She needs a woman who can work with her anger." And then there is Eve, who tells me that, now that she is out of hospital and able to choose her analyst, there is no question that she wants a woman. When I inquire into this choice she, like my colleague, has trouble explaining why.

I have begun to explore the issue of the analyst's gender as an important variable that can facilitate the expression of certain aspects of the patient's experience of masculinity and femininity (Ceccoli,

1999). Analytic listening is filtered through gender; the differences between men and women reveal themselves at the level of listening (see, e.g., Amigorena, 1996).

This essay addresses the contribution of women analysts to the analyses of women, particularly as regards the construction, elaboration, and integration of female desire and sexuality. It argues that women's subjectivity is influenced by the multigenerational legacy of the maternal function (Parker, 1995), as well as by the individuality of each particular woman who mothers. I elaborate the view that the psychic representation of sexual difference, and the maturational unfolding of physical femininity has particular developmental consequences for sexual subjectivity and desire. Moreover, both sexuality and aggression are experienced in gender specific ways. Women analysts can offer women a pathway to becoming desiring subjects through their active containment and processing of aggression, envy, hate, and love. Although a maternal transference can develop regardless of the gender of the analyst, women analysts can offer other women a gendered container for these affects and their meaning.

> *". . . and one does not stir without the other"*
>
> *Luce Irigaray*

THE SPECTER OF THE MOTHER

Whereas Freud made feminine sexuality out of male libido, he occluded the role of maternal desire and its influence in the shaping of female sexuality. Olivier (1989) notes that a baby's sex is never a matter of indifference with respect to the desire of the adult responsible for its care. Our first erotic teacher is our mother. It is her touch, her smell, her voice, and her physical management of us that introduces us to our bodies. Her desire forever casts a shadow on our sexuality and has different implications for women and men. What ensues between infantile libido and parental libido helps to establish individual male or female constitution.

Contemporary women analysts have taken up this question with great originality. Benjamin (1988, 1996) has argued that a mother's recognition of her own desire is key to the establishment of her child's separate subjectivity and sense of agency. Fathers have traditionally served as the figure representing subjectivity, but Benjamin has shown that mothers who can claim their own desire can serve as "subjects of desire" for both sexes. Kristeva (1989) views the mother's subjectivity in terms of her desire for another, other than her child, and elaborates this idea as the imaginary father within the mother. In her view, it is not the desire for a concrete penis but mother's desire for another, outside the mother–child dyad, that creates a space for the child's subjectivity and the development of mature sexuality, the sense that she too is a subject and can desire other than mother.

Irigaray (1985a) has argued that the lack of adequate cultural representation of the feminine and the female intensifies the conflictual nature of the mother-daughter relationship, which then speaks symptomatically through the body. It is the unspoken and unsymbolized that reverberates through generations of mothers and daughters. But we can also think of each new generation of women as holding the potential for finding those silenced words and that women analysts can provide space for the development of this feminine voice. Irigaray argues for a feminine language (écriture féminine) that can locate sexuality at the site of origin–a return to the maternal body. Naming the unnameable is itself a cure, providing a way to process and metabolize what Kristeva (1982) calls the maternal "thing," thus birthing a dialogue between two separate voices.

Lessana (1999) also views the mother–daughter relationship as a passionate attachment that resists analysis because it is not symbolized in language, making it necessary to use the female body as an imaginary source of identity. She conceives of the mother–daughter relationship within the Lacanian (1965) notion of *ravissement,*[1] wherein the mother "captures" the daughter with her illusion of their similarity and "confiscates" her in an ongoing debate on feminine identity that cannot be spoken and thus takes place at the level of shared skin. It is a debate based on an image of femininity that does not yet exist, that remains to be constructed.

Lessana suggests that mother and daughter are locked in an ongoing enactment regarding difference and similarity vis-à-vis femininity. Without adequate language, mothers and daughters are deprived of the means for a rigorous, relational exchange. They are thus conflictually bound together under the sign of an idealized, abstract femininity. Their "debates" become enacted at the level of the body and the skin, a fraught embodiment that fills in for the absence of symbolic categories to represent feminine agency and desire.

In Lessana's view the daughter is "ravished" by the mother, who embodies an ideal of femininity that the daughter cannot achieve. The daughter must articulate a personally realized feminine identity of her

[1] Lacan (1962) elaborated this in his essay "Hommage fait à Marguerite Duras du ravissement de Lol V. Stein," a discussion of the novel by the same name. Through Lacan's eyes, the novel deals with a young woman who, after being jilted by her fiancé for another woman, becomes fascinated and persecuted by the image of her rival. The image of the other woman both ravishes and ravages her, binding her in a cyclical struggle that consumes her identity and sexuality.

own, one that must be constructed through the working through of this relationship. Mother's ideal image is both ravishing and fascinating as well as ravaging and persecutory, as the daughter will always fall short. Its resolution requires a female corporeality to represent and symbolize the ravishment.

"WHERE DOES A WOMAN BEGIN?" —Helene Cixous

"I really think I am gay," Sara tells me, crumpled on the chair, barely audible. The distress this statement causes her is visible. "I am always looking at other women's bodies, their breasts, their legs, how they dress. It makes me so nervous, I am afraid I am going to reach over and touch their breasts, you know. I have this obsession with women and their bodies, its all I think about. I don't know what it means to be a woman."

Her confusion about sexual identity comes from living in a body that is female and alien, a body that did not develop on its own and has left her wondering exactly what she is. Sara suffers from Primary Ovarian Failure, her womanliness having arrived late in her early 20s and only as a result of hormonal treatment. " I am a construction," she tells me, "my femaleness created and sustained by the hormones they give me. This does not come *naturally* to me. I take it in a pill every day." Having had a hard, muscular, asexual body throughout her adolescence, a body that did not menstruate or change, she has learned to think of herself as an anomaly, not man and not woman. She experiences her curiosity about women, their bodies and rituals, as a sign that she is gay. Yet she is more comfortable with men because they *treat her like a woman*. Sara's dilemma is that she exists in "a woman's body," but she does not know it from the inside out; it is an object without subjectivity. She has looked to men for a definition of femininity, but this search only confused her. With me, she attempts to see herself in a mirror. Her wish is to create her femininity through her work with me. She exemplifies Benjamin's (1988) early statement that "the psychological integration of biological reality is largely the work of culture" (p. 90).

"Largely the work of culture," *but not entirely*. Montreley (1993) suggests that the tension between the biological realities of being female and its cultural and social construction make up the feminine unconscious. Post-Lacanian writers such as Cixous (1994), Irigaray (1985a, b), Kristeva (1982, 1989), Montreley (1993), and Lessana (1999) highlight sexual difference by remapping the feminine onto the sexed body of the female, arguing for its prediscursive status (see Brennan, 1989). By contrast, Anglo-American psychoanalytic feminists like

Chodorow 1978, 1995), Dimen (1991), Goldner (1991), and Harris (1991, 1997), view sexual difference as grounded in the internalization of prevalent social and cultural practices and also as multiply determined and fluid. A middle position is offered by Italian feminists (see DeLauretis, 1994, and Bono and Kemp, 1991), for whom sexed biology constructs psychic identity and is also reinterpreted psychically on the basis of varying social and cultural circumstances.

The literature on primary femininity (see Stoller, 1976; Mayer, 1985; Silverman, 1987; 1995; Richards, 1996; and Elise, 1997) views the development of female gender identity as grounded on a girl's early experiences of her body, particularly her female genitalia. A girl is aware of what she has (a vagina) and eventually of what she does not have (a penis). The awareness of her body as both complete and different is the starting point. There is a dramatic intensification of these experiences at puberty. The intense psychic experience of bodily changes also change the way others look at her. The girl now becomes the conventional object of male desire and of the male gaze, and she is now culturally perceived as her mother's equal and rival. Now she begins to develop a complex relationship to her newly sexualized body. But, as Sara reminds me, her relationship to her female body is more complex still. Looking at her now shapely figure, she says sadly, "This does not come *naturally* to me."

Sara's experience of herself as a girl could not carry her into adolescent femininity. This created an identity crisis around the issue of her sexuality. When her menses did not arrive, she felt she had been robbed of her femininity. In her work with me, she attempts to integrate cultural beliefs, missed developmental experiences, and needs with her recently acquired physique. She chose a woman as her analyst so that she could develop a language with which to articulate her femininity. Her own mother remained distant and silent, largely owing to her own fears about Sara's condition, and was not available as an object of identification or as a subject of articulation. In the transference, I became her teacher, someone whom she saw as a "natural" woman in contrast to her "constructed" woman-self. In the treatment matrix, I confront my own history as a "woman" with how I arrived at and inhabit my femininity and sexuality.

Sara remained a "girl interrupted" having to assimilate and create experiences for herself even though she looks like a woman. She knows the developmental stories but did not live them and is looking to my embodied history as a girl, a teen, and a woman as a way to map her own. She relies on it to fill in her own developmental gaps and normalize her experience. "I kept waiting for my breasts to look like everybody else's and stared at the other girls, wondering why I was not like them," she tells me on one occasion. "Then I would go home and pull on my nipples hoping that something would happen, some magic." "Many girls are anxious about the changes in their bodies in adolescence. You were anxious about the lack of change," I suggest to her. "Really?" she reacts with genuine surprise and some relief. On another occasion, after I have cut my hair very short, she looks at me and is visibly shaken by the change but is unable to talk about it. Over the course of many sessions, her fear that perhaps I am gay comes up. "And if that were the case?" I ask her. "Well, it of course scares me because I don't want to be," she answers. "But it also makes me curious because you are so feminine. It makes me question whether I am like you." (Note that here again sexual orientation is holding the space for gender anxiety.)

In Lessana's (1999) terms, Sara is struggling with the ravishing fascination of the feminine image as well as its persecutory and ravaging components, stemming from the "illusion of our similarity," the notion that there is one feminine archetype embodied by the mother, here embodied in the analyst.

THE MATERNAL BODY

Braidotti (1994) speaks of the maternal body as the site of origin and of primary repression, a container that escapes representation. Kristeva (1982) represents mothers as dissidents, as representatives of impossible borders, the maternal breast transgressing the border of sexuality and maternity. She sees the maternal body as a passageway that must be "abjected," given up with violent intensity in order to prevent a fusion with the specter of maternal chaos. The maternal figure promises and threatens identity itself, creating an instability of boundaries.

Rachel looks at me incredulously when I ask her if there is any pleasure in her life. "Pleasure? I don't dare. I have contempt for it. It was always beneath her [mother]. Only one kind of woman was permissible, and she is smart, acerbic in her humor. Stoic. And she doesn't wear heels either!" A writer, Rachel narrates her desire from the male point of view—as a he, she can fuck the other. In sex, she creates a psychic penis for herself and sees her lovers taking it in. In her experience, sex is the domain of men, which reduces women to orgasmic hysterics. Thus psychic masculinity has been her sexual solution, but it cannot be fully owned.

She too wants to work with a woman, knows that she has unfinished business as a woman, and is looking for a woman to talk with about it, a particular woman, despite her acknowledged contempt for everything feminine. "Well, at least you're not one of those really petite women," she tells me, with a sneer, on our first meeting. "You look substantial enough, and you have a sense of elegance." A quick recovery from the first of many aggression-filled quips, which have become opportunities to discuss her envy and, underneath that, her desire.

A mother who cannot claim subjectivity is unable to tolerate, let alone encourage, her daughter's sexuality. This leaves the daughter to become an object for the desire of others, much like the mother's experience of herself. Such a mother may instead focus on the regulation of her daughter's sexuality or unconsciously on its extinction. This can often produce a sense of alienation around gender issues, since daughters of such mothers have no gendered container for their embodiment. These daughters continue in constant search for validation, often through the male gaze as the object of their desire, but also through other women, who become mirrors that reflect their lack or become the object of envy, jealousy, and competitiveness, because such women seem to own their femininity.

A mother who does not narcissistically demand her daughter's identification with her, who is a sexual subject herself, can tolerate, and perhaps even celebrate, a daughter's differentiation from her. Steinberg (1993) speaks of nonrivalrous oedipal mothers who can liberate daughters through creative identification, because they have built a psychic life of their own. In psychoanalytic treatment, a woman analyst can create a transitional space for women patients to confront the repudiated aspects of their mother's desire which have become ravishing. Through the analytic process, women patients can birth their own desire.

Rachel came to see me one year following the death of her mother. "What kind of woman was she?" I ask. "Surprising," she tells me, "I've only recently discovered how passionate a woman she was from her diary. She never showed it. I had no inkling. She was always so intelligent and witty, quick with words, literate, but angry. And sensible, you know, no heels, no makeup, army pants. It seems there was a time when she was very beautiful and smart, fashionable, when she was crazy about my father and their life together."

What emerges is a portrait of a woman who was betrayed by her husband and who buried her passions so deeply that Rachel is only now uncovering them, wondering if she is entitled to any of her own, frightened of where they might lead her. In my work with Rachel, I often find myself sitting with that part of her who identified with her mother–an articulate, powerful woman who renounced her sexuality and femininity and now looks at me with contempt and cynicism when I inquire about her desire, her body, her fantasies. I can see and feel the hatred and envy, the fascination, when she eyes me up and down, taking in my body, my clothes, my lipstick, my high heels. I experience my own discomfort, my difficulty in tolerating her stare, my desire not to lose my words, to be smart *and* beautiful. Slowly I start to realize my own competitiveness and wonder if I am also holding it for both mother and daughter.

At other times, I find myself articulating Rachel's mother's pain, her sense of betrayal and sadness at the loss of her husband's love. The depth of her passion is revealed to me in a clinical moment when I become a woman forlorn, left lonely with her growing daughter, too pained by obsessive love to fix her a meal or be interested in her changing body. A crack in the omnipotent mother with whom Rachel entwined herself. At such times, Rachel is surprised at the emotion that rises up within her, at the memories of M&M dinners she fixed for herself. Then she is able to speak the swallowed words of her girlhood.

The mother–daughter relationship is characterized by conflicting needs to identify and separate. Parker (1995) suggests that ambivalent feelings on both sides are central to the maintenance of a loving linkage, where hatred protects against excessive identification and love supports separation. For Parker, the experience of maternal ambivalence provides a woman with a sense of her independent identity and makes that possible for her daughter as well. The ability to tolerate and contain, let alone use, ambivalence presupposes symbolization: a language and voice with which to identify and name love, hate, and everything in between. When my patient Sara searches for a maternal subject, she is looking for a woman, not necessarily a mother, with whom to untangle her sexual identity. For Rachel, the search is for a woman with whom she can develop a feminine language.

WHEN OUR LIPS SPEAK TOGETHER . . .

These lines from Irigaray's (1985b) famous poem about daughters and mothers are a metaphor for the analytic entwinements that emerge between women patients and their analysts. There is a tension between merging and separation that takes a unique gendered form in these treatments. When our lips speak together–oh, what joy! Who would want to leave such a place of jouissance? On the other hand, knowing the joys of subjectivity, who would want to stay? These analytic entwinements oscillate between fascination and persecution because the gender of the woman analyst stirs up particular desires for the woman patient. What lies between them is the "image of woman," which circulates in the treatment until it is resolved (Lessana, 1999).

Here is Eve: "Sex? I don't want it in my current incarnation. Women like you have sex, probably even good sex. That's why you want me to have it. Just because you do doesn't mean I have to." Eve's envy of what she imagines to be my sexual life pushes her away. She abdicates her carnal self, leaving me to have sexuality and joy. Splitting off her desire, she remains stuck in all areas of her life but joined in a conflictual union with me.

When Eve looks at her body, she finds herself wanting; she considers herself unformed. When she looks at me, she wants to identify with me and also hates me for being what she "is not." In my incarnation of the maternal image, I fascinate and persecute her. For my part, I struggle to keep my voice and remind her that we can be two women, separate in our desire, without either of us having to give ourselves up.

Envy exemplifies one way in which aggression is a revolt against the other's subjectivity, a precondition for becoming a subject, for separateness, for womanhood (Benjamin, 1996; Harris, 1997). Viewed in this way, hostility between women can be seen as aimed at asserting separateness and individuality. Being able to transform hate into aggression in our daily lives frees us from the persecution of the image. The issue for the woman/child is to confront the persecutorial image that ravages and ravishes her. Depression becomes the symptomatic alternative: a way of remaining close to the maternal body, entwined, silent and good, and thus to avoid feelings of competition. This depressive stance in the service of attachment is, in Kahane's (1995) terms, eroticized so that the maternal presence paralyzes the narrative subject. Silently entwined forever.

Eve tells me, "Well, yes, there is my vagina. Who wants to talk about that?! The [male] doctors that treated me before you so they could dissect me in their staffing. I shut that door tightly then, and now you want me to open it—to talk about my vagina, about sex. *Well, I don't feel anything during sex, not a thing*. I watch my body go through the motions, and a part of me thinks, What's the big deal about?" Later, when we have revisited her body as a little girl's, her vagina a source of both pleasure and shame, when she has begun to reintroduce herself to her adult, womanly body, and it now comes easily to her, with pride and sometimes even joy, that sex is a *big deal,* Eve becomes convinced that her mother will die, that her own breasts will rot with cancer, and, worse, that Eve herself has caused it. In her dreams, I too become depressed and dead, not able to tolerate her sexuality and emerging desire. She is torn between going forward and remaining at my side so that we may both stay forever entwined. She hates my separateness and longs for it.

Eve gets right to the point. She despises and loves our sessions together. Sometimes shutting me out, other times swallowing me up, and on good days able to see me as the woman she loves and hates. "So, have you ever written anything?" she asks me pointedly at a time when she herself is writing. Her question a mix of curiosity, envy, and hope. I hear it and immediately think of my own struggles with voice.

She is asking about my voice as a woman, the first seeds of her separation from me. If I have written, how can she compete with me—she might be more articulate than I—can she survive outdoing me? Can I? If I haven't written, how can she possibly entertain the idea for herself? Who can help her make the leap if not I? (I am reminded that in my own analysis I could not bring myself to remember anything my analyst wrote—she is a prolific author—until well on my way to termination, when suddenly I was flooded with knowledge, hers and my own.)

In her own struggles with voice, Eve's fears of injuring me and of my retaliation become evident. She prefers to love me and see me as capable of everything she wants, to feed it to her through unmediated closeness. Entwined forever. "And what is the problem with that?" she taunts me. "Why can't I remain the little girl/woman?" Sometimes in an effort to compromise, she tries to steal the goodies from me (do as I do), but then she is unable to use them because they are mine and not hers. We remain entwined. There is only one solution: to continue talking.

Kahane (1995) suggests that hysteria occurs when, suspended in an oedipal moment, a woman turns her rage against herself in a kind of "narcissistic biting of the tongue" so as to not use it aggressively against the other (p. 37). Benjamin (1996) notes that, for women, failures in struggles for recognition cannot be fully repaired by using a male identification to revolt against the mother, as in the case of my patient Rachel. Lessana (1999) goes further, arguing that feminine subjectivity must be elaborated through corporeality, a female skin to embody and to separate from.

If this confrontation cannot take place with mother, then another woman is needed. Thus the value of female friendships and female mentors, as well as the accoutrements of femininity: creating and recreating opportunities for confrontation and integration, they circulate the ideal image among women.

The consulting room is another place for women as psychoanalysts to function as figures of symbolic mediation for female patients. The Italian feminists have referred to such a relationship as one of *affidamento* (entrustment) (see DeLauretis, 1994). Such a notion embraces the many ways in which women can make use of each other on their journey toward elaborating their desire.

REFERENCES

Amigorena, H. (1996), In: *She Speaks, He Listens,* ed. E. H. Baruch & L. J. Serrano. New York: Routledge, pp. 113–124.

Benjamin, J. (1996), *Like Subjects, Love Objects*. New Haven, CT: Yale University Press.

——— (1988), *Bonds of Love*. New York: Pantheon.

Bono, P. & Kemp, S. (1991), *Italian Feminist Thought*. Oxford: Basil Blackwell.

Braidotti, R. (1994), Mothers, monsters, and machines. In: *Writing on the Body: Female Embodiment and Feminist Theory,* ed. K. Conboy, N. Medina & S. Stanbury. New York: Columbia University Press, pp. 59–79.

Brennan, T. (1989), *Between Feminism and Psychoanalysis*. New York: Routledge.

Ceccoli, V. (1999), Beyond milk and the good breast: Reconfiguring the maternal in psychoanalytic dyads. *Psychoanal. Dial.,* 9:683–694.

Chodorow, N. (1978), *The Reproduction of Mothering*. Berkeley: University of California Press.

——— (1995), Gender as a personal and cultural construction. *Signs,* 20: 516--544.

Cixous, H. (1994), *Hélène Cixous Reader,* ed. J. Sellevo. London: Routledge.

DeLauretis, T. (1994), The essence of the triangle or, taking the risk of essentialism seriously: Feminist theory in Italy, the U.S. and Britain. In: *The Essential Difference*, ed. N. Schor & E. Weed. Bloomington: Indiana University Press, pp. 1–39.

Dimen, M. (1991), Deconstructing difference: Gender, splitting, and transitional space. *Psychoanal. Dial.,* 1:335–352.

Elise, D. (1997), Primary femininity, bisexuality, and the female ego ideal: A reexamination of female developmental theory. *Psychoanal. Quart.,* 56:489-517.

Goldner, V. (1991), Toward a critical relational theory of gender. *Psychoanal. Dial.,* 1:249–272.

Harris, A. (1991), Gender as contradiction: A discussion of Freud's "The psychogenesis of a case of homosexuality in a woman." *Psychoanal. Dial.,* 1:197–224.

——— (1997), Aggression, envy and ambition: Circulating tensions in women's psychic life. *Gender & Psychoanal.,* 2:291–326.

Irigaray, L. (1985a), *Speculum of the Other Woman*. Ithaca, NY: Cornell University Press.

——— (1985b), *This Sex Which Is Not One*. Ithaca, NY: Cornell University Press.

Kahane, C. (1995), *Passions of the Voice: Hysteria, Narrative, and the Figure of the Speaking Woman, 1850–1915*. Baltimore, MD: Johns Hopkins University Press.

Kristeva, J. (1982), *Powers of Horror: An Essay on Abjection*. New York: Columbia University Press.

——— (1989), *Black Sun*. New York: Columbia University Press.

Lacan, J. (1965), Hommage fait à Marguerite Duras du ravissement de Lol V. Stein. In: *Marguerite Duras,* ed. P. Connor. San Francisco, CA: City Lights Books, 1987, pp. 122–129.

Lessana, M. (1999), The ravishment between mother and daughter. Seminar presented at April meeting of Après Coupe, New York City.

Mayer, E. L. (1985), Everybody must be just like me. *Internat. J. Psycho-Anal.,* 66:331–348.

——— (1995), The phallic castration complex and primary femininity: Paired developmental lines toward female gender identity. *J. Amer. Psychoanal. Assn.,* 43:17–38.

Montreley, M. (1993), Inquiry into femininity. In: *The Gender Conundrum*, ed. D. Breen. New York: Routledge, pp. 145–165.
Olivier, C. (1989), *Jocasta's Children: The Imprint of the Mother*. New York: Routledge.
Parker, R. (1995), *Torn in Two: The Experience of Maternal Ambivalence*. London: Virago.
Richards, A. K. (1996), Primary femininity and female genital anxiety. *J. Amer. Psychoanal. Assn.*, 44:261–281.
Silverman, D. K. (1987), Female bonding: Some supportive findings for Melanie Klein's views. *Psychoanal. Rev.*, 74:201–215.
Steinberg, Z. (1993), The still another, other mother: Janine Chasseguet-Smirgel's Freud and female sexuality. Unpublished manuscript.
Stoller, R. J. (1976) Primary femininity. *J. Amer. Psychoanal. Assn.*, 24:59–78.

Mothers, Monsters, Mentors

Adrienne Harris, Ph.D.

In this essay I explore the difficulties many women have in creative work and the relation of this difficulty to conflict with relations to mothers and to women mentors.

I am going to begin by looking at some excerpts from Sylvia Plath's (2000) recently published journals. I find these writings fascinating, appalling, mesmerizing. Plath seems simultaneously familiar and dazzlingly *sui generis*. For any woman with a memory of the prefeminist 1950s and 1960s, Plath's journals will pull you toward a harrowing and relentless mirror. There is, for example, in the young college-age Plath's writing an exploding, impossible, histrionic determination to wield power over men. We see the fiendish delight in a young woman's fascination with her own sexuality and its impact on others. At the same time, men are endowed with such magic: "If I were a man, I would write a novel about this, being a woman why must I only cry and freeze, cry and freeze" (p. 177). Plath returns over and over again to a quandary she cannot work out: she must save herself through writing but only a man will save her. It is a testament to her complex, inverted sense of her own power that she is always looking for a big man, and sometimes a doubled dose of masculinity, a man with a good father. Here is a poignant entry written during her honeymoon: "Ted is working at the main table. . . . Living with him is like being told a perpetual story: his mind is the biggest, most imaginative I have ever met. I could live in its growing countries forever. I also feel a new pouring of energy into my own work" (p. 249). The honeymoon diaries record, among other readings, Plath's immersion in *The Joy of Cooking*, an involvement in domestic pleasure but always a pleasure she experienced in relation to the appetites of her husband.

From a certain point of view, the Plath journals illuminate the mid-20th century, Western woman's impossible tangles with her own agency. And yet Plath also fought against so many of the cultural forces designed to spoil a woman's creative ambition. You cannot smugly say, "Oh well, this is all prefeminist" because Plath, in these journals, *is* ambitious, pragmatic, powerful with words, determined to write. She was also tortured and woman hating. From other sources we know she came to understand that she was hated for her insistent sexuality (Rose, 1991).

Plath, armed with a kind of psychiatric imprimatur, pours out pages of hatred of her mother. "I give you permission to hate your mother." She is quoting her therapist (a woman), who has, with this mantra, provided an elixir Plath calls "as intoxicating as cocaine." These words were "better than shock treatment," and she hurls back her response: "I hate her, doctor. So I feel terrific. In a smarmy matriarchy of togetherness it is hard to get a sanction to hate one's mother. . . . I don't imagine time will make me love her. I can pity her. She doesn't know she is a walking vampire" (p. 429).

Plath's list of reasons she hates her mother is long and contradictory. She hates her mother for marrying her father, for killing him, for giving Plath an old father, for hating sex, for sacrificing for her children. "I hate her because he [her father] wasn't loved by her. . . . Now this is what I felt my mother felt. I feel her apprehension, her anger, her jealousy, and her hatred"

(p. 432). Plath catalogs her own sins of disobedience, mostly centering on sleeping with bad boys and ignoring nice ones.

> I have done practically everything she said I could not do and be happy at the same time and here I am, almost happy. . . . So how do I express my hate for my mother? I think of her as the enemy, somebody who killed my father . . . she is a murderer of maleness. . . . I'd kill her so I'd kill myself [pp. 430–431].

The melding of murderous hatred and identification could not be more clearly put. I quote from Plath's journals to explain neither her creativity nor her suicide nor her distortions nor her white-hot experience of her mother and her own situation. For me, this material is interesting and important for its misogyny, a misogyny that is internal, external, relational, social and intrapsychic, real and imaginary. Plath's journals reveal the particular heartbreak of women's misogyny: the gloomy difficulties women have with self-love, self-esteem, and the cache of disgust and shame that adheres to many women's experience of femininity.

Exploring misogyny would take us onto a wider, more dangerous minefield than space in this paper affords. Woman hating can be curled around many phobias about femininity; it can provide a deep, odd form of attachment (hatred as linkage and binding); and it can be implicated in processes of separation. Homophobia and misogyny can seem to be dark twins (Brennan, 1993; Corbett, 1993). We do not always know which form of fear is in the driver's seat. I have explored elsewhere (Harris, in press) the core function that misogyny plays in the formation of any subject; misogyny functions as a kind of midwife to individuation. In the complex flash points of mother–daughter interactions, misogyny may be the residue of shame and impossible, forbidden desires (an accompaniment to maternal seduction). Here I try to do some deconstructive work on this phenomenon and its destructive undertow to women's creativity and public voice.

We are all by now too knowledgeable about the difficulty, even the impossibility, of locating or fixing the source of the black hate Plath writes of. In the mother, in the culture, in the daughter? It is everywhere. We know that experiences are sometimes intersubjectively flowing and in play and that boundaries between people are often permeable. A hectoring, harsh voice, once heard in vivo, can in dialogue become seamlessly a part of the self. Feeling attacked becomes lurid self-attack; hatred becomes paranoia and persecution. In contemporary psychoanalysis, we think that there is "an ebb and flow of interiority and exteriority" (Schafer, 1968). Sometimes the flux of interpersonal effects and intrapsychic ones is delicious and playful. In the mother–daughter dance it is too often an activity of lethal and mutual terrorization.

Projection is bidirectional; mother and daughter are both fantastical and real objects for each other; and there are enigma and indeterminacy in hatred's sources and agendas. We cannot finally decide just whose hate this is. We do not really, finally, know whether this hate is the residue of frustrated love or destructiveness. But we do know the object of this hate: the feminine, in particular the maternal figure.

Allow me to set a problem. One way to situate the conflicts in female creativity is to see that a woman's relationship to aggression, ambition, and agency is often inevitably connected, in fact or in fantasy, to a conflictual relationship to her mother. Out of this problematic connection (and, of course, hate is a potent attachment) we do our work in defiance of mothers, in attempted disidentification with them, and we often set at their feet our failures and inhibitions as loyalty or destructive triumph. Although this cannot be some new universal aspect of femininity formed outside of context and situation, it is pervasive because, I believe, the roots of women's difficulties with creativity and ambition lie along a historic bed of constricted and inhibited life experiences. Gender differences, even if socially constructed, can seem generic and the asymmetrical conditions in men's and women's lives can anchor these differences to a startling degree.

Aggression often seems to be a potent bastion of gender differences, as evidenced in a number of social and biological-science disciplines. (Fausto-Sterling, 1992, 2000). But a psychoanalytic perspective allows us to see that the real distinction between men's and women's aggression is probably not the amount of aggression but access to it. Women very often report consistent difficulties in social and self-tolerance when intensity, passion, potency, and creative agency are prominent. Women too rarely make clear distinctions between agency and destructiveness, excitement and damage to others, competition and a feeling of or wish to murder.

Women can exhibit stunning creativity in the forms of their undoing and self-damage. Writer's block, postproduction meltdown, depression, orchestrated unhappiness, and self-attack before, during, and after creative work or in public professional life—the undertow for many women is astonishing. And, if a woman does find a clear line through to creative work, all too often one may trace the (conscious or unconscious) hand of some paternal force in this achievement. It is rare for a woman to feel and use a connection to a maternal imago that is full and rich or to a real-life mother who seems authorized and fully subject and who can therefore be safely killed in fantasy and so outdone or joined with in reality.

Women's conflicts around creativity and public agency may be related to separation issues, to oedipal victory, or to loyalty to damaged or fragile others. I have written about women's conflicts with ambition (Harris, 1998) elsewhere so let me only summarize the argument to which many people in psychoanalytic feminism across many theoretical orientations have contributed.[1]

If gender development goes in a more or less prescribed way, a girl's progress to individuation and autonomy may be compromised by incomplete separation. In different theoretical views, this incompleteness has a number of different meanings or understandings. The girl may be less fueled toward differentiation, as gender is usually not at stake. Masculinity, since Stoller, has been viewed as constituted by way of

[1] Benjamin (1988, 1993), Bassin (1996), Coates (1991), Corbett (1993), Persons (1999), Goldner (1991), Harris (1990, 2000a), Elise (1997), Dimen (1991, 1995), Chodorow (1976, 1999), and the Ur-figures (Kestenberg, 1956, 1982; Bernstein, 1993; Dinnerstein, 1996), and—even earlier—Lampl-de-Groot (1933) and Horney (1933).

disidentification with the mother. Gender is part of the securing of bounded identity, and vice versa. It is assumed that these boundaries bleed a little between mother and daughter. In women, it is argued, the pulls for fusion and relatedness overcome the less driven and less sanctioned push for independence (Chodorow, 1976; Bernstein, 1993). The capacities for robust separation may depend on both the access to a maternal object and its pleasures and some bedrock of activity.

Yet there is some contradiction for many young girls and women. Accompanying the guilt at individuation there is a press for a kind of pseudomaturity so that many girls take on relational duties too early. Chodorow's (1976) early work focused attention on the very early reproduction of relational and emotionally related functioning, conditions that underwrite mothering. Olesker's (1990) observations on gender differences in early separation focus on the toddler girl's greater social relatedness along with her self-management. I think it is possible to examine these early styles or modes of relatedness for their potential for precocity and for demands on care of the other that can threaten to disrupt or sidestep care of the self.

The gender differences around relatedness or attunement and around aggression are often subtly interpreted as temperament, or they are given a kind of sociobiological reading. A young girl taking on relational tasks like empathy is often seen as more mature or more self-regulating than is a boy of similar cohort. These capacities are often seen as rooted in her "nature." Many feminist analysts (e.g. Flax, 1990; Brennan, 1993; Dimen, 1995; Chodorow, 1999) have deconstructed this knot of ideas and passions around the "nature" of women. I would like to consider that what we call temperament is an intersubjective, relational partially socially constructed phenomenon. Assesments of temperament usually involve judgments about levels of activity, irritability, or reactivity in an infant. It is possible that such judgments may not be entirely objective but reflect subtle expectations in the viewer. Scoring differences do arise when the assessment is done by a parent or by a stranger. Our scale of what constitutes levels of irritability or reactivity may carry subtle biases, which are informed by our feelings and beliefs about gender, for example. We might think that young girls are often subject to the pressure to develop ego precocity, a pressure of the sort Corrigan and Gordon (1995) and Winnicott (1949), among others, have seen as compromising development.

A central idea in considering ego precocity is that it is a forced demand to be self-regulating and self-containing long before body, psyche, and internal world have the structural capability to bear such self-management. With inadequate external containment, the mind or body-ego must somehow cobble together capacities and structures that can hold the self and transact self–other interactions. But this precocity always exacts a price. There are many potential strains, anxieties, and fragilities that can produce a kind of brittleness that accompanies early hypermaturity. Not all children are called on to self-manage in an inappropriately mature fashion, and not all children faced with a demand for escalated maturation can rise to the occasion.

I believe, though, that there is a complex interaction that may be constructed in the lives of many girls in which the demand for mature self-management becomes connected to some early physiological maturational lead. The outcome is a capability for relatedness orchestrated with self-containment that eclipses not just autonomy but an earlier stage of steady containment by another. Simply put, if a girl is pressed toward precocity, the attendant difficulties are both in the experience of dependency and in independence. This paradox–needing and not needing help and containment–might help us to think about how many women, simultaneously experience fusion and depletion in relation to their mothers.

Thus a girl's progress toward individuation may be too brittle or too tentative and particularly compromised in regard to the expression of aggression. What emerges, then, for some girls may be a burdensome and constricting fantasy of omnipotence. Very familiar in clinical work is the woman who carries the feelings that her needs or wishes are dangerous and that the environment, particularly the relational environment, is not robust or supportive enough to tolerate her. This belief retards creativity and mobility precisely because it stifles fantasy and the ability to play constructively and destructively in a kind of mental play-space.

A second, but deeply related constellation of difficulties that women have with creativity and public voices, involves envy and its impact as an actual and as an imagined experience. Envy works its black magic in either of two forms: passive or active. Envious feelings can seem shameful and debilitating and can constrict creativity through one's angry immersion in deprivation, neglect, and fear of dependence. But being envy's object carries another kind of unique toxicity, which is often deep in women's psychic life. It is the fear of being envied.

The fear of being envied, with its particular brake on women's zest and creativity, leads me back to the problem of the *maternal imago*. As others have argued (Benjamin, 1993; Bernstein, 1993), I think that the destructive virulence or greedy devouring of this figure marks many dark and wild fantasies we develop as individuals and as a culture with regard to female, and in particular maternal, power. Plath (2000), musing to herself writes:

> But with your father dead, you leaned abnormally to the "Humanities" personality of your mother. And you were frightened when you heard yourself stop talking and felt the echo of her voice, as if she had spoken in you, as if you weren't quite you, but were growing and emanating in her wake, and as if her expressions were growing and emanating from your face [pp. 64–65].

As she explores her conflicts in writing as conflicts around spiting her mother and over the question of ownership of her work (hers or mother's), she traces the flow of hatred between them and in herself: "How can I get rid of this depression: by refusing to believe she has any power over me, like the old witches for whom one sets out plates of milk and honey" (p. 447).

I believe that mother–daughter dyadic life is too often a kind of ground zero of misogyny. One manifest symptom of the problematic struggles in dyadic female life is envy. Envy, I believe, carries within it both aggression and desire. Both are thwarted in open exchange. I have written about the particular struggles many women have with envy and being envied (Harris, 1998, 2000b). We are most familiar with the stings and vicissitudes and baleful hurts coiled around envy. A rich elaboration of envy's spot in our psychic life is one of the staples of Kleinian work (Klein, 1977). There envy is a kind of outcropping in reaction to deprivation, and its destructive and rageful components are stressed. I, wanting to explore the shadowy presence of desire in envy braided around aggression and retaliatory fantasy, would see longing thwarted and spoiled. In regard to aggressive feelings or desirous ones, envy packages its affects in covert form, its passions hidden or disguised.

Another way to approach the complexity and contradiction in woman-hating is through the intricate dance between homophobia and misogyny. Let me elaborate this idea, which depends on applying gender theory to the work of Laplanche (1989) and others on maternal seduction, the enigmatic seduction. Many authors have noted the tendency to de-eroticize the preoedipal mother (Kristeva, 1982; Elise, 1997, 2000). Others have welcomed the revival of Laplanche's work on maternal seduction, rendering as it does a view of sexuality as limenal, as on the mysterious, partially unconscious borders between persons (Stein, 1998; Dimen, 2000). Desire must be instantiated in any individual, and desire complexly fused and unfused from its objects enters personal life from the beginning.

In fact, clinicians consider that the effects of neglect can be as powerful as the effects of attack. Fonagy and Target (1995) have argued that the effects of violence and of neglect on a child's mind and affects can seem almost indistinguishable. Maternal detachment shapes attachment but does not prevent it, and so we want to see the fates or effects of love, libidinization, fusion, and the range of other emotions and anxieties they may accompany as mother and daughter live in the intimacy and individuality of dyadic life. How can a mother's capacities to libidinize her daughter and empower her be compromised? Disturbances in mother–daughter life and love could emerge in a variety of forms. For instance, is there anxiety about homosexual desire in regard to daughters? Is desire gendered in this way? Does the mother carry shame and anxious fantasies about the feminine body experienced as a self-state or projected onto the daughter? Do fear and anxiety cohere to their aggression regarding anyone?

Loewald (1949) described the earliest experience a child has as a primary density out of which self and object precipitate. But when we consider the contribution of the adult to this experience—the mother, specifically—we wonder what affective states are mirrored or function as kinds of contagion in the parent–child environment. How much does gender experienced in the parent or projected into the child carry anxieties, longings, conflicts, loves, or hatreds that become elements suspended in the solution in which the child swims? These affect states precipitate out into and through communicative interaction that becomes internalized, incorporated, or introjected by the child. States of being and feeling, patterns of experience, both social and solitary, all become part of what the cognitive developmentalists term "procedural knowing," a knowing that is primarily secret, preconscious, and unconscious. Over time theses modes of knowing self and other become the stuff of later narratives and fantasies, the origin lost and enigmatic. The story-telling constructions take on a life of their own.

I might think of women's troubles with envy and aggression as a sign that gender development and construction can be a kind of intergenerational transmission of trauma. The trauma is both the historical conditions in which women live (including generations of constriction and sanctioning) as well as the particular inalienable conditions of infant vulnerability and fantasy. Trauma as a term is used in a rather elastic way, I realize. Taking advantage of the current work on intergenerational transmission of trauma, I suggest that quite gross or particular phenomena (women's health conditions, work possibilities, self-esteem conditions that are social and intrapsychic) may enter the subtle, often nonverbalized transactions between parent and child and so may be carried as unconscious and encrypted memories later absorbed into self-representations.

Bernstein (1993) has written very evocatively of the problem of the maternal imago as an aspect of the superego. The presence of an internal, archaic representation of mother leads to acute and virulent forms of conscience, attack, and self-reproach that seem sharp in female life and acutely destructive to women's creative life. These ideas are developed in the work of John Steiner and his colleagues (1990), Elizabeth Bott Spillius (1993), and Rita Frankiel (2000). The more I think about the maternal imagery the more paradoxical it appears to be. One reading of this figure, often a merged primal couple where the maternal figure has devoured all, including the father and his penis, comes from Klein (1977). A big, full, sexual mother inspires envy in the little girl and threatens dangerous retribution if the daughter dares to want or to act. But equally often this figure's danger is in her envy, in the powerful destructiveness that is felt to emanate from her despair, her dependency, and her depression. Empty or overwhelming, the maternal imago is no help. It can apparently do none of the work that the ego ideal or the superego is supposed to support, that is, to underwrite mastery, effort, agency, goals, and projects.

Plath, reading Freud and going to her therapist, is constructing an understanding of her work struggles. She can thrash around in conflict and hatred, in depression and block as a complex triumph over her mother and what she imagines as her mother's wish to own her work and with it her. But she is beginning to get a glimmer of another truth–that there is longing, for love and approval and what she feels to be the hopeless but still persistent task of gaining access to maternal care and love. Yet, throughout these journals, maternal potency remains conflictual and problematic; and perhaps, even in the wake of becoming a mother herself, this possible source of potency failed her.

This paradox has many difficulties attached to it. There is the issue of mentoring as a matrilineal process. Hence my title–mothers, monsters, mentors. Among the difficulties of women being mentored by women is that none of the structures of hierarchy and deferment built into male oedipal formations translate easily for women. Granted that the intergenerational transactions between men can be fraught and deeply conflicted, there is, at least in principle, a structure of inheritance. Much as one would hope that maternal transferences might be manageable in professional or institutional settings, I think a psychoanalytic inquiry into these matters has to include an acknowledgment that unconscious forces, in particular archaic, preoedipal maternal transferences, can play powerfully and not always constructively.

A lot of work has been done on the great advantage a woman acquires through her father's identificatory love. Benjamin (1988, 1993) has developed the most elaborate argument on this matter. It is important to remember that in her analysis it is the father's capacity to identify with the daughter that creates conditions of sponsorship and agency. Identifications are initiated by the child but authorized or potentiated by the receiver. Bassin (1996) has been pursuing the effects of cross-sex identifications in postoedipal development. I have been thinking about "masculinity" in women in my work on tomboys (Harris, 2000b). One interesting quandary is how to keep differentiated the advantages of identificatory love from the father and the disadvantages of being an oedipal victor. Although these two forms of attention from a father are conceptually distinct, there are many women for whom they get muddled, either in fact or in fantasy. Plath's early history included what, in her view, was a powerful though eventually enigmatic connection to her father, from whom she felt early on a special sense of being the favorite, the chosen child. But in a very fascinating passage in the journal she records a dream of her mother's in which she (Sylvia) is a prostitute who steals the father. One senses this dream to be, among other things, a shared fantasy between mother and daughter. Sylvia is the oedipal winner who must feel shame and disavowal at her illicit or incestuous power to win father from mother.

We still have to wonder how much female agency is dependent on some access to phallic agency, whether it comes through a man or a woman. The power of many women is tied to men, sometimes in actual alliances, sometimes in identificatory process.

Masculinity, in some form, real or intrapsychic, is still viewed in the culture and in our theories as a kind of vaccination against the maternal undertows. Or riptides. Do we still gender the kind of agency that is actually effective, and do we still render feminine power too dangerous? Or, to pursue the matter in a different way, how far can revenge on the mother take you? If you can't get the monster, a.k.a. mother, out of your mentor, how are women to become publicly generative and privately creative. Or, perhaps another way to get at this, how can our fantasized monstrousness become useful and interesting to us, fueling work, not defaulting to self-attack? We do not have good or clear-cut ways to found female power as a lineage. Generativity, that ostensive mark of the feminine, remains too often thwarted and self-thwarted when power, public success, and goods in the world are at issue.

As long as women's power remains, for many women, more albatross than talisman, I fear that women will be caught in an undertow of negation, particularly when the journey takes them away from the domestic domain and into the world. The still tragic truth is that, for too many women, power in the world, power in the domestic world, and power in the psychic world are deeply awry. Dinnerstein (1976) made this one of her themes 30 years ago. Like her we will need both feminism and psychoanalysis to fully excavate and transform this paradox.

REFERENCES

Bassin, D. (1996), Beyond the he and the she: Toward the reconciliation of masculinity and femininity in the postoedipal female mind. *J. Amer. Psychoanal. Assn.*, 44S:157–190.

Benjamin, J. (1988), *The Bonds of Love*. New York: Pantheon.

——— (1993), *Like Subjects, Love Objects*. New Haven, CT: Yale University Press.

Bernstein, D. (1993), *Female Identity Conflicts in Clinical Practice*. Northvale, NJ: Aronson.

Brennan, T. (1993), *History After Lacan*. London: Routledge.

Chodorow, N. (1976), *The Reproduction of Mothering*. Berkeley: University of California Press.

——— (1999), *The Power of Feelings*. New Haven, CT: Yale University Press.

Coates, S., Friedman, R. & Wolfe, S. (1991), The etiology of boyhood gender identity disorder: A model for the integration of temperament, development and psychodynamics. *Psychoanal. Dial.*, 1:481–521.

Corbett, K. (1993), The mystery of homosexuality. *Psychoanal. Psychol.*, 10:345–357.

Corrigan, E. & Gordon, P. E. (1995), *The Mind-Object.* Northvale, NJ: Aronson.

Dimen, M. (1991), Deconstructing difference: Gender, splitting and transitional space. *Psychoanal. Dial.,* 1:335–352.

——— (1995), In: *Disorienting Sexualities,* ed. R. Lesser & T. Domenici. New York: Routledge.

——— (2001), Perversion is us? Eight notes. *Psychoanal. Dial.,* 116:825–860.

Dinnerstein, D. (1976), *The Mermaid and the Minotaur.* New York: Beacon.

Elise, D. (1997), Primary femininity, bisexuality and the female ego ideal: A reexamination of female developmental theory. *Psychoanal. Quart.*, 66:489–517.

——— (2000), Bye-bye to bisexuality. *Studies in Gender & Sexual.* 1:61–68.

Fausto-Sterling, A. (1992), *Myths of Gender: Biological Theories about Women and Men.* New York: Basic Books.

——— (2000), *Sexing the Body.* New York: Basic Books.

Flax, J. (1990), *Thinking Fragments: Psychoanalysis, Feminism and Postmodernism in the Contemporary West.* Berkeley: University of California Press.

Fonagy, P. & Target, M. (1995), Understanding the violent patient: The use of the body and the role of the father. *Internat. J. Psycho-Anal.,* 76:487–503.

Frankiel, R. (2000), Fear of difference. Presented at meeting of the American Psychoanalytic Association, New York City, December.

Goldner, V. (1991), Toward a critical relational theory of gender. *Psychoanal. Dial.*, 1:249–272.

Harris, A. (1998), Envy and ambition: the circulating tensions in women's relation to aggression. *Gender & Psychoanal.,* 2:291–325.

——— (2000a), Envy's excitements. Presented at meeting of American Psychoanalytic Association. New York City, December.

——— (2000b), Gender as a soft assembly: Tomboys' stories. *Studies in Gender & Sexual.* 1:223–250.

——— (in press), Misogyny: Hatred at close range. In: *Hatred in the First Person Plural* , ed. D. Moss. New York: Other Press.

Horney, K. (1933), The denial of the vagina–A contribution to the problem of the genital anxieties specific to women. *Internat. J. Psycho-Anal.*, 14:57–72.

Kestenberg, J. (1956), Vicissitudes of female sexuality. *J. Amer. Psychoanal. Assn.*, 4:453–476.

——— (1982), The inner genital phase: Prephallic and preoedipal. In: *Early Female Development: Current Psychoanalytic Views,* ed. D. Mendel. S. P. Medical & Scientific Books, pp. 81–126.

Klein, M. (1977), *Envy and Gratitude and Other Works 1946–1963.* New York: Delta Books.

Kristeva, J. (1982), *Powers of Horror: An Essay on Abjection.* New York: Columbia University Press.

Lampl-de Groot, J. (1933), Problems of femininity. *Psychoanal. Quart.*, 2:489–518.

Laplanche, J. (1989), *New Foundations for Psychoanalysis.* London: Blackwell.

Loewald, H. (1949), The ego and reality: In: *Papers on Psychoanalysis.* New Haven, CT: Yale University Press, 1980, pp. 3–20.

Olesker, W. (1990), Sex differences during the early separation-individuation process: Implications for early gender identity formation. *J. Amer. Psychoanal. Assn.*, 38:325–346.

Plath, S. (2000), *The Unabridged Journals of Sylvia Plath,* ed K. Kukil. New York: Anchor Books.

Person, E. (1999), *The Sexual Century.* New Haven, CT: Yale University Press.

Rose, J. (1991), *The Haunting of Sylvia Plath.* London: Virago Press.

Schafer, R. (1968), *Aspects of Internalization.* Madison, CT: International Universities Press.

Spillius, E. B. (1993), Varieties of envious experience. *Internat. J. Psycho-Anal.,* 74:1199–1213.

Stein, R. (1998), The poignant, the excessive and the enigmatic in sexuality. *Internat. J. Psycho-Anal.,* 79:259–268.

Steiner, J., Feldman, M., O'Shaughnessy, E. & Britton, M. (1990), *The Oedipus Complex Today: Clinical Implications.* New York: Brunner/Mazel.

Winnicott, D. W. (1949), Mind in relation to psyche-soma. In: *Collected Papers.* New York: Basic Books, 1989, pp. 243–254.

Lost in a Fog, or "How Difficult Is This MOMMY Stuff, Anyway?"

Maura Sheehy, LCSW

Private Practice

Interpellation is not only a function of public life. It is also at home. Here Maura Sheehy works with Melissa, a young mother, who, just like her analyst, struggles with the multiple interpellations of motherhood. Abjected as well as idealized, motherhood produces both exaltation and utter confused misery for both. As the treatment proceeds, we witness analyst's and patient's common search for intelligibility, a parallel process in which the analyst finds/sees how both her patient and she locate themselves in and wrestle with discourse, an engagement that effects change in both.

Melissa began our first session perched on the edge of the couch and turned toward me at an uncomfortable angle, leaving herself both unsupported and off balance. She had two daughters, she said, ages 3 1/2 years and 8 months, and was feeling sad and overwhelmed due to what she assumed were "postpartum weaning issues." She said she was sorry to be giving up the symbiotic breast-feeding connection with her infant but also glad to be freed up from the constant nursing demands. Rather than enjoying her new freedom, however, she felt panic and loss. "They're growing up, I haven't done the baby books, I'm not recording what's happening, my older daughter never talks to me about herself, it's all slipping away," she said, tearing up.

Simultaneously, she felt she should be getting back to work. An Ivy League educated architect, Melissa had designed and directed the building of their whole apartment while pregnant and now expected herself to perform a similar virtuosity of multitasking. But she couldn't finish even the tiny lobby design she'd been hired to do by her co-op board and felt a mounting sense of failure and shame. She wondered if she could ever return to architecture after seeing the angry, viciously competitive older women at the firms she'd worked at, who never saw their families. She wondered why she couldn't find a way to balance her life "like everyone else."

Everything in Melissa's life seemed to be where it was by default rather than by choice. Chaos reigned. Despite having a full-time babysitter she was often late to sessions, having been derailed by some relative trifle like her daughter's tantrumy mind changes about who would take her to school. She longed for time to herself but couldn't separate for fear her girls would suffer somehow, but if she did break away she busied herself with mindless chores. When she did spend time with her children it never seemed terribly satisfying, despite her initial complaint, because she was so anxious about how the interactions and activities should go. She admitted that sometimes the babysitter's presence made her feel "like I'm on an IV drip in the back room," but nevertheless the babysitter was omnipresent, even at the, in their case, not-just-mommy-and-me classes. Yet every night she was bedeviled by the thought, "What do I need to do tomorrow to be a good parent?"

Melissa felt a general sense of exile in motherhood, as if she'd been dismissed from the world and was like "a peg that didn't fit." She imagined her former colleagues assuming she "couldn't hack it" and snickering at her retreat into motherhood, the co-op board laughing at the little mother who couldn't get the job done, and the ultratrendy professionals in her neighborhood greeting her stroller-pushing presence with a disapproving "What are YOU doing here?" But she couldn't connect with the other preschool mothers for fear of what they'd think once they found out she had a full-time babysitter, house cleaner, and a SoHo loft and wasn't working—again, she'd be dismissed. Above all, she felt she had no right to complain–about anything. As her husband asked whenever she voiced a need, she imagined everyone wondering, "What do you DO all day?"

I was struck by Melissa's near-complete lostness—as if she could not find comfort in any part of her identity or the world—and her lack of definition was evident in her wandering, overgeneralized, contradictory associations. She felt "lost in a fog," and so did I. Nothing we did seemed to get at what was really "slipping away" or to provide much relief. And then I began to dismiss her, too. After all, she was easy to dismiss: a wealthy, White, educated, stylish woman, rolling in help and lost in an abundance of options. Were the voices of censure that bedeviled her not somehow deserved, not perhaps a symptom of her privilege?

My fantasies of a meaty attachment-related analysis devolved into disappointment as once again she brought in one of the self-help slash parenting books she studied hungrily and recited their simple revelations. Our sessions began to feel like mommy coaching 101 and my mind became cluttered with reductive prescriptions such as "She needs to cut back on that babysitter so she can feel more connected to her kids, and then we'll help her get back to work part-time." Impatiently, dismissively, I kept wondering, "Where is the second-time mother with her game in place, why can't she get control of those kids, set the schedule, send her sitter on errands, do what she wants?" As I reflected on what was at the base of my impatience, I heard a voice say, "How difficult IS this 'MOMMY' stuff, anyway?"

Dimly, I was aware that something about this reaction was off. All my own mother chaos, ambivalence, trouble balancing all the desires and needs—my own and my children's—was disavowed. My confidence wavered. I couldn't stop wondering if I was reacting to her as a mother or analyst (and what exactly the difference might be), prescribing my own biased cures or meeting her needs. The identifications and disidentifications were disorienting. I was only back to work 4 months since having my second child and felt my mother self to be barely hidden behind a too-shaky hologram of my analyst self. It felt reductive to be thinking of her, and myself, at such a binary dead end in terms of a self that was independent, separate from children, and defined by work, or as a mother self, as if it were possible to separate our desire and identities into neat piles. I felt stuck but could not see what was I was stuck in. So I resolved for a while to examine her history more closely—an analytic fallback position, to be sure, but somewhere that I hoped would anchor us.

As we peeled back the historical layers we found the mother who was a poster child for prefeminist domestic enslavement and the father who was a first-generation immigrant grooming Melissa for greatness, teaching her to leave play for after work and to be anything but her mother. Her early talent for painting had been immediately commodified into a product to be bought by her father or his friends and then pushed aside for ''real'' work. But the work was never done, until she finished graduate school and realized the mountain she'd climbed to the cutting-edge career ''was really,'' she said, ''just a cliff'' that led to more endless work, no play, no time for family. Now she feared she'd pour herself in to her daughters, they would use her up like a commodity, and then eventually they would dismiss her as everyone else in the world did.

Around this time, I wrote an essay for a writing group of analysts exploring my own conflicts over separation from and connection with my children, my heated desire for both, and the elemental fears that could arise from either state during the course of a day. I related my search through the attachment, object relations, and relational canons to find something that spoke to MY experience—MY maternal identity—rather than only my effect on my child and my child's maternal experience. To my utter surprise, someone said they didn't get why I had to read books at all, why didn't I just know what I wanted and then do it? It was the voice I'd heard in myself in response to Melissa, now coming from outside: ''How difficult is this 'MOMMY' stuff, anyway?'' Mothers were supposed to KNOW how to manage motherhood, not flip around like a fish out of water or talk about their own desire. While writing I had noticed the feeling that revealing my mother self felt humiliating and inappropriate outside the home sphere, not worthy of intellectual inquiry, just mommy talk, mommy crap. Now it seemed confirmed, and as I went home suffused in shame I felt a sudden surge of identification with Melissa. As Melissa and I answered society's hailing as mothers, had we, as Judith Butler (1993) has suggested, taken our new, maternal identity in as a ''reprimand'' that had repressed other parts of ourselves in return for offering us recognition as mothers?

Still seeking to clean up my countertransference and return to some supposed ''solid'' analytic stance toward Melissa, I brought Melissa's case to an all-female supervision group. To my surprise, they reacted to the case with pained anxiety and identification with the patient as all their unresolved conflicts about their work and motherhood choices and their shifting sense of their own subjectivity surfaced. I began to see how filled we were with negative maternal images and impossible expectations of ourselves. How little we understood the forces at work upon and within us. How we blamed ourselves for our own confusion and inability to find balance, thinking we had so many choices. But did we?

According to a Harvard University study by the Project for Global Working Families, out of 173 countries the United States is 1 of 5 that doesn't provide paid maternity leave (Heymann, Earle, and Hayes, 2007). The others are Lesotho, Swaziland, Liberia, and Papua New Guinea. And our access to basic supports such as family sick leave, national childcare standards, and affordable health care coverage not tied to a full-time job lag far behind those of most developed countries. Judy Warner (2005), in her book *Perfect Madness*, has made a strident argument that the lack of social policy supporting families has made it impossible for women not to feel betrayed, as Melissa does, by the message that we can have it all—work and motherhood—and develop a fairly stable and positive maternal identity when in fact we can't, easily if at all.

But Melissa's case opened my eyes to an even more insidious set of internal obstacles to the development of a maternal subjectivity that includes a sense of agency. First, the tendency to think in binaries—work versus motherhood, good mother versus bad, separate versus connected. Reflecting and reproducing the bifurcated social structure within which women try to be both workers and mothers, these binaries leave women without any psychic in-between territory for exploration or creation of a maternal subjectivity that doesn't, still, contain shame.

Melissa's personal financial and class advantages had blinded me to the more universal conflicts she, and I, were caught in and had anesthetized me to her real anguish. But as we unpacked her maternal shame, I found my own. I had thought myself very different from her, less ambivalent about my delight in the maternal experience. But there I was, feeling my maternal identity was something to hide and wanting to solve her confusion as it reminded me too painfully of my own. I realized how lost I was in the confusing web of social constructions of women and mothers that no amount of feminist reading or consciousness-raising had been able to free me from, despite how enlightened, and therefore immune, I had thought myself.

I began to wonder about this self-hating mother introject and how it prevents women from taking their own maternal desire seriously. By maternal desire I mean not only what Daphne de Marneffe (2004) has called the profound, drivelike need to have physical and emotional contact with one's children but also our maternal subjectivity in the larger sense—who we become and what we desire for ourselves when we become mothers. There is almost no way to think about ourselves as having aching desires for deeply intimate relationships with our children while also remaining connected to the larger world and to ourselves. We are only taught to think about ourselves in two absolutely opposed categories: as maternal facilitators and holders who can have no desire but to respond to our children's needs and not our own or as women who can clearly and consistently individuate away from the maternal role (which, we are told, is good for us and them). But individuate too much, desire too much in either direction, and one is a bad mother: engulfing, engulfed, regressed, or too separate.

I no longer felt that our conversations about motherhood texts were beside the point. After all, where else was discussion of a mother's experience to be found but in those steerage-class, self-help regions of the bookstore, or in the work, usually memoir, of women writing from and about the same binary- and shame-defined confines we were stuck in. I also didn't cringe when Melissa saw an article I'd written for *Child* magazine (Sheehy, 2004) in which I revealed some of my messy maternal process, or when my bag tipped over and a sea of Cheerios skittered across the floor, or when she asked me how I'd figured it all out. "What makes you think I have?" I answered. "I'm struggling too, doing what you are: reading, talking with other mothers, looking for mentors and models. There is no other way."

One night around this time Melissa went to hear a panel of artists discuss their process, and the next day she came to session feeling inspired to resume her painting. Then she announced triumphantly that she knew why her oldest daughter wasn't sharing anything about herself: "I'm not talking to her about my process, my secrets!" said Melissa, "so she's not talking to me about hers." I was struck by Melissa's use of the evening's gift and my decision to share my maternal "secrets." She wasn't just following the healthy development script of Mother separating from her children in order to fulfill herself, finding identity in separation and individuation. Rather, in finding more of her own voice she found more of a voice as a mother, too—the parts of herself not opposed in a binary but intertwined.

AUTHOR BIO

Maura Sheehy, LCSW, is a psychotherapist in private practice in Brooklyn, NY.

Part II: Maternal Subjectivity

Oi Mother, Keep Ye' Hair On! Impossible Transformations of Maternal Subjectivity

Lisa Baraitser, Ph.D.

Motherhood is commonly referred to as a transformational experience. Where the psychoanalytic literature articulates the maternal subject and her development, transformation is figured as a working through of infantile issues prompted by the psychic crisis that motherhood represents. Juxtaposing recent autobiographical accounts of the transition to motherhood with the work of Irigaray, and using my own experiences of early motherhood, I look at the way motherhood as a transformational experience is represented as either the movement from unity towards fluidity, or its reverse, the movement from fluidity to the hardening of desire around the unity of the child. I use a discussion of wigs to show how transformation itself is caught by its own material effects, inevitably failing to pass itself off as the magical movement from one state to another. The transition to motherhood is understood as both the painful and playful realisation of the impossibility of transformation itself.

PART I: MATERNAL SUBJECTIVITY

> When I spoke to new mothers, it seemed to me that although a child and new love has been born, something else within them had passed away, and the experience was made harder because, at some level, underneath their joy in their babies, these women were quietly in mourning for this part of their earlier selves [Wolf, 2001, p. 6].

In *Misconceptions*, Naomi Wolf's disturbing account of giving birth in North America, she writes with some surprise at the profound changes that occur for women when they become mothers. Her focus by the end of the book sits squarely within a discourse that understands these changes in terms of the social, political, and economic realities that structure motherhood. However, she seems elsewhere to be genuinely surprised by the extent and sheer arduousness of the psychological work that accompanies this shift from womanhood to motherhood–the quiet mourning, for example, that she detects in so many mothers' accounts of this oddly painful transition.

Although her "Mother's Manifesto" (Wolf, 2001, p. 243) is full of the usual call for changes in working patterns and child-friendly facilities, things that are vital in returning to women the hard-won independence they achieved before having children, a kind of despair infusing the personal stories seems to undercut the possibility of such a return. There is a quiet acknowledgment that perhaps things will not be the same again. Although one gains a child, one loses, I think she suggests, the irreplaceable clarity of the borders of the self. From now on one's "self" is crucially changed by the presence of this particular "other" who is one's child. Wolf writes that it is a "messier, more inter-dependent new maternal self" (Wolf, 2001, p. 6) that emerges.

This discourse turns on the supposition of an earlier independent, solitary, unitary self that must yield to a more fluid self capable of bearing a much more porous relation to another. Motherhood, it appears, is a condition in which the self budges up to make room for another self and is radically changed in the process. The self undergoes a fundamental transformation from one state into another; from something solid, unified, singular, to something messy, interdependent, and altogether more blurred.

A unity/fluidity dialectic, my starting point for tracking the psychological work entailed in transforming woman to mother, belongs to the highly contested notion of feminine identity that informs any discussion, whether feminist or psychoanalytic, of the maternal subject. Psychoanalysis has long troubled the notion of a clearly boundaried self, working instead at the very border of self-knowledge that would ground such a concept. We are, according to Lacanian psychoanalysis, constantly undone from within, carrying with us, under the sign of the unconscious, our own self-dissolution. The unitary "I" was always a fiction anyway—one we glimpsed in a jubilant moment of misrecognition and that we absurdly mourn as if we once had. Rather than a discrete substance as such, the psychoanalytic subject is understood to be under constant maintenance because of these inherent threats to its real or imagined stability, a shifting process of negotiation between material conditions and unconscious desire. And the feminist analysis of such a position has assiduously uncovered the gendered split in this dialectic, pointing out how the masculine usurps the position of unified subject and relegates the feminine as the necessarily unthematizable excess, which serves to give the masculine its consistency, form, and visibility.

My concern, however, is this: If the old independent self/new messy maternal self are refigured as two poles of the same unity/fluidity dialectic, it is the maternal, instead of the feminine, that is now being relegated beyond unity. Maternity, containing the messy and unthematizable excess signified by femininity, produces retroactively the old (feminine) self as a fictional unitary subject that must be mourned and then given up. Contemporary accounts of motherhood that articulate the confused and painful movement from one state to the other do so by (perhaps necessarily) misrecognizing the feminine as a lost unitary fiction. Cusk (2001) writes:

> The vision of myself that I ... glimpsed in the park—unified, capable, experiencing "the solidarity of life"—is one that I will continue to pursue over the coming months. It proves elusive ... To be a mother I must leave the telephone unanswered, work undone, arrangements unmet. To be myself I must let the baby cry, ... forestall her hunger or leave her for evenings out, ... forget her in order to think about other things. To succeed in being one means to fail at being the other. The break between

> mother and self was less clean than I had imagined ...for later, even in my best moments, I never feel myself to have progressed beyond this division. I merely learn to legislate for two states, and to secure the border between them [p. 57].

The "unified capable" self is retroactively glimpsed, only to be lost again under the weight of the child's demands.[1] "Ah," we seem to be saying, "only now I can see, too late, what I was, now that I must give up this version of myself for a more interdependent version, one that is premised on being able to make room for another." Ironically, here the feminine takes up a position under the unified sign of the masculine, at the point that the mother gives way to the true demands of the other: her child. Imbued with both loss and shock, the maternal emerges in these popular accounts as the most confusing of subjective positions, full of fissures and splits, illusions and hopes, broken apart by violent emotions.

The cost of the psychological work involved in moving from womanhood to motherhood is beginning to be recognized in the psychoanalytic literature too. With it is an acknowledgment of the debt psychoanalysis owes to the mother as a key model who has been plundered for metaphorical significance and then abandoned when it comes to applying psychoanalytical insights to helping mothers understand their complex reactions to mothering. Kraemer (1996) has argued persuasively that, as psychoanalytic constructions of the mother have shifted from Winnicott's rather idealized good-enough mother to a more subjectively complex one, she now risks being valorised both "for her resilience and for her ability to play easily with her feelings of hate and aggression towards her baby" (p. 765). The mother, in other words, is now seen to be able to move fluidly in and out of intense emotional states, with no apparent consequences to her mental health.

Kraemer (1996) claims that reidealizing the mother in such a way misapprehends what experiencing intense hate, aggression, envy, and sadism towards children feels like and what it does to mothers. Yet again, the complex and, at times, treacherous process of "claiming oneself" (p. 775) as a subject is replaced with a fantasy mother

[1]For similar autobiographical accounts, see Figes (1998), Buchanan (2003), and Enright (2004).

who can simultaneously claim herself and navigate her baby's needs. However, Kraemer contends, "interdependence" is not some easily attained fluidity. She refocuses us on the important question of "how the mother feels about what she feels and what she does with how she feels" (Kraemer, 1996, p. 765), and in particular, what she feels about her own destructiveness in relation to the baby. The mother in her view has to bear her subjectivity, not by gracefully juggling with constant tensions, but by tolerating very difficult, and largely unconscious, feelings: hatred, ambivalence, failure, shame, self-hatred, and remorse. This juggling exacts a price, and at times causes us to go under.

Crisis and Transformation in Maternity

There appears to be a need to understand maternal subjectivity as a fundamentally changed state, a state at or beyond the border that we once would have recognized as a self-boundary and from which we may glimpse ourselves anew. On the one hand, transformation, with its magical overtones, tends to gloss over the profound struggle with overwhelming experiences that motherhood prompts. On the other, like all experiences that put the subject "on-trial" (to borrow Kristeva's, 1975, phrase), it alludes to the way motherhood can create substantial shifts in both material and semiotic conditions, prompting a renewed configuration of self. Hence Kraemer's (1996) reminder that transformation can exhilarate as well as daunt, that mothers can find satisfaction in anger and aggression as well as feel crushed by them and that part of a complex notion of maternal subjectivity must include the mother's relation to creativity and hope.

Recent work suggests that motherhood's transformative potential resides in its ability to cause a kind of psychic crisis in the lives of women. If crises can prompt breakdown, they can also allow a reconfiguration of our relation to new and necessary fictions of who we once were, are, and would like to be. Parker's (1997) notion of maternal ambivalence, a counterpart to Klein's infantile ambivalence, concentrates on the creative potential of holding in tension our love and hate for our children. She notes the way maternal ambivalence can call forth new resources within a mother that contribute to a renewed self-experience. Raphael-Leff (2003) speaks about the ways having children causes us to revisit and rework the "wild things" from our infantile lives (Raphael-Leff, 2003, p. 54). In Stern's (1998) view, pregnancy and the period directly following birth cause a fundamental psychodynamic shift in which the Oedipal configuration, as the major organizing structure, gives way to what he calls the "motherhood constellation," a new psychic organisation with its own set of "action tendencies, sensibilities, fantasies, fears and wishes" (Stern, 1998, p. 171).

Ethics and Subjectivity

The psychic crises of motherhood unveil maternity's relation to ethics. Cusk (2001), we have seen, voices mothers' commonly felt experience of having to choose between their own and their child's needs. "Choice," however, becomes an ethical problem in the context of the particular openness and responsiveness to the other embedded in this new, interdependent, porous relation. For Ruddick (1989), maternal practice, understood as a discipline in which the mother develops intellectual capacities, judgments, attitudes, and values, becomes a moral choice. The mother, in her view, attains an ethical subjectivity through her ability to deal with the uncertainty and conflict inherent in child rearing with grace and good will.

As Oliver (1993, p. 15), however, has shown, the maternal subject, understood as "in-process/on-trial" (Kristeva, 1975), calls ethics itself into question. Ethics is usually deemed to be a set of relations between stable autonomous subjects and objects. However, a subject "in-process" is by its very nature ethical, because this subject brings with it its own disruptive force, its own negativity or otherness. Kristeva posits negativity as both the drive, that which is heterogeneous to the symbolic, and, in the case of maternity, the otherness within the mother that puts both the symbolic and our relation with others on trial.

In other words, motherhood not only presents us with ethical dilemmas but also challenges our notion of subjectivity itself, causing us to radically rethink who we are. Motherhood is a practice that interrogates the subject, due to the daily demands of the otherness "without"—that is, the mother's relation with her actual child. Kristeva's (1977) notion of "herethics" (p. 185) understands this being-for-another not as a description of a self-abnegating masochistic femininity but as the name for the subject whose ability to put herself aside inherently challenges the whole symbolic system. Maternity, in Kristeva's scheme, becomes the figure for the border territory between the symbolic and semiotic, agitating the split, making us think again about what grounds us.

The dilemma of choosing between one's own and the child's needs has been voiced within feminist psychoanalysis as a tension between the psychical and social mother, the mother that psychoanalysis has told us plays such a vital role in the child's developing internal world and the mother who is a desiring subject in her own right. An emphasis on reciprocity and recognition, particularly in Jessica Benjamin's work, has softened this polarity. Benjamin (1995) argues persuasively for the need to recognize the mother's subjectivity as a locus of self-experiencing beyond that of the child. If the child does not have a mother whose subjectivity is recognizable, then the child cannot hope for recognition herself. In its crudest form, the mother can finally be thought of as having a life of her own. The choice is no longer cast as either/or but the holding in tension of both mother and child's needs and desires.

However appealing at an egalitarian level, there is a danger that reciprocity glosses over the skewed nature of the relationship between mother and child and gives way to the characteristic collapse of the maternal subject in the face of the needs of the fragile and developing child. It is the child who is seen to benefit from a mother who has a life outside of the child's sphere. In the process, I believe we lose sight of the way maternal subjectivity is structured through the relation to the child. I would argue, instead, that one's subjectivity as a mother is precisely what emerges through this real and imagined relation. The positioning of maternal desire as that which goes beyond the child may be necessary to protect the child from what Kristeva (1987) terms "the caring and clinging mother" (p. 34). It does not, however, necessarily help us understand maternal desire itself.

A return to the binary mother–infant relationship is clearly problematic and prompts a reconsideration of the role of the third, though this time from the mother's perspective. It is possible that the child's otherness can function as a third term for the mother and, therefore, prevent the regressive pull of the mother–infant dyad whilst allowing us to understand her desire as the desire for the child. When Kristeva (1987) poses the question "What does a mother want?" (p. 41), the answer she provides is that she wants her own mother, even in the figure of the child. All desire, in other words, is understood as desire for the lost mother, including our desire for our children. But surely the mother also has a relation to the child that at times escapes this repetition.

Psychoanalysis variously configures maternal desire as the desire for the missing penis, the longed-for union with the imaginary mother, or the desire for the "father" (or lover, work, politics–whatever takes the mother away from the child) that plays a vital function in breaking up the dyad with the child. If the focus shifts from the child's psychic health to the mother's, it may be possible to consider how maternal desire, proceeding from the direct encounter with the child, fundamentally changes the way we mothers feel and think about our partners and lovers, work and politics, mothers and ourselves. In other words, although we constantly allude to the felt experience that we are "transformed" through our relations with our children, we are perhaps fearful of dwelling on how or why, because in doing so, we may jettison the precious connection we have with the world beyond our babies. We fear we will fall into a regressive symbiotic relationship with our children, to their and our own detriment.

PART II: "MOTHER-WRITING"

Juhasz (2003) has attempted to posit maternal writing as a site for structuring maternal identity, an argument that I want to use to situate my own writing. Juhasz discusses how maternal subjectivity can be achieved through the creation of points of coherence within what she terms "mother-writing" itself (Juhasz, 2003, p. 395). Mother-writing is seen as a creative space that can promote recognition for the mother–author who uses writing to navigate a plurality of self-positions, for the reader who also acts as surrogate mother to the mother-writer and for the text itself. By bringing together multiple maternal identities within the same textual space, she argues a "grammar" (p. 400) can be established and, with it, the possibility of viable relationships among different maternal positions, creating a potential point of connection for the mother.

Although Juhasz (2003) emphasises multiplicity, creativity, and recognition, her account rests on a core notion of "self" onto whom these "multiple identities" are pinned. She explicitly rejects positions that valorise decentredness. She argues instead that maternal work consists of the twin tasks of caring for the child and simultaneously trying to organize diverse aspects of the self so that they "seem coherent, viable, or to possess continuity" (p. 406). Writing, she believes, can create a semblance of coherence out of the self fragmented by splitting due to ambivalence and help the mother recognize the work she does to hold in tension disparate facets of herself.

In contrast, my own mother-writing, beginning in the next section, issues from the murky area between unity and fluidity. Whilst finding Juhasz's (2003) emphasis on maternal recognition very helpful, I am arguing that we understand maternal subjectivity to put the subject on trial. I emphasize motherhood's radical potential to disturb the self, rather than the need to create the semblance of coherence by patching the self's fissures. Sitting uneasily between the academic and the autobiographical, I have tried to retain some of the indigestibility of maternal experience by leaving small, uncohered, autobiographical "chunks" of maternal writing within the more formal academic reflections. Mindful of Blau DuPlessis' (1990) dry observation about feminist autobiography, "but (and) many people have reinvented the essay" (p. 175), I nevertheless find myself nostalgic for the possibility of writing that mirrors Kristeva's subject in process. Rather than providing a space for multiplicity to cohere, writing as process attempts to keep multiplicity open, resisting points of coherence in favour of the negativity that pushes coherence to its very limit. Blau DuPlessis writes of a "writing as writing. Writing as praxis. Ongoing. Curious. Situated. Rapid. Rabid. Marked with one's markings. Not uniform. An exposure. Incomplete. Unsafe. Even deplorable" (p. 61). Such writing, writing as praxis, does not simply describe or stand in for experience, but may be said to enact or engender it through the very process of writing.

PART III: TRANSFORMATION

I have restricted my comments on transformation to the very early stages of maternal development. To be sure, later developments in the trajectory of the maternal subject are as important, and the transition begins way back in pregnancy and even before, in the unconscious fantasies about babies carried from early childhood into adulthood. The transition from maternal narcissism to the experience of the baby as a new object begins with the "quickening" (Bibring et al., 1961, p. 15.), when women feel the baby's first movements at around four months. But the momentous transition from woman to mother is often experienced in the first days, weeks, and months after the birth of a baby—a time that women are most prone to maternal depression, when the "transformation" really kicks in.

Transformation is an induced or spontaneous change from one element into another. In common usage, it describes what happens when something is changed utterly, like the miraculous metamorphosis of runny egg whites into those elusive "stiff white peaks" of children's recipe books. Perhaps transformation's fascination lies in our difficulty in deciding when the egg whites really are standing up on their own, knowing that, if you beat for a moment too long, they disastrously dissolve back into their runny form. In Eric Carle's timeless children's book, *The Very Hungry Caterpillar* (Carle, 1969), transformation itself is not depicted. The caterpillar disappears into the brown cocoon and magically emerges as something completely different. The children squeal in disbelief. In this sense, transformation mines our never fully relinquished belief in magic. We know the change has taken place but missed the point, the exact moment when one state slipped into the other. Inherent then in the notion of transformation is a blurred boundary and a questioning of limits or edges.

"Transformation" has least two other intriguing etymological meanings. First, it has roots in the theatre, describing "a sudden and dramatic change of scene on stage" (*Oxford English Dictionary,* 1989). Whether via the sudden dropping of a backdrop from the fly bar or a piece of scenery flown in from the wings or the visible moulting of characters into the pantomime figures of Harlequin and Columbine, the scene supposedly transforms before our very eyes. With a dull thud of Hessian, we move from inside the witch's hovel to the lakeside at twilight. We will ourselves to believe what we see, despite the noisy clunk as the backdrop hits the floor.

Second, and wonderfully, transformation is an archaic term for "a woman's wig" (*Oxford English Dictionary,* 1989). Conjuring dilemmas of mind and matter, this odd definition contains a constellation of interrelated meanings about performance and mimicry, and by association, female sexuality and madness. It also holds a double allegiance to materiality: When the caterpillar becomes a butterfly, or the runny whites turn stiff, is that a change of state or of stuff? Whilst transformation wants to pass itself off as the magical movement between one state and another, it finds itself caught by the coarseness of its own material effects. Just as the backdrop's clunk can never be completely edited out, so the wig's synthetic nylon never fully convinces. Even a "real" human hair wig does not pass itself off as anything other than a wig. In fact, the closer the wig gets to looking "real," the more we seek to examine it, to touch it, to ascertain its credentials, and inevitably the more drawn we are towards its ultimate artificiality.

Perhaps we can conclude that transformation contains its own impossibility. A paradox, transformation simultaneously signals a movement towards change and exposes its own mimetic strategy, showing itself up as a fake.

Motherhood is the pitilessness of the present tense. Reflective space is obliterated. This relentless and infinite present destroys all that is subtle, indeterminate, unknowing in one's thinking. It's not that mothers stop being able to think. It's that we think in another order–the order of immediacy. Ha! Is this what is meant by maternal instinct? That we are forced into a kind of survival mode, a chronic crisis, the endless horror of Groundhog Day? In this immediacy, I am brought face to face with the patched over, broken bits of myself, the cracks in relations with mother, lover, siblings, friends. Everything is challenged, like in analysis, painfully peeled back.

During the days and weeks after the birth of my first son, in the grip of a mute and helpless grief, I feel chained to this tiny creature, chained by an invisible thread, a shadow of the umbilicus, in oh so many subtle ways restricting the movement of my very being. Movement, as Irigaray would have it, is the being of woman. Is this why so many women feel such terrible loss after the birth of their first child?

It is the first day I leave the house alone after giving birth. My son is perhaps two or three days old. He is sleeping, his face set like a tiny Celtic high priest, sleep draining the colour from his cheeks, in a deep, lost place. And I am in search of a maternity bra, so unprepared am I for the trappings and paraphernalia of new motherhood. As luck would have it, there is a famous bra shop on the Whitechapel Road. Its name is Carol's. Carol says her family members have run a lingerie shop there for generations. Plump and matronly, she swishes around, breathing womanly secrets, as she measures and hoists, clasps and tugs. She is aghast, horrified that I am out of bed, that I show no visible signs of having given birth three days ago other than my tender leaking breasts. She views me with a faint whiff of irritation.

But despite my body's refusal to let on, I know that everything has changed. I am unsteady, dizzy, like I'm relearning to walk after a long illness. I imagine a war has taken place while I've been away. I look for the signs. I can't understand that no one else has noticed. I want to rush up to the thin stream of Bangladeshi men, moving up and down Brick Lane, and confer with them, join them in their huddled groups to discuss in hushed voices the catastrophic shift that's taken place. I stand on the curb waiting to cross the road, fearful should anything happen, conscious of needing to protect myself in a way that has never occurred to me before. Not trusting that I know what to do, I waver, looking left, then right twenty, then thirty times, still unable to propel myself off the curb. I have to stay alive. I am two. Maybe more. I don't know myself. Severed from myself, like the cut end of a worm, I am disorganized, stunned.

PART IV: IRIGARAY, FEMININITY, MATERNITY

Irigaray (1985a) claims that indeterminate being, being as a state of transformation itself, is the very scene of "woman." I want to reread this claim through Judith Butler's *Bodies That Matter* (Butler, 1994), which draws together a knot of ideas about femininity, maternity, materiality, and mimicry embedded in the notion of transformation itself. I will then turn to Irigaray's reading of the placenta as "first veil."

For Irigaray (1985a), woman is neither closed nor open:

> She is indefinite, in-finite, *form is never complete in her* .... This incompleteness in her ... morphology, allows her continually to become something else, though this is not to say that she is ever univocally nothing. ... But she is becoming that expansion that

she neither is nor will be at any moment as definable universe [p. 229].

In Irigaray's terms, woman (which appears close to Levinas', 1969, concept of infinity) is that which overflows its own idea. Irigaray takes the notion of the feminine as unthematizable excess and runs with it, pushing it to its limit without losing sight of the necessary function and origin of its exclusion.

Likewise, Butler (1994) shows us that Irigaray's version of the feminine-as-other exceeds those binary pairings within which it is usually located–male self/female other, matter/form, body/rationality. Both displaced by and produced by them, the feminine as excessive otherness–a name, that is, for radical alterity–is necessary for these dichotomies' ontological status and internal coherence. The feminine does not, however, possess an autonomous ontological existence of its own. Produced at the point it is also excluded, the feminine becomes the necessary outside, which is always already inside, showing up "within the system as incoherence, disruption, a threat to its own systematicity" (p. 152).

In her critique of Irigaray, Butler seeks to problematise the way "matter" is figured as irreducible, prior to discourse, and used to ground claims about sexual difference. Matter itself is, she argues, already imbued with discourses on sexuality, reproduction, and signification that prefigure and constrain its nomination. In addition, matter as category is founded on a set of violations or exclusions that shadow its use. She argues that although feminist scholars have worked to reveal the link between women and materiality, especially the body as matter, Irigaray's strategy is more subtle, showing how matter within philosophical discourse is both a substitution for and a displacement of the feminine. The displaced feminine is positioned beyond or excessive to matter. It is the feminine that therefore cannot be figured within the terms of philosophy proper, because it is the necessary exclusion of the feminine from philosophy that enables philosophy to speak itself.

Irigaray's critique of the origin of matter in philosophy and its consequences for the feminine occurs in her discussion of the receptacle, or *chora*, in Plato's *Timaeus* (Irigaray, 1985a, pp. 168–179). I will draw on Butler's elegant account of Irigaray's strategy in order to tease out the troubled relation between femininity, maternity, matter, and transformation. I will be arguing that, in the main, Irigaray reinstitutes femininity at the expense of maternity.

Briefly, Plato's *chora* or "receptacle" is the site of transformation, where matter, through its resemblance to a Form, comes to be recognizable as a material object. Referring to this place as the "receiving principle," Plato (1977) uses the analogy "nurse" or "mother" (pp. 67–69). Because it is the place in which shapes take on their Form, this receptacle cannot itself have shape. Because its function is only to receive and effect transformation, it cannot transform itself. The *chora*, figured as the mother/nurse, is entered, but cannot enter: She conceives form but lacks form herself. In this sense, the receptacle escapes definition and can only be known by the analogy mother/nurse.

Interpreting Irigaray, Butler usefully distinguishes between the "specular figures" of mother/nurse and the "excessive feminine," which is what is displaced by such figures. The mother/nurse represents the feminine within the binary pair form/matter, both of which are subsumed under the masculine and work to displace the feminine (I am tempted to say the "feminine proper," whilst falling into the same difficulties with nomination that Butler comments on) at the moment they purport to represent it. In this sense, Butler argues:

> This receptacle/nurse is not a metaphor based on likeness to a human form, but a disfiguration that emerges at the boundaries of the human both as its very condition and as the insistent threat of its deformation; it cannot take a form, a morphe, and in that sense, cannot be a body [p. 154].

On this reading of Irigaray, the maternal becomes the lesser feminine. Just as the receptacle exceeds its metaphorical figures (mother/nurse), so femininity exceeds the receptacle as the "impossible yet necessary foundation of what can be thematized and figured" (p. 154). If the maternal is a specular figure for the feminine, one that, when (mis)taken for the feminine, exacts its erasure, then the maternal always threatens the feminine, and in particular, the feminine's fluidity. The maternal becomes one of Irigaray's names for the fixing of femininity. Butler writes, "taken as a figure, the nurse-receptacle *freezes* the feminine as that which is necessary for the reproduction of the human but is itself not human" (p. 155; emphasis added). Elsewhere, Irigaray (1985a) writes, "And for her the risk of maternity is that of limiting (herself and her desire) to the world of *one* child. By closing herself up over the unit of that conception, by curling around that one, her desire hardens" (p. 229, original emphasis).

If the feminine is thus understood as that which exceeds the maternal and at the same time makes the maternal possible, the maternal subject is left in a difficult position. Irigaray's claim stands as an interesting theoretical counterpart to women's more personal articulations of the difficult move from femininity to maternity, as recounted by Wolf (2001). The maternal, made possible by this "other" site of the feminine, is left by Irigaray as a "disfiguration,"the poor imitation of the excessive feminine, the other to the male same. The maternal is like a poor relation, suspect and threatening to constrain the feminine. Under the very sign of transformation, the maternal restricts movement, oddly coming to be appropriated, this time, by the masculine. This demotion then reverses the assumptions made, as we have seen, about maternal transformation as a process of moving from independence to interdependence, unity to fluidity.

Irigaray might be read to mimic the exclusion of the feminine in order to point towards the exclusion already evident in Plato and, hence, within phallogocentric discourse as a whole. In my reading, however, Irigaray reinstalls the feminine at the expense of yet another shadow, that of the maternal. Elsewhere, seeking to reverse the unacknowledged matricide on which Western culture is based, she deliberately collapses the distinction between woman and mother. For example, her positing of woman as never complete can be read as a mimetic response to the mother's body, which she describes as having been "torn to pieces" between fathers and sons, leaving her fragmented and unable to speak her difference (Irigaray, 1991, p. 38). Her mimetic strategy is then a jubilant articulation of multiplicity in order to both reveal and reverse this fragmentation. The "maternal-feminine" (Irigaray, 1993a) becomes its own kind of fluid entity, irresolvable into one or the other, at all times both.

But this account erases the specificity of the maternal as a subject position. To make this point, I will draw on Irigaray's important treatment of the underrepresentation of the umbilical cord, the placenta, and the moment of severance between mother and child. Because the cut from the umbilicus marks her entry into motherhood, obscuring it leaves a specific void for the mother herself. The cut may, of course, restimulate infantile fantasies of guilt and abandonment, as well as prompt intense identification with the mutilated body of her own mother. But it also represents a specific loss for the mother; of an intimate connection with the fantasy-other within her. The child, Irigaray reminds us, is left with a kind of scar, an irreducible mark of birth in the form of the navel (Irigaray, 1991, p. 38). But the mother is left with no mark of the cut at all, nothing to represent her entry into this new intimacy. Perhaps her stretch marks and scars hint at this loss, but these marks of absence seem only to reinforce the cut's lack of representation. Irigaray reminds us not to collude in matricide. But remembering our mothers comes too late if the mother's "birth" has already been forgotten.

Perhaps this erasure is part of the vague unspeakable loss she experiences immediately after birth, and that haunts the early weeks and months of motherhood?

Moments after the birth, I feel a huge sense of elation. I want to run around the corridors telling people what I've done. I want someone to congratulate me, to be as astounded as I am at what I have achieved. I need to eat and then sleep. My labouring work is done. So preoccupied am I with the event of the birth itself that I struggle to remember that something was produced with all that labouring. I am shocked when the nurse wakes me up to inform me that the crying baby lying in the plastic tub by my bed is my baby, that this is disturbing the whole ward, and would I mind, by any chance, feeding it. I think why is she waking me? What I need most in the world now is to sleep. This is not my responsibility. Isn't someone supposed to take the baby away? As far as I am concerned, the baby has passed through me. I housed him, accommodated him, made space for him as an act of hospitality, a profound gesture of generosity. And then I birthed him. The cord was cut. My work was done. What more did he want of me?

Let us imagine the mother's "birth" from a kind of originary state of transformation by tracing the umbilical cord back to the placenta, called by Irigaray (1993b) "the first veil." Schwab (1994) explicates the connection of this metaphor with the early work of the feminist biologist, Hélène Rouch. Upturning our simplistic notions of the placenta as the organ that nourishes only the foetus, Rouch (1987) describes how the placenta benefits mother too, regulating her immune system so that the embryo is not rejected, whilst providing high enough levels of immunity to protect her from disease. In doing so, the placenta mediates, establishing a unique relationship between mother and foetus by maintaining a connection that is characterized by neither separation nor fusion.

From this view, the placenta holds both mother and foetus in tension, unresolved in terms of their boundaries, their beginnings and ends. What is more, the placenta is made of the genetic and cellular material of the embryo itself. In fact, most of the so-called "preembryo's" cells go toward creating the placenta and the membranes that surround the foetus, with the embryo itself forming from a tiny mass of cells known as the primitive streak. When the umbilical cord is cut, the baby is, strictly speaking, cut not from the mother's body, but from the placenta, something that was already part of itself. So the foetus was always already other within the mother. Passing through.

Cutting the umbilical cord for the mother terminates an intimate dialogue, one she will have to painstakingly rebuild with her child.

> My 10-day-old child talks to me. Really he does. Back and forth, back and forth, ahhhghoo, ahhhghoo, ahhhghoo. It's a secret. No one believes us, so we keep it that way. No, we are not dancing. We are speaking. Nor is this a manifestation of our sticky bond of love. He speaks to me. He pushes a sound out into the space between us and I receive it, and send it back. We're both delighted. It's so clear and simple. Sound moving across a space. That vital 10 inches that we need to focus. He's 10 days old. Really he is.

PART V: OI MOTHER KEEP YE' HAIR ON: FROM VEIL TO WIG

To sum up so far, writing about the transition from woman to mother seems to draw on metaphors about excess and otherness that have been previously used in discussing femininity and masculinity. On the one hand, the current popular literature unwittingly figures the feminine as the lost unified subject, and maternity as the messy interdependent excess, with transformation producing both a "new self" as well as prompting a kind of mourning for the "lost self." Here the lost feminine comes to be figured as a unified subject, traditionally associated with the masculine, while maternity is understood as excessive, messy, and interdependent, covering over the loss of what we think we once had.

But to call this process "transformative" smooths over a very rough passage. "Transformation" suggests a magical movement from one state to another. But the transition to motherhood entails a certain horror; disintegration–the birth of a state of being excessive to unity, of being a subject-in-process/on trial–is not exactly pleasant. Yet this unpleasant state also has creative potential, as we saw in Kraemer's work, who articulates this in psychoanalytic terms, as well as Kristeva.

It is logical then to turn to Irigaray. For one thing, she uses the notion of transformation to figure the feminine itself. For another, her whole strategy is to try to release the creative potential of restrictive practices and discourses through engagement rather than critique (you could say this is what mothers do on a daily basis!). At the same time, however, Irigaray runs this argument the other way, which I believe does not necessarily help. Although she works hard to rescue mothers from their silenced and unrepresented position, I think she ends up associating motherhood with the unified (which in her terms means ossified and also masculine) figure, against femininity which is seen as a kind of jubilant excess. Of course, through her mimetic strategies, Irigaray's celebration of excess is not entirely a simple valuing of one thing over the other. It is her way of doing something creative with what little we've got, in order to reveal the paucity of a space and language left for women to operate in. But when the maternal is associated with ossification, lack of fluidity or movement, it is left even more unrepresented than before. Although Irigaray does not address the process of becoming a mother from the perspective of the mother (hers is mostly a daughter's perspective) or moving from singularity to a relation with the child, she uses notions of transformation as a way of articulating the maternal-feminine–a kind of composite woman-mother who must resist the pitfalls of motherhood in order to retain a relation with fluidity (i.e., femininity). So something is left unspoken in her work about maternal subjectivity, about the transition to motherhood, and about loss.

We need, I am suggesting, to move away from a simple reliance on the notion of transformation as a way of dealing with the transition to motherhood. Keeping in mind that, as I said earlier, "a transformation" is an archaic term for "a woman's wig," I want to use wigs as a metaphor to address the problem of holding onto the intransigent or resistant aspects of transformation—the way it contains the notion that we both can and can't change and also of going over the same ground as a way of bringing something new into being, much in keeping with Irigaray. To do so, I first return to Irigaray's reading of the placenta as a veil and then move from veils to wigs. Her use of the term veil is, of course, a reappropriation of that which has for centuries been a site for the control of women's sexual desire. As a covering for women's hair in Judaism and Islam, it has signaled modesty, sexual maturity, and consent to the patriarchal order that makes woman man's possession (Koppelman, 1996).

> Some years of my childhood are dominated by my sister's hair. It is matted, unruly, knotted, wiry, rude. My mother runs after her with a comb in her hand. Her daughter must be brought under control. Her hair is the site of the family's shame. Her Jewish hair. How beautiful it is now. Soft, silky, naturally streaked blond. Her hair assimilated all by itself! Mine, like Christopher Robin's, so straight and compliant, has grown a little ruder over the years. I have allowed it to recently, since having children, and as they say, "letting myself go." It no longer needs to be cropped, canceling out a passing comment that still festers; that I don't look like anything in particular, just the Jewish girl next door.

In her analysis of veils and wigs in Jewish history, Leila Bronner (1993) locates the moment in the 16th century when Jewish women stopped veiling their hair and donned wigs instead. The challenge to veiling came from the women themselves. Wanting to emulate French fashion, they convinced the upholders of rabbinical law that wearing a wig was the same as wearing a veil. (After the resulting controversy, some of the most orthodox women took to wearing wigs, which they then covered with a veil—just to make sure.) In some ways, this push towards the acceptance of wig wearing within Jewish law could be seen as assimilation to the dominant cultural practices at the time. But there is something equally delightful about the notion that Jewish women, whose hair was seen within their own cultural context as dangerously sexual, found a way around this suppression by covering their hair with someone else's hair, "fake" hair to mimic their own. So long as their own hair was discreetly hidden, they could flaunt someone else's, as it wasn't technically hair.

Unlike the veil, the wig, thus historically situated, then allows us to play with the notion of transformation itself and to return to that difficult binary: femininity/maternity. Like masks, wigs are odd cultural objects, working their effects not through a suspension of disbelief but through an engagement with their artificiality. We are not asked to believe that the wig is "real hair," but we engage with it as if it were real all the same. The "me/not me" quality of this play is reminiscent of the function of Winnicott's transitional object. The wig does its work through the ability to get close to real hair and the simultaneous exposure of its own fakeness. Wigs, therefore, allow a process of mimesis to occur.

"One must," writes Irigaray (1985b, p. 76), "assume the feminine role deliberately." Mimesis defines her strategy of reappropriation, as opposed to "just playing the game,""which means already to convert a form of subordination into an affirmation and thus to begin to thwart it...To play with mimesis is thus, for a woman, to try to recover the place of her exploitation by discourse, without allowing herself to be simply reduced to it" (Irigaray, 1985b, p. 76). Mimesis is close to parody, in which parroting becomes a commentary on what is being parroted, not merely a misguided reappropriation. At another level, however, mimesis can also be understood as allowing a new way of being to emerge, through the parodic imitation of a tired discourse, just as both actors and children can "go through the motions" in order to bring on an "authentic" emotion. Mimesis, exceeding that which is being parodied, could be understood as a more anarchic reappropriation, a subversion that allows something altogether different to emerge.

In its mimesis, can motherhood also subvert? Among the various discourses on maternity, there is, I have been saying, a dialectic that understands motherhood as either a movement from unity towards fluidity, or the opposite, the moment that fixes fluidity in relation to the unity of the child. Wanting to move beyond matter, whilst being caught by this impossibility, I have tried to show that transformation itself contains this double allegiance to materiality. Like the transformation from veil to wig, the shift to motherhood may fix or free, trap or liberate. In all likelihood, it does both. If mimesis produces a kind of creative excess, as it seems to in wig wearing, then transformation points towards something that is excessive to this dialectic: the woman becoming mother. In liberating as it binds, motherhood is perhaps closer to the repetitive but also creative motion of mimesis than to the magical transformation of caterpillar into butterfly.

REFERENCES

Benjamin, J. (1995), *Like Subjects, Love Objects: Essays on Recognition and Difference.* Cambridge, MA: Harvard University Press.

Bibring, G. L., Dwyer, T. F., Huntington, D. S., & Valenstein, A. F. (1961), A study of the psychological processes in pregnancy and of the earliest mother-child relationship–I. Some propositions and comments. *Psychoanaly. St. Child,* 16:9–24.

Blau DuPlessis, R. (1990), For the Etruscans. In: *The Pink Guitar: Writing as Feminist Practice.* New York: Routledge, pp. 1–19.

Bronner L. L. (1993), From veil to wig–Jewish women's hair covering. *Judaism.,* 42.4:465–477.

Buchanan, A. J. (2003), *Mother Shock: Loving Every (Other) Minute of It.* New York: Seal Press.

Butler, J. (1994), Bodies that matter. In: *Engaging with Irigaray,* ed. C. Burke, N. Schor, & M. Whitford. New York: Columbia University Press, pp. 141–173.

Carle, E. (1969), *The Very Hungry Caterpillar.* New York: World Pub.

Cusk, R. (2001), *A Life's Work: On Becoming a Mother.* London: Forth Estate.

Enright, A. (2004), *Making Babies: Stumbling Into Motherhood.* London: Jonathan Cape.

Figes, K. (1998), *Life After Birth.* London: Viking.

Hogue, C. (2004), *To Go Back to the Idea of Process: Form, Feminism and Kathleen Fraser's Poetry.* Rutgers, NJ: The State University of New Jersey. 21 May 2004 <http://english.rutgers.edu/fraser.htm#N_7>.

Irigaray, L. (1985a), *Speculum of the Other Woman,* trans. C. G. Gill. New York: Cornell University Press.

_____ (1985b), *This Sex Which Is Not One,* trans. C. Porter & C. Burke. Ithaca, NY: Cornell University Press.

_____ (1991), The bodily encounter with the mother. In: *The Irigaray Reader,* ed. M. Whitford, trans. D. Macey. Oxford: Basil Blackwell, pp. 34–46.

_____ (1993a), *An Ethics of Sexual Difference,* trans. C. Burke & G. Gill. Ithaca, NY: Cornell University Press.

_____ (1993b), *Sexes and Genealogies,* trans. G. C. Gill. New York: Columbia University.

Juhasz, S. (2003), Mother-writing and the narrative of maternal subjectivity. *Studies in Sexuality,* 4: 395–425.

Kraemer, S. (1996), "Betwixt the dark and the daylight" of maternal subjectivity: Meditations on the threshold. *Psychoanal. Dial.,* 6:765–791.

Kristeva, J. (1975), *Desire in Language,* trans. T. Gora, A. Jardine, & L Roudiez, ed. L. Roudiez. New York: Columbia University Press.

_____ (1997), Stabat Mater. In: *The Kristeva Reader,* ed. T. Moi. Oxford, England: Blackwell, 1986.

_____ (1987), Freud and love: Treatment and its discontents. In: *Tales of Love,* trans. L. Roudiez. New York: Columbia University Press, pp. 21–56.

Koppelman, C. (1996), The politics of hair. *Frontiers,* 17.2:87–88.

Levinas, E. (1969) *Totality and Infinity: An Essay on Exteriority,* trans. A. Lingis. Pittsburgh, PA: Duquesne University Press.

Oliver, K. (1993), Julia Kristeva's outlaw ethics. In: *Ethics, Politics, and Difference in Julia Kristeva's Writing,* ed. K. Oliver. New York: Routledge, pp. 1–22.

Oxford English Dictionary. (1989), 2nd ed. Oxford, UK: Clarendon.

Parker, R. (1997), The production and purposes of maternal ambivalence. In: *Mothering and Ambivalence,* ed. W. Hollway & B. Featherstone. London: Routledge, pp. 17–36.

Plato. (1977), *Timaeus and Critias,* trans. D. Lee. Harmondsworth, London: Penguin.

Raphael-Leff, J. (2003), Where the wild things are. In: *Parent-Infant Psychodynamics: Wild Things, Mirrors and Ghosts,* ed. J. Raphael-Leff. London: Whurr, pp. 54–69.

Rouche, H. (1987), Le placenta comme tiers. *Languages,* 85:75.

Ruddick, S. (1989), *Maternal Thinking: Towards a Politics of Peace.* London: Women's Press.

Schwab, G. M. (1994), Mother's body, father's tongue: Mediation and the symbolic order. In: *Engaging With Irigaray,* ed. C. Burke, N. Schor, & M. Whitford. New York: Columbia University Press, pp. 351–378.

Stern, D. (1998), *The Motherhood Constellation.* London: H. Karnac (Books) Ltd.

Wolf, N. (2001), *Misconceptions: Truth, Lies and the Unexpected on the Journey to Motherhood.* London: Chatto & Windus.

Centre for Psychosocial Studies
School of Psychology
Birkbeck, University of London
Malet Street
London WC1E 7HX

What Exactly *Is* the Transformation of Motherhood? Commentary on Lisa Baraitser's Paper

Daphne de Marneffe, Ph.D.

Baraitser's novel articulation of the "unity/fluidity" dialectic permits a rethinking of the ways that maternal desire has been oversimplified in both psychoanalytic theory and cultural life. In this discussion, I reflect on how Baraitser's various innovative arguments contribute to a fuller, more complex account of maternal subjectivity. In particular, via the metaphor of veil and wig, she explores the simultaneously freeing and constraining aspects of motherhood and casts new light on the question of how a mother's encounter with her child radically changes her relationship to herself and others.

Lisa Baraitser, in her paper "Oi mother, Keep Ye' Hair On! Impossible Transformations of Maternal Subjectivity," has shown us a number of directions in which psychoanalytic thinking about motherhood now needs to go. First, she has identified a powerful theme woven throughout contemporary conversation about motherhood, which she calls the "unity/fluidity dialectic." Second, she has raised important questions about psychoanalytic views of maternal subjectivity. Third, through her vivid metaphor of veil and wig, she has given us a suitably complex way to think about the simultaneously binding and freeing aspects of mothering and about psychological change itself. Parsing these themes under the light of her subtle and generous intellect, Baraitser helps us to apply them to our work with patients and consider their impact on the wider social situation of mothers.

Baraitser begins by identifying a tendency in recent mothers' memoirs, by Naomi Wolf and Rachel Cusk among others, to see the move to motherhood as a move toward formlessness. In these accounts, the premotherhood feminine self is characterized by clear boundaries and a solidity that the interdependent "messier" maternal self lacks. The firmly boundaried prematernal self is solid only in retrospect–indeed, created only in retrospect–and becomes the focal point of mourning and a sense of loss.

Central to Baraitser's point is how mobile such characterizations are. Past feminist and psychoanalytic writings have at times treated motherhood as something of an end of development, static and nonprogressive. By contrast, in the newer twist on the unity/fluidity dialectic, "it is the maternal, instead of the feminine, that is now being relegated beyond unity" (p. 219, this issue). The familiar gendered attribution of unity to male and fluidity to female also shifts; now women, like men, are construed as clearly boundaried, and it is mothers who are seen as "unthematizable excess."

In our eagerness to install maternity at one end of the fluidity/unity spectrum, Baraitser suggests, we oversimplify the nature and complexity of maternal desire. Baraitser asserts the "need to understand maternal subjectivity as a fundamentally changed state," involving "substantial shifts in both material and semiotic conditions" that prompt "a renewed configuration of self" (p. 221, this issue). Recent feminist psychoanalytic theorists have rightly recognized a mother's needs and desires as separate and separable from the child's. But in Baraitser's view, in our focus on these separate interests, we may unwittingly "lose sight of the way maternal subjectivity is structured through the relation to the child." "I would argue instead," she writes, "that one's subjectivity as a mother is precisely what emerges through this real and imagined relation" (p. 10).

How might we understand the maternal subjectivity that emerges through this real and imagined relation? Baraitser spends the rest of her paper reflecting on that question in various ways: contemplating the function of "mother writing" in the construction of a maternal self, mining pregnancy (the placenta, the umbilicus) for images that capture the mother's unique position vis à vis her child, and investigating the transition from woman to mother in light of the metaphor of veil and wig.

At its core, it seems to me, Baraitser is saying that a mother's relation to her child structures a different consciousness, and this has to do with the way in which the mother experiences her desire to relate to her child *as her own desire.* A mother does not abdicate her personality and melt into her child. Nor does she continue to identify her "self" so cleanly with her independent goals and desires. She comes to experience fulfilling and satisfying her *child's* desire as one of her most powerful desires *for herself.* Kristeva (1986) "understands this being-for-another not as a description of a self-abnegating masochistic femininity, but as the name for the subject whose ability to put herself aside inherently challenges the whole symbolic system" (p. 223, this issue). I'm not sure "put herself aside" entirely covers it. It is also the way her love for the child makes her *want* to put herself aside, and the way that putting herself aside to care for her child *paradoxically fulfills her.* But Kristeva's point, with which Baraitser and I both agree, is that having a child changes a woman's relation to herself and others in a way that has implications for how we think about the self.

One psychoanalytic truism about the mother–child relationship is that it requires a third to break up its hothouse intensity and introduce the child to reality itself. As I have discussed at length elsewhere (de Marneffe, 2004), this view reflects biases about a mother's inability to negotiate varying psychological positions in a way that provides her baby or child with the experience of difference. In an important passage, Baraitser reflects:

> Psychoanalysis variously configures maternal desire as the desire for the missing penis, the longed for union with the imaginary mother, or the desire for the 'father' (or lover, work, politics–whatever takes the mother away from the child) which plays a vital function in breaking up the dyad with the child. If the focus shifts from the child's psychic health to the mother's, it may be possible to consider how maternal desire, proceeding from the direct encounter with the child, fundamentally changes the way we mothers feel and think about our partners

> and lovers, work and politics, mothers and ourselves [p. 224, this issue].

I have found that even in feminist iterations of the need for the third, where the father is no longer the crucial player, a mother is enjoined to hold fast to her independent aims ("work, politics–whatever takes the mother away from the child"), so as not to be lured into a disorientingly regressive merger with her child. Into this discussion, Baraitser injects an innovative possibility: "the child's *otherness* can function as a third term for the mother, and therefore prevent the regressive pull of the mother-infant dyad whilst allowing us to understand her desire as the desire for the child" (p. 224, this issue). Here Baraitser draws upon a little-theorized but powerful aspect of what women experience when they become mothers, that is, the stunning otherness of the baby. We have an overwhelming sense that the baby has come from somewhere, but we don't know quite where. Before we become familiar with states of melding love or blissful synchrony or even disruption and repair, we come face to face with another person to whose care we need–and desire–to bring our personal ingenuity and resources. A woman's experience of *wanting* to care for her child changes *her.* Baraitser rightfully contests the notion that the mother's desire for the child can be summed up as a "regressive pull" and searches for a way to conceptualize maternal subjectivity that does justice both to the mother's sense of adult autonomy and utter interdependence, her love and aggression, freedom and constraint. Baraitser has not entirely worked out how a mother's subjectivity is structured through the relation to the child–who among us has?–but she has offered some very useful insights to pursue.

A maternal position that embraces contradictions, as Baraitser notes, is a difficult one for many women to occupy. She writes:

> [A]lthough we constantly allude to the felt experience that we are "transformed" through our relations with our children, we are perhaps fearful of dwelling on how or why, because in doing so, we may jettison the precious connection we have with the world beyond our babies. We fear we will fall into a regressive symbiotic relationship with our children, to their and our own detriment [p. 224, this issue].

The very rhetoric of transformation can conceal a resistance to change, Baraitser suggests, and obscure the truly radical shifts that motherhood brings on. We not only fear that we will fall into a regressive (unhealthy, insular) relation with our children. We are also confused about what or who our "self" is now that our energies and values are fundamentally redirected. We wonder whether we will be the same people, happy in the same jobs or marriages or priorities, if we fully open ourselves to experiencing the changes we sense are occurring.

In this light, the move from unity to fluidity described by Wolf or Cusk can function to organize and contain, to place in a progressive narrative, the unforeseen and destabilizing changes in perception and consciousness that accompany becoming a mother. Certainly, it is via the very construction of a previous "solid" self that we create the mothering relation as regressive abyss. And that construction serves a defensive function, subtly devaluing the real changes we experience. Those given to construing these dilemmas in purely political terms take this narrative of the move from solidity to chaos as a basis for calls for political changes that will result in the restoration of lost autonomy. In my view, political changes can never fully solve the problem of mother's lost autonomy, precisely because motherhood also involves an inward psychological change in orientation. At the same time, the larger social, economic costs of motherhood are glaringly apparent to women. Sociologists have documented that the impediment to advancement is no longer gender but parenthood (Hochschild, 1997; Crittenden, 2001). If a woman is willing to do "what a man does" in the workforce, she largely escapes discrimination. Thus, in a very real way, one can maintain one's "unity," one's solid (masculine or feminine) self, as long as one doesn't disrupt one's economic or psychological condition by becoming a mother.

Faced with such social conditions, women try to find a way to mother that does not compromise their standing as workers or as autonomous adults. The boundaried feminine self of which Baraitser writes provides one way to consolidate a sense of autonomy. At times I've wondered if the invidious comparison of the now "messy, interdependent" mother to the formerly independent woman plays itself out in women's images of their bodies. I am struck, for instance, by the contemporary anxiety about "losing one's sexuality" when one becomes a mother. This is a frequent topic in glossy magazines, but research studies document it too (Bell, 2005). Implicit in this narrative is a vision of desirable femininity, of assiduously maintained feminine shape, which exists in sharp contrast to the shapeless mass of the maternal body. Those things that a woman fears she's lost when she becomes a mother–self-control, self-determination, unitary focus, sleekness, activity–are precisely those things prescribed to cure her of her maternal body shape. The idea that a maternal body might be sexually desirable or desiring is scarcely entertained. Yes, many women temporarily lose their sex drive and their figures in the hazy aftermath of a baby's birth, but there is this notion that without extraordinarily *hard work,* without a disciplined regimen for *regaining what one has lost,* a woman falls off the edge of the sexual earth, never to return.

The tendency to identify motherhood with a sort of formlessness also contributes to the almost defensively individualistic way in which some women come to view themselves (see Layton, 2004, for a fascinating description of "defensive autonomy"). They feel a sense of pride and accomplishment at not feeling too needy or desirous of a partner or children, as if they have mastered a female weakness. One patient, Caroline, felt torn between what she perceived as "mature, goal-directed activity (work) on the one hand versus an amorphous mass of feelings (motherhood) on the other" (de Marneffe, 2004, p. 58). To some women, the desires associated with wanting to mother feel uncontrolled, overwhelming, and regressive, emotionally and politically. This is an issue I have tried to understand in my own clinical and theoretical work, and Baraitser's articulation of the unity/fluidity dialectic provides a compelling explanatory framework.

In discussing the transition of woman to mother, Baraitser's most original contribution may be her use the metaphor of the veil and wig. Baraitser voices reservations about Irigaray's treatment of specifically maternal subjectivity, but she demonstrates that the latter's approach is well suited to characterizing the contradictions of transformation. Irigaray's "whole strategy is to try to release the creative potential of restrictive practices and discourses through engagement rather than critique." As Baraitser trenchantly observes, "you could say this is what mothers do on a daily basis!" (p. 234, this issue).

Irigaray's concept of mimesis gives us a position from which to subvert the politically loaded feminine role, even as we engage in it.

It addresses the feminine—and feminist—quandary of how a person can play the role of mother while retaining her freedom of thought. For me, the implication of parody or parroting in the idea of mimesis is not its most important feature, at least where motherhood is concerned. The more interesting question is how we assume biological, historical, and social roles and make them our own; how we use structures creatively to express vital, authentic aspects of personality. Here, I may be straying from Baraitser's intention, because I sense there is something important to her about the parroting aspect—the way, for instance, that transformation "simultaneously signals a movement toward change and exposes its own mimetic strategy, showing itself up as a fake" (p. 227, this issue)—that I haven't quite grasped. Still, at the risk of sounding a bit too earnest for what Baraitser had in mind, I want to explore some potential clinical and social implications of her work.

As I understand it, in taking on motherhood, we don, like a wig, an array of sedimented ideas about who we are without having the slightest notion, yet, of who we ourselves are as mothers. We "mime" motherhood, we act the part, and the part requires the adoption of certain roles—caretaker, diaper changer, breastfeeder, walker-of-the-floors at night—which are saturated with ideological and historical meanings about mothering, womanhood, nurturing, self-sacrifice, and so on. At the same time, in the process of becoming mother, a new way of being emerges, attended by duress and disorientation, discovery and pleasure, aliveness and growth.

It is exactly in the personal experiencing of given social forms that meaning is created. Psychic development itself fundamentally involves the working over of old forms to bring new organization and experience into being. Loewald's (1980, 1988) writings portray this aspect of growth more eloquently and persuasively than any others I've read. A new mother's life is narrowed to a repetitive round of care-giving tasks and a constricted universe of preoccupations. She is also taking her place in an entire sociocultural history and biological cycle of motherhood. But it is what she does with those conditions, in their specificity and in the new, creative relation with her child, that gives rise to her individual experience of mothering—its subjective quality, its meaning, its contribution to her further development, and as Baraitser movingly alludes to, her sense of creativity and hope.

If there is anything that is lost in the attention to mimesis's aspect of parody, it is the intense *affect* involved in becoming a mother, or for that matter, in displaying one's feminine charms in a wig. "The challenge to veiling came from the women themselves ... Jewish women, whose hair was seen within their own cultural context as dangerously sexual, found a way around this suppression by covering their hair with someone else's hair" (p. 236, this issue). This creative use of available cultural forms simultaneously fulfills social expectations of modesty *and* expresses an intense, fleshly desire to be attractive, to be fashionable, to be noticed and responded to. That is the very genius of the solution. Similarly, the transition to motherhood inevitably involves a woman in various cultural scripts, but it also provides a means for expressing her individuality, interests, and desires.

In Baraitser's article, affect comes to the fore in her passages about birth and the postpartum phase. If there is one thing I might have wished for, it is that Baraitser had brought her discussion of transformation's "double allegiance to materiality" back around to her own experience of becoming a mother. That said, her descriptions stand on their own as beautifully conveyed moments of lived experience. Through them, she seeks both to capture the power of her experiences and to question the goal of their containment in a coherent written form.

In this connection, Baraitser discusses Juhasz's concept of "mother-writing." I don't find Juhasz's goal of writing to organize a maternal self that seems "coherent, viable, or to possess continuity" (p. 225, this issue) to be as suspect as Baraitser does. "Coherence" need not signify the staking out of "an" identity; it can also signal a narrator's desire to relate her experience in a way that is comprehensible and helpful to the reader. One could argue that Juhasz's goal of coherence prematurely forecloses "motherhood's radical potential to disturb the self," but this is a matter of degree. Some texts assert the coherence of maternal identity, just as some refuse any narrative coherence at all (the multitude of mothering blogs on the Internet provide a ready example). Different mother-writers may have different needs for conceiving of what they do in terms of coherence, but all are trying to make meaning of their situation, engaging in the psychological task of standing apart from their immediate experience at the same time they are immersed in it.

This is akin to what we aim for in therapy. Analogous to the therapist, the writer's ability to navigate porousness and closure helps the reader. If complexity is sacrificed to coherence, the reader can't trust the writer. That is the problem with so much pop psychology; the reader knows the world isn't so simple. But if the writer assumes too little authority, the reader is left dangling. For me, what is useful in Baraitser's paper, as in Kristeva's (1986) "Stabat Mater," is seeing how a thinker navigates the passage from her own powerful physical and emotional experience to an understanding of it. Their writings give me a map and an inspiration for making a similar passage myself.

Baraitser's essay provides a psychological angle on some of the same insights that more politically inclined writers are also grasping toward. Recently Judith Stadtman Tucker, the editor of The Mothers' Movement Online, wrote an essay entitled, "The New Future of Motherhood" (2005). She argued that activists in the mother's movement should move away from the narrative of motherhood as a "job." Instead, she suggests,

> looking at motherhood as a *relationship* [emphasis mine] could shift the dialog in the right direction. Unlike jobs, relationships aren't results oriented–they're process oriented; they evolve. So instead of looking at child-rearing as a project and children as blank slates on which mothers inscribe the lines of success or failure, we can begin to consider the ways children are active participants in their own upbringing. Also, it's safe to assume all relationships are unique, since every relationship encompasses all the unique qualities and personal histories two individuals bring into the mix–in other words, it's unrealistic to suggest that all caring mothers should and do feel exactly the same way about the same things, even though they all share the experience of being in relationship with children.

I am heartened that mainstream political discussion has begun, finally, to incorporate the emotional complexity of maternal subjectivity and the mother-child relationship. Tucker (2005), like Baraitser, is concerned with the question of *what* exactly changes when women become mothers. Both are concerned with the ways that motherhood has its freedoms and its constrictions, psychological and social. And both ultimately point us toward the value of an individual's creative act of making meaning, and the impossibility and undesirability of prescribing its form. As we question more static pictures of motherhood–whether as "job," or "identity," or even as "fluidity" or "unity"–we open up a political and psychological conversation guided less by prescriptions and linear developmental norms and more by individuality, play, and paradox. This is a conversation to which Baraitser has added, with great charm and intelligence.

REFERENCES

Bell, L. (2005), Objects of Affection, Subjects of Desire: Twenty-Something Women and the Contradictions of Sexuality. Unpublished doctoral dissertation, University of California at Berkeley.

Crittenden, A. (2001), *The Price of Motherhood: Why the Most Important Job in the World is Still the Least Valued.* New York: Metropolitan Books.

Cusk, R. (2001), *A Life's Work: On Becoming a Mother.* New York: Picador.

de Marneffe, D. (2004), *Maternal Desire: On Children, Love, and the Inner Life.* New York: Little, Brown.

Hochschild, A. (1997), *The Time Bind: When Work Becomes Home and Home Becomes Work.* New York: Metropolitan Books.

Kristeva, J. (1986), Stabat Mater. In: *The Kristeva Reader,* ed. T. Moi. New York: Columbia University Press, pp. 161–86.

Layton, L. (2004), Working Nine to Nine: The New Women of Prime Time. *Studies in Gender & Sexuality,* 5:351–69.

Loewald, H. (1980), *Papers on Psychoanalysis.* New Haven, CT: Yale University Press.

_____ (1988), *Sublimation: Inquiries into Theoretical Psychoanalysis.* New Haven, CT: Yale University Press.

Tucker, J. S. (2005), The New Future of Motherhood. *Mothers Movement Online.* 1 Jun. 2005 <http://www.mothersmovement.org>.

Wolf, N. (2001), *Misconceptions: Truth, Lies, and the Unexpected Journey to Motherhood.* New York: Doubleday.

Reply to Commentaries

Lisa Baraitser, Ph.D.

I am grateful to Daphne de Marneffe for her sensitive and informed reading of my paper. She takes what is both emergent and latent in the piece and clarifies my argument, strengthening a tentative through-line that seeks to illuminate how maternal consciousness is structured, in part, around a relation with a child, before extending its implications to the wider social situation of mothers and to the psychotherapeutic project of psychic and emotional change. It is a rare pleasure to have one's thoughts understood, clarified, and extended in such a way.

De Marneffe helpfully summarizes the contribution of the paper as falling into three discrete areas: the deconstruction of the "unity/fluidity" dialectic as a contemporary way of speaking about the transition to motherhood; my discussion of psychoanalytic notions of maternal subjectivity that I believe run into difficulties when the mother is unwittingly returned to her function as object in the developing world of the child, or her subjectivity is figured as precisely what lies beyond her child; and my use of the metaphor of the wig as a way to understand the essential paradox of maternal transformation.

I am grateful, in particular, for her inventive reformulation of mimesis towards the end of her commentary, as a way in which we inhabit biological, social, and historical roles, whilst making them our own. My figure of the wig was underdeveloped. I had an intuitive sense that it might be useful but was unable to fully work through how it could be utilized to help think about maternal transformation. In de Marneffe's view, the constrictions of various representations and constructions of motherhood obviously cannot be ignored or easily sidestepped. The task, however, is precisely not to seek to get around such representations but to engage them head on, so that they can convey, in her words "vital, authentic aspects of personality" (p. 247, this issue). I liked, especially, her fleshing out of the idea that we don, like wigs, an "array of sedimented ideas about who we are without having the slightest notion, yet, of who we ourselves are as mothers" (p. 247, this issue). This comment gives a tragic–comic spin to motherhood, capturing some of the desperate absurdity of embarking, as so many of us do, on an encounter that is of such vital importance to the child, without having any idea of what we are doing and who we are in the doing. However, going through the motions of motherhood, which may include engaging with activities traditionally invested as "feminine" (nurturing, self-sacrifice), can force through a new way of being ourselves, without this "newness" being uncoupled from the ideological and historical meanings that motherhood has accrued. In other words, something new does emerge in the process but "forced" by a relation to what is already available for identification. This exactly encapsulates my attempt to articulate the dual freeing and constraining aspects of "transformation" and pushes my rather abstract formulation through to an engagement with the concrete tasks of mothering. I share with de Marneffe an understanding that it is through the very mundane tasks and roles of motherhood ("caretaker, diaper changer, breastfeeder, walker-of-the-floors at night" [p. 247, this issue]) that new subjectivities emerge.

De Marneffe also extends my thinking by picking up on the social manifestations of the tension I have tried to identify between representations (including self-representations) of women as unitary and mothers as fluid or the other way around. Observing that "desires associated with wanting to mother feel uncontrolled, overwhelming, and regressive, emotionally and politically" (p. 246, this issue), she looks at the pressures women feel to regain control over the boundaries of our bodies after childbirth, as if acquiescing to them might shore up the edges of the self. My sense is that whilst this effort expresses one pole of the dialectic I tried to identify, motherhood is also shadowed by the other, doubled pole: Irigaray's marking of the maternal as a "hardening" around the unity of the child and the feminine as the condition of transformation itself. The experience of motherhood as messy interdependence is paradoxically coupled with a profound sense of restriction and loss of movement. As de Marneffe says, many women who become mothers fear they have lost "self-control, self-determination, unitary focus, sleekness, *activity*" (p. 246, this issue, emphasis added). This state of mind is a mixed bag in which many of the anxieties about femininity (am I singular or multiple, unitary or fluid, self-determined or relational?) surface through the shift in subjectivity that motherhood prompts. These anxieties are perhaps defended against through reidentifying as quickly as possible with a "feminine" body shape in which a fantasy that one can both have edges *and* be infinitely fluid can be maintained. In my view, motherhood threatens to give the lie to such a fantasy, which is one reason why it can be such an enormously emotional and distressing period in a woman's life.

I would like to use the remainder of this space to think through in more detail one of the core issues de Marneffe identifies in my paper. It appears to me that we share a concern with articulating a specifically maternal subjectivity that needs to be thought of in relational terms; through a relation, that is, with the child. I put forward a suggestion that the child's otherness can function as a third term for the mother, allowing her access to otherness that also gives rise to the possibilities of an emergent maternal subjectivity. de Marneffe rightly notes that I have not entirely worked out how the mother's subjectivity is structured through the relation to the child, and although she kindly acknowledges "who among us has?" (p. 244, this issue), I would like to risk it and have another go. What I am attempting to do here is think again about how the child's otherness may function for the mother and what the implications are for maternal love, maternal desire, and, ultimately, maternal subjectivity.

de Marneffe focuses on a notion of maternal desire, in which the "mother experiences her desire to relate to her child *as her own desire*" (p. 243, this issue). If I have understood her correctly, the mother's subjectivity neither disappears in relation to her child's developing subjectivity nor needs to be rigidly shored up through the mother's relation to the world beyond her child. Instead, her desire to relate to her child can be recuperated "as one of her most powerful desires *for herself*" (p. 243, this issue). In reclaiming this desire as her own, the implication is that the mother can emerge as a desirous subject in her own right, but without losing sight of the role of the child in structuring such a subjectivity. It is not that the mother's desire is premised on the third term, the "father," but her desire to be with the child, to mother the child, gives rise to a desiring maternal subject. This, I believe, is the main theme of de Marneffe's recent book, *Maternal Desire: On Children, Love, and the Inner Life* (de Marneffe, 2004). I would, therefore, like to briefly explore the implications of such a notion of maternal desire by thinking through the distinction between maternal love and maternal desire. In doing so, I hope the issue of the child's "otherness" is addressed more thoroughly than in my original paper, as maternal subjectivity becomes impossible to imagine without an experience of what I would call "maternal alterity" (a mother's experience of the other that is her child).

I start from the perspective that we have become anxious about articulating both maternal love and maternal desire. As soon as the mother is thought about as a loving subject, she appears to lose her precious status as a desirous, speaking subject with access to the symbolic. She appears to fall into a romanticized and sickly union with her child. And yet, as soon as she is configured as desirous, we seem to lose hold of our ability to articulate maternal love as something stemming from the child and forming a core part of maternal subjectivity rather than a manifestation of either narcissism or love for our own idealized mothers. In other words, we miss the point that both love and desire require a relation to an other rather than an internal object that the other always stands in for.

Some of the difficulty arises out of an inevitable confusion and conflation of love and desire. And yet, from a psychoanalytic viewpoint, these key elements of subjectivity (and sexuality) are seen to unfold at different points and are structured differently, prompting a need to distinguish, perhaps between maternal love and maternal desire in adult life.

In my understanding, psychoanalysis counts one, two, three. Three is the figure for the Oedipal moment of desire. Two is the figure for the dyad, for love, which appears through primary narcissism and identification. One is the figure for either the autoerotic infant or the fantasy of wholeness through union or merger with the mother. Both love and desire require a gap, what Kristeva calls an "emptiness" (Kristeva, 1987, p. 24), suggesting that the not-yet-self must encounter a not-yet-other of some kind in order for either love or desire to arise. There must be a notional "two," a self and an other, for identification, even narcissistic identification to occur. Love is distinct from desire in that it is a dyadic condition that operates either through self-love or identification with the Other. In Lacanian terms, it is an imaginary phenomenon (Lacan, 1953–1954, p. 142), prior to entry into the symbolic. Desire is the product of a triadic structure, and signals, in Lacanian terms "the desire of the other's desire" (Lacan 1964, p. 235). It is the fact that the other desires (i.e., desires another) that gives rise to my desire.

I am aware that despite my wish to keep love and desire distinct and separate, it is not so easy. In fact, although Lacan appears to give us one of the most comprehensive accounts of the aetiology of love and desire, there is an entanglement between the two that can be seen in his work. He wants to figure love as belonging to the imaginary and desire as belonging to the symbolic. However, given that, in his view, we love only in order to be loved (Lacan, 1964, p. 253), we chase the fantasy of union with the loved one as much as we desire to become the object of the Other's desire. Both are an impossibility. In addition, as Evans has pointed out, given that desire is born out of the remainder between need and demand, and demand is always ultimately a demand for love, desire is the element of demand that cannot be satisfied, *which we may term love* (Evans, 1996, p. 104). So, love has a way of suffusing desire. Three has an uncanny way of becoming two.

Where is maternal desire and maternal love in all this? When de Marneffe talks of "maternal desire," she is describing the mother's desire to relate to her child. My sense is that we would need to understand what constitutes the third term in this configuration if we are to stay with the terminology of desire, rather than describing the mother's pull towards her child as a loving impulse.

When it comes to maternal desire in the psychoanalytic literature, it is certainly premised on the mother's relationship with a third term (be it actual or fantasized), articulated as the mother's desire for the phallus (as in Lacan), for her own mother (as in Kristeva), or other symbolic relations that take the mother away from the baby (as in Benjamin). Lacan describes the kind of love a woman feels for a child as the same as the masochistic jouissance that the female subject attains through gratifying another. Woman is always and only man's Other. She cannot have the phallus. She can only pretend to be the phallus, the object of man's desire and gratification (Lacan, 1958, p. 84). In other words, there is only maternal desire. In this reading, women desire to have children so they can continue to gain masochistic pleasure from being the object of another's desire. The child is the symbolic substitute for the missing penis that does not really satisfy her desire, despite having the child (Evans, 1996, p. 118). There is therefore no articulation of the specific loving feelings a mother has towards a child, only an articulation of her desire that is never satisfied by the actual child.

In Freud, we do see a clearer distinction between maternal love and maternal desire. Freud saw all parental love as deeply narcissistic (Freud, 1914, pp. 89–91). Parental love becomes a socially sanctioned form of narcissism, without the requirement to move to full object love. Desire for a child in women, on the other hand, is his well-known formulation of the desire for a substitute to make up for the longed-for penis (Freud, 1931, 1933). So we can see that a Freudian/Lacanian trajectory broadly understands love for a child as love for the self and desire for a child as the endless desire for the phallus. Either way, the child is a substitute for something else. Furthermore, I would argue, the child's alterity is not accounted for. If the child cannot be understood as an "other," then the mother also loses her access to maternal alterity and, I would argue, maternal subjectivity. For what is subjectivity if it has no relation to an other?

Kristeva comes closest to holding onto both identificatory love, desire, and otherness. She posits a "good" loving mother as a desiring mother, as the third term is necessary to rescue the child from a dangerous entanglement with the loving mother who looks only to her child. Kristeva (1987) famously warns:

> The loving mother, different from the caring and clinging mother, is someone who has an object of desire; beyond that, she has an other with relation to whom the child will serve as go-between. She will love her child with respect to that other, and it is through a discourse aimed at that Third Party that the child will be set up as "loved" for the other [p. 34].

The loving mother must "love" an other in order that the child can feel loved and can go on to love in their own right. The aetiology of love is made possible only through desire. In other words, the child will come to be able to love so long as the mother's "love" is actually desire for an another. However, although she is termed the "loving" mother, it is her ability to be a "desiring" mother, desiring of a third party and not the child, that is the factor that saves the child from being devoured by the clinging and caring mother. To this degree, love is love to the extent that it occurs through desire. For Kristeva, this comes about because of the mother's curious straddling of the biological and social. She exists at the border of the two, enabling her to make a commitment to the engendering of the species whilst also necessarily existing as a speaking subject.

However, although Kristeva is surely right in insisting that the mother must be understood as desirous in order that she exist within the symbolic at all, this again leaves love in the realms of either narcissism or idealization. Maternal love, therefore, gets folded back on itself as either love for the self or love for (ultimately) one's own mother, thereby collapsing the distance between mother and child. Again the child's alterity is negated and with it the specificity of maternal love for a child. Because desire is always chasing something unrecoverable that the other stands in for, both the child and maternal love in its specificity slip out of sight. For me, this slippage begs the question "why love a child?" Why stay alongside this crying, tantruming, questioning, demanding, enigmatic, unpredictable other, when we could find plenty of other stand-ins for our narcissism and idealization?

My suggestion, when I refer to the child's otherness as standing in for the third, is that we hold onto a notion of love that can be thought of "otherwise" than a discourse of narcissism and idealization in order to account for the peculiar ethical commitment maternal love entails. Perhaps maternal love can provide a bridge back to the mother's self-experience but via her specific relationship with the child as other. From this view, the child's alterity offers the mother something. But contrary to the notion that through love we try to attain "wholeness" by closing the gap between self and other–in itself a hopeless attempt to close the inherent split on which subjectivity is founded–perhaps we can work this idea the other way round. Perhaps we can think about how, in moments when the inherent splitting of the self is experienced, something we may call maternal love can emerge. Through the mundane tasks of mothering that de Marneffe listed in her commentary, through the moments of despair

Kraemer (1996) alludes to in the middle of the night, when the mother not only deals with the child's projections but with her own feelings about not being able to contain them and her guilt when she knows she has shoved them back to the child to deal with–in these moments, I believe, something we could call maternal love can appear.

My formulation would be as follows: through the numerous painful and unsettling moments of motherhood, I am punctured by my child's otherness. In these moments, despite their austerity, I love you (other) because you (in your radical alterity) provide me with an experience that I may be able to take back as my own: a momentary experience of myself as a self, emerging out of an experience that there are always already two of us. This, for me, is maternal subjectivity that arises out of a relation with a child.

I am grateful, again, to Daphne de Marneffe for her thoughts and for providing a spur to a renewed effort, albeit another partial one (who indeed among us has worked this out!) to think about how the mother's subjectivity is structured through the relation to the child.

REFERENCES

Benjamin, J. (1995), *Like Subjects, Love Objects: Essays on Recognition and Difference*. Cambridge, MA: Harvard University Press.

_____ (1998), *Shadow of the Other: Intersubjectivity and Gender in Psychoanalysis.* New York: Routledge.

de Marneffe, D. (2004), *Maternal Desire: On children, love and the inner life.* New York: Little Brown.

Evans, D. (1996), *An Introductory Dictionary of Lacanian Psychoanalysis.* London: Routledge.

Freud, S. (1914), On narcissism: An introduction. *Standard Edition,* 14: 67–102. London: Hogarth Press, 1974.

_____ (1931), Female sexuality. *Standard Edition,* 21: 221–243. London: Hogarth Press, 1974.

_____ (1933), Femininity. *Standard Edition,* 22:112–135. London: Hogarth Press, 1974.

Kraemer, S. B. (1996), Betwixt the dark and the daylight of maternal subjectivity: Meditations on the threshold. *Psychoanalytic Dialogues,* 6:765–791.

Kristeva, J. (1987), Freud and love: Treatment and its discontents. In: *Tales of Love,* trans. L. Roudiez. New York: Columbia University Press, pp. 21–56.

Lacan, J. (1953–54), *The Seminar of Jacques Lacan, Book I: Freud's papers on technique, 1953–1954,* trans. J. Forrester, ed. J-A. Miller. Cambridge, UK: Cambridge University Press, 1988.

_____ (1958), The Meaning of the Phallus. In: *Feminine Sexuality: Jacques Lacan and the Ecole Freudienne,* eds. J. Mitchell & J. Rose. New York and London: W.W. Norton & Company, 1982.

_____ (1964), *The Seminar. Book XI. The Four Fundamental Concepts of Psychoanalysis,* trans. A. Sheridan. London: Hogarth Press and Institute of Psycho-Analysis, 1977.

Mum's the Word: Intersubjectivity, Alterity, and the Maternal Subject

Lisa Baraitser, Ph.D.

Where motherhood and ethics are brought together, it is usually under the rubric of an "ethic of care," with the mother-child relationship figured as a paradigmatic example of such an ethic. In this article I make use of Levinas' account of ethics as first philosophy to flesh out a notion of "maternal alterity" as an alternative to a maternal ethics based on the various complex mental and emotional tasks that make up care. This represents an attempt to recuperate something for the mother out of her often bewildering encounter with the enigmatic otherness of her child. Situating Levinas alongside a dialogue between Jessica Benjamin and Judith Butler on intersubjectivity, I attempt to disentangle maternal subjectivity from the developing subjectivity of the child and offer an account of the maternal subject as an ethical subject situated, perhaps, "otherwise" to a discourse of care.

To say something in one's own name is very strange, for it is not at all when we consider ourselves as selves, persons or subjects that we speak in our own name. On the contrary, an individual acquires a true proper name as the result of the most severe operations of depersonalisation, when he opens himself to the multiplicities that pervade him and the intensities which run through his whole being [Deleuze, 1977, p. 114].

In the attenuated moments after giving birth, while the bloodbath is mopped up around me, in those first blinking, thinned-out moments, as I realize the pain has miraculously stopped as inexplicably as it began, and I lie stunned, and empty, someone asks me if I have decided on a name. What? A name? A name for what? A name for the baby, the same someone says. "Now what?" I think. "Not only must I birth the baby, but I must author it too?" My partner and I look at each other. No, we haven't decided, but this seems like an inadequate response to the enormity of the question; a question that begs so many other questions about belonging, memory, culture, taste. So I say, I mean I just slip it out ... "Joel." I just say it, and then it is his name. My partner nods to me. Like all names, it is the best of a bad bunch. It is not quite right, but it will do. It is at the top of our not-quite-right-names list. Saying it makes it his name, but does not yet make it right. The name is too big for him. Any name would be. I find myself embarrassed saying it. As I say it again and again over the coming weeks, until eventually his name sticks to him, until it becomes, through use, his right name, I retain this discomfort. A whiff of embarrassment lingers in the gap between the child and his name. The child is a stranger to his name. He doesn't respond when I call to him. It hangs around him, as the nappies hang around his tiny bum, like ill-fitting sacks. It is inconsequential to him. He didn't choose it. I elected it as his name, so quickly, so arbitrarily. And I am deeply implicated in making what is strange in him familiar, in fixing him in language before he even knows what language is.

What is this discomfort I have with saying his name? Have I still not come to terms with the arbitrary relation between signifier and signified? It comes back to me like a mantra that I realize I have repeated endlessly without understanding at all. My notebooks are full of badly drawn trees and odd-looking toilet doors, but this is nothing compared with the actual responsibility of assigning a name for the first time to the unnamed and watching it stick. Yes, naming both claims him as my child and fixes him in the Other, the symbolic, the order of language. Once stuck, he is simultaneously mine and given over to the Other, same and strange. But for a few weeks, he is neither. His otherness appears to be his very own.

At some point in his fifth year, Joel, the named one, starts to call me by my first name. Initially I thought he had learned a clever way to get my attention. Realizing that I no longer responded to "mum," I would at least lift my head if I heard "Lisa." But later, I thought that perhaps he was retaliating, or just playing with that same making-strange experience that I had had with him. As far as he was concerned, my name was "mum." That was the name that stuck to me. By renaming me "Lisa" he renews my strangeness, opening a gap between myself and who he elects me to be. Again, for a few weeks I experience an uncanny sensation, only this time myself made-strange, until, eventually, his election of me as "Lisa" resticks itself to me and the gap closes.

INTRODUCTION: MATERNITY, ETHICS, AND THE OTHER

Sara Ruddick once called a child an "'open structure' whose acts are irregular, unpredictable, often mysterious" (Ruddick, 1980, p. 352). These qualities–irregularity, unpredictability, mystery–structure the child as an enigma, an other who is constantly changing, defying our attempts to "fix" such otherness through processes of knowing. Mothers, however, are usually given the unenviable task of being in the position of the one supposed to know. From Winnicott and Bion on, mothers have been imbued with capacities for empathic understanding, attunement, reverie, mentalization; capacities that supposedly allow mothers to make sense on the infant's behalf of their confusing, stricken, and contradictory internal world, and so return to them their thoughts and feelings in a more digestible form. As more complex accounts of maternal subjectivity have emerged (e.g., Benjamin, 1995, 1998, 2004; Kraemer, 1996; Raphael-Leff, 1996, 2003; Lombardi, 1998; Juhasz, 2003; de Marneffe, 2004; Parker, 2005; Hollway, 2006) the naturalness and ease of these maternal mental processes have been brought under scrutiny. In these accounts the focus shifts from purely how the infant uses the mother toward how the mother experiences her mothering role, her tasks, and her changing identities, as well as her shifting internal object relations, and how this may impact, in turn, on a mother's capacity to relate to her child. However, although we have begun to tentatively ask ourselves the hair-raising question "What is it like to be alongside a child?," an account of "maternal subjectivity," as opposed to a description of mothering, would in part entail imagining what it is like to be in close proximity to the "open structure" that is a child. This would mean thinking more deeply about women's child-rearing experiences from the perspective of being responsible for a child who remains ongoingly irregular, unpredictable, and essentially unknowable, and the pressures and strains as well as the generative potential that this may have on the maternal psyche.

This article seeks to think maternal subjectivity and ethics together. It suggests that maternal subjectivity can be thought of as an ethical subjectivity through providing an account of maternal alterity–maternal encounters with an inassimilable otherness, seen here in the figure of a child. It is not at all unusual to bring together the terms "mothering" and "ethics." Some early work on the ethics of care theorized mothering as a particular kind of ethical work by dint of it revolving around the tasks Ruddick (1980) originally highlighted–those of fostering life and promoting the growth and social acceptability of the child. This led on an exploration of an ethics of care that could draw on the mother-child model as a way of describing an ethical sphere that was not purely governed by autonomy, independence, and justice (Gilligan, 1982; Ruddick, 1989; Noddings, 1984; Tronto, 1993). Mothering was seen as a paradigmatic type of caring relation, one that involved empathic understanding, interdependence, flexibility, relatedness, receptivity, responsiveness, attentive and preservative love, nurturance, and training. These types of qualities, with their "feminine" overtones, were valorized by early theorists, in part as a way of elevating maternal work to the status of ethical work (this is particularly evident in Ruddick's work), and in addition, opening up a debate about care and justice in the social and political sphere. "Care" became a trope used to both soften up moral philosophy with its traditional concerns with justice and to indicate new modes of social and political transformation (Tronto, 1993; Sevenhuijsen, 1998; Hollway, 2006). Williams (2001) identifies a paradigm shift in the of work on the ethics of care that seeks to move beyond the binary, care versus justice, with its connotations of public versus private and masculine versus feminine. Here care breaks free from associations with the mother-child model and can be seen instead to structure all human relationships (Sevenhuijsen, 1998). This universalist paradigm (Williams, 2001) sees the earlier reliance on the mother-child relation as a model for care as problematic, as it reduces concern with the ethics of justice and of social equality and is also highly normative (Roseneil, 2004). Mothering in the ethics of care literature seems to have been drawn on and then, to some degree, left behind as the focus has broadened to include other models of care such as friendship (Roseneil, 2004).

My purpose here is to try to move the account of the ethical nature of the mother-child relationship away from its reliance on notions such as flexibility, relatedness, receptivity, and responsiveness–notions that are closely bound up with traditionally defined "feminine" attributes–but without jettisoning the project of mapping out a specifically maternal ethics. My interest is in the maternal rather than "care." Instead of "borrowing" from the mother metaphorically to help us understand something of our relations to others (as much psychoanalytic literature has done in order to help understand the relationship between analyst and analysand), my purpose is to return to the mother-child relation itself to probe the complexity of a specifically maternal ethics–of the kinds of relations established between mothers (understood here as those women who are involved in the practice of parenting) and those others we "elect" to be our children (be they biological, fostered, adopted, community, or members of an extended family or friendship group). To do so requires understanding maternal ethics as less to do with an unstinting commitment or caring attentiveness toward an other and more to do with the way otherness structures and infects human subjectivity. This implies understanding not only the ways otherness figures in the developmental trajectory of the child but crucially in a mother's own developmental process too. This would go some way toward recuperating something for the mother out of her often bewildering encounter with a child, which could then be used to shore up the notion of a specifically maternal subjectivity (Baraitser, 2006).

To do this, I bring a different strand of ethics to bear on the maternal subject, one drawn primarily from the work of Emmanuel Levinas (1961, 1974, 1985). Levinas' philosophy proceeds from the assertion that subjectivity is not a given. There is no individual human subject describable as an ontological entity prior to our responsibility for others. First and foremost there is the Other. Subjectivity is seen to emerge through a relation to this radical alterity, or otherness. I argue that, in fact, the maternal could be seen as both an emblematic and enigmatic formation of this subjectivity "called into being" through the relation to an "other" who, in this case, is a child. I contend that an interrupting, tantruming, crying, demanding, changing, questioning, loving, unpredictable, and ultimately unknowable other that is a child is a particular kind of other, the response to whom calls us, as maternal subjects, into being.

Having said that I will draw on Levinas, I must declare from the outset that I am no philosopher. I certainly have no training, credentials, or background in philosophy. To this degree I have no rights to lay claim to philosophy. I am predominantly a clinician, a psychotherapist who has worked specifically with mothers over a number of years. But I must declare also that despite drawing heavily on psychoanalytic theory in my clinical work, I am not a psychoanalyst either. I come to my three chosen practices, those of philosophy, psychoanalysis, and mothering, as a willing amateur. However, it may be fair to say that philosophy, psychoanalysis, and mothering all lay claims on me. If, as the quote from Deleuze suggests, to philosophize is to attempt to write the autobiography of a spiritual automaton, then perhaps this piece could be thought of as a kind of philosophising. And in ways that I hope to substantiate as I go along, maternity shows up the limit of psychoanalysis, calling psychoanalysis into question at the point it gives way to ethics. So, although I come to philosophy as a willing amateur, I am impelled to look there for different answers than psychoanalysis can provide to the questions I have, and where I find philosophical answers, I am impelled to loop back to psychoanalysis as my own "first philosophy" to reinterrogate them from a perspective that always reminds us to hold the developing child in mind. My hope is that in placing itself in proximity to both psychoanalysis and philosophy, this piece overcomes the limits of its own specialization, that of maternity, as well as using maternity as a model to challenge the limits of both psychoanalysis and philosophy.

It makes some sense, then, to begin with a discussion between psychoanalysis and philosophy, one staged between Jessica Benjamin and Judith Butler around different readings of intersubjectivity, drawing, as they both do, on the work of Hegel to try to understand how we come to have relations with others at all. Part of this discussion involves the status of the Other as radically other as opposed to another subjectivity or ego.[1] As I understand it, at the core of this debate is whether difference can be thought of in the same terms as alterity–whether being other to me, beyond my control, and thereby

[1]As far as possible I have used the term "other" to denote other person or ego and "Other" for radical alterity, a transcendent other, although it is not always possible to make such a clear distinction, particularly in Levinas' work.

recognizable as another, like me, can be thought of in the same terms as being radically Other and thereby beyond notions of "me-ness." This is perhaps already a dialogue in different registers, psychoanalytic and philosophical. If Levinas' position is useful, it is perhaps because of his assertion that there is no me before or beyond the Other. Subjectivity is understood as emerging through particular relations with alterity–the Other shown up as "face" in the child, persecutor, stranger, brother, lover, neighbor.[2] As we shall see from the following discussion, the child in Benjamin's account of intersubjectivity emerges through relations to the other, but the account is reliant on the mother as the ultimate site of otherness that structures notions of both self and other but without articulating maternal experiences of alterity. Without figuring the child as essentially an enigma, a stranger who calls the mother to ethical responsibility, it is difficult to see a way of theoretically sustaining maternal alterity, and without a relation to alterity, I believe the mother will always be in danger of being co-opted to serve the child in all her classic manifestations: object, abject, container, receptacle, mirror, or absent "Thing" (Kristeva, 1987).

In the second half of this article I engage with Levinas' work to look in detail at his figures for the "paternal" and "maternal," suggesting a reworking of his notion of "paternity" in order to help with a sustained account of maternal alterity that engenders subjectivity. Finally, I briefly return to the anecdote that this article opened with in an attempt to hold onto a maternal subjectivity that emerges through the mundane details of lived experience–a particular and situated encounter with a particular other who is one's "child."

JESSICA BENJAMIN AND THE INTERSUBJECTIVE TURN

Intersubjectivity has become a major theoretical addition to psychoanalysis, emerging largely within the relational tradition through

[2]In Levinas, the encounter with the Other occurs in the "face-to-face," the position also of language. The "face" is the exteriority of the Other, through which the Other is revealed to the self. However, what is revealed is what goes beyond whatever idea the self has of the Other. The face-to-face is the situation in which the Other's infinite alterity is expressed.

the work of Benjamin, Mitchell, Aron, and others (Mitchell, 1988, 2000; Aron, 1996; Benjamin, 2004). In Benjamin's work it is through her account of reciprocity, recognition, and intersubjectivity that she arrives at how we experience otherness (Benjamin, 1990, 1995, 1998, 2004). Benjamin moves away from psychoanalytic formulations that seek to understand how the infant internalizes real and fantasized interactions in the interpersonal domain and which, through the dynamics of projection and introjection, come to shape, in their turn, that domain. Instead, she holds out for an understanding of intersubjectivity that is more than merely internal object relations and that exists in tandem with the interpersonal. In this sense Benjamin keeps in sight a distinction between the interpersonal and the intersubjective, or the object and the other. She writes,

> If we take the tension between recognition and omnipotence to be the inner conflict that shapes the interpersonal world, then I think we are taking the intersubjective to be an axis that cuts across intrapsychic and interpersonal [Benjamin, 2000, p. 297].

Benjamin's notion of the intersubjective rests on an otherness that remains beyond one's control, resistant to the pressures of an internal split complementarity governed by omnipotence. If omnipotence is the condition in which the subject attempts to control the other by forcing the self and other into complementary polarized positions, then the other is reduced to the status of internal object and the distinction between other and object is destroyed.

One inherent aspect of our psychic world, Benjamin argues, is the defensive structure that involves splitting and is governed by the need for omnipotent control or independence, the philosophical roots of which can be seen in her use of both Hegel's master-slave model and Freud's notion of narcissism (Benjamin, 1995, p. 36). Another aspect of our psychic functioning, however, is what Benjamin calls "intersubjective space," in which it is possible to identify with the other's position without losing one's own. This space is characterized by mutual recognition, in which the self can recognize the other as a like subject and in turn be recognized by such a subject. Mutual recognition is achieved through a process in which the other survives destruction, albeit in fantasy, and is thereby established in the subject's mind as beyond omnipotent control. Benjamin here draws heavily on Winnicott's ideas about the "use of an object" (Winnicott, 1969), where he marks out a developmental phase that comes after object relating and involves object use, which is made possible through seeing that the object survives unconscious destruction. The object in question is the mother, and "survival," in Winnicott's terms, describes the mother's ability to respond in a nonretaliatory manner to the infant's unconscious attacks. In intersubjective space, both reflection and analysis become possible on the mother/analyst's side because the infant/patient experiences the other as truly external through survival of its own destructive impulses. And it is through this process that the mother/analyst attains subjectivity in the mind of the infant/patient. When intersubjective space breaks down (when destruction is truly destructive, if you like, when the other does not "survive" but instead retaliates or abandons), there is a return to the complementary positioning of internal objects. In Benjamin's view there is an ongoing and endless cycle of the establishment of mutual recognition followed by its negation, constituting a never-ending tension between complementarity and mutuality, between relating to the other as object or like subject.

Benjamin's position clearly has implications and consequences for the mother and her own relation to otherness. There are some important points in Benjamin's theorizing when she specifically addresses the issue of the mother's subjectivity in relation to the child (Benjamin, 1995). Given that she is concerned with tracing the development of our capacity to experience otherness, as well as wanting to accord the mother a subjectivity of her own, Benjamin maintains that the mother's subjectivity is necessary for the development of the child's separate experience of self. She asks some crucial questions pertaining to the development of maternal subjectivity starting back in childhood:

> How does a child develop into a person who, as a parent, is able to recognize her or his own child? What are the internal processes, the psychic landmarks, of such development? Where is the theory that tracks the development of the child's responsiveness, empathy and concern and not just the parent's sufficiency or failure? [Benjamin, 1995, p. 32].

In many ways this looks promising. Here the capacity for recognition is seen as a developmental achievement in childhood and is later extended to the new child of the child-now-parent. Recognition is not something the mother just does naturally or altruistically for the child. However, what Benjamin does with the mother in this early work is complex.

First, as we can see from the aforementioned quote, what interests her in terms of the mother's subjectivity is the mother's capacity to recognize the child. Second, although she argues passionately for the importance of mutual recognition of maternal subjectivity, she relies on the maternal subject's ability to respond benignly to the child's attacks as the cornerstone for the child's development of the capacity for recognition. However, mothers are not always able to do this. More often than not, they find themselves failing to maintain any sense of separate or autonomous "self" in the face of the dramatic and relentless onslaught of the child's needs and demands, especially their needs to destroy their mother's separateness (Kraemer, 1996). In addition, they must then contend with the sense of failure, hopelessness, and despair that arises from their awareness that they have not "survived." Although it could be argued that this is a form of survival in its own right–the capacity to contend with these feelings and to evolve in the face of regularly "losing it"–Kraemer argues that this amounts to a reidealization of motherhood, just at the point that it appears that we have become able to think about maternal ambivalence. Mothers live with strong, normative social and cultural messages that remind us that, although we all have a range of powerful and conflicting feelings about our children, we still need to act responsibly in the face of infantile ruthlessness for the sake of the developing child.

One of the examples Benjamin gives of the mother's "survival" is her ability to set firm but not too rigid boundaries during the child's second year of life, as the child becomes consciously aware of the mother's separateness and stages a battle against it. The battle is one in which the child attempts to destroy the mother by attacking her difference; when the child cries "want what I want," it is the mother's otherness that is under attack. If a mother, attempting to leave the protesting child to go to work, for instance, still leaves but communicates to the child that she misses him or her, the child comes to realize that the mother is outside of the self, an other who cannot be coerced, and paradoxically, as Benjamin claims, through omnipotence the child comes to experience otherness. The child can later identify with the mother who misses the child and repair the breakdown in recognition (Benjamin, 1995, p. 92).

I think, however, that although it appears that we have kept our eye on the maternal subject throughout, she has, in fact, slipped out of the frame. Benjamin's account suggests a reworked version of a "good-enough" mother who will bear the destruction and deal with it creatively in order for this to happen. She writes,

> Let us imagine a mother who gives in to the child and never leaves. The child feels she or he has succeeded in controlling Mother, and this means "Now Mommy is still my fantasy, Mommy is also afraid, and I can never leave Mommy without great anxiety either." Thus, even as the child loses contact with the real independent mother, the omnipotent fantasy mother fills the space. ... If alternately, the mother leaves and returns, followed by a happy reunion, the child feels that the danger—the projection of his own anger onto Mother—was not real [Benjamin, 1995, p. 91].

The mother must, in other words, have the capacity for depressive position functioning. However, in Benjamin's account, the mother who is able to do this must be drawing on her own childhood experience of intersubjective space in order that she now has the capacity to relate to her child as other rather than purely as object. The mother's abilities to set boundaries, to experience her child as separate, to know not to cave in, and to manage to do this consistently without burdening the child with her own distress or despair, is presumably a mother who had a mother who managed the crisis brought on by separation. Now a mother in her own right, she is the one who can maintain herself in the face of the child's demands because she can experience her child as another locus of subjectivity rather than purely an internal object. This, in its turn, allows her child an experience of her as a subject and therefore an experience of intersubjective space.

One of the questions this circularity begs is how we account for those who have not had such "good enough parenting" but who go on to parent as adults effectively and with imagination and skill. The notion that good-enough parenting begets good-enough parenting presents a highly deterministic view of human development. Moreover, it has implications for a mother who is struggling to overcome inadequate parenting, perhaps through the very task of parenting a child herself (Raphael-Leff, 2003). In addition, how do we account for those who have had good-enough parenting but when faced with their child's omnipotence, still cave in? And who is to really say that caving in is wrong? As Frosh (1997) writes movingly of fathering in a clinical vignette,

> Sam's father has stayed at home with Sam since his mother died, not sending the boy to school. "I want to be everything to him now," he says, "but people tell me he will cope with the separation; they say I should send him to school." I think, I wish nobody had to go to school. Perhaps people's criticism of Sam's father reflects their discomfort with–and their envy of–his decision not to act in accordance with what Sam might "cope" with, but with what he and Sam want [p. 47].

It is interesting, perhaps, that Sam's father holds out against the criticism that he should be sending the boy to school. Frosh, as the therapist here, supports the father's resistance to external pressures, supports his "caving in" to the demands of the child. One wonders if such support would have been maintained had it been the father who had died and the mother who decided to keep the child home with her.

Finally, though Benjamin does talk about how the mother may experience the demanding omnipotent child as a disillusionment (Benjamin, 1995, p. 89), causing her to relinquish the fantasy of both the perfect child and herself as the perfect mother, her subjectivity is not seen to stem from the negotiation of the feeling states that this provokes. The mother is expected not to throw a tantrum, after all. To assign the mother her own subjectivity, Benjamin then looks to the mother's engagement with what is not her child: her work, lover, political activity, and interests outside of the child's sphere. As de Marneffe has powerfully argued, there is a need to articulate how caring for children might itself express autonomous desires rather than impede them (de Marneffe, 2004, p.75). Equally, at a theoretical level, the mother is required to shore up the development of intersubjective space without attending to how this positioning affects her capacities to sustain both subjectivity and alterity in relation to the child.

JUDITH BUTLER AND THE "REALITY" OF NEGATION

One of the questions Judith Butler raises in relation to Benjamin's work has to do with the way recognition, in facilitating the transformation of object into other, itself becomes valorized, figuring as both a norm and an ideal form of communication (Butler, 2000). Against the ideal of recognition, destruction becomes an "occasional and lamentable occurrence" (Butler, 2000, p. 273) and one that can be reversed and overcome through therapeutic dialogue. According to Butler, although recognition and destruction co-exist in tension in Benjamin's schema, it is only by overcoming destruction, by moving through it and realizing that the destroyed object is still there, that recognition, and thereby an experience of otherness, is made possible.

The question that is then raised by Butler is what is destruction, if the whole point is that it does not destroy? Benjamin works with a notion of destruction in fantasy, drawn from Winnicott but at the same time bringing it alongside Hegel's account, which is closer to a murderous impulse toward the other. Hegel imagines a fight to the death between two subjects struggling for a self-consciousness, which requires recognition from the other (Hegel, 1807). Butler argues that Benjamin wants to make a distinction between destruction and negation, where destruction must be continually survived as negation, so that eventually destruction is overcome. But what Butler goes on to argue is that in Hegel's famous "master-slave" model in *The Phenomenology of Spirit* (Hegel, 1807), the encounter with the Other is seen as encompassing self-loss as well as the possibility for recognition. Butler's reading is that in Hegel

> whatever consciousness is, whatever the self is, it will find itself only through a reflection of itself in another. To be itself, it must pass through self-loss, but when it passes through, it will never be "returned" to what it was [Butler, 2000, p. 286].

This, according to Butler, leads to an inherent ambivalence in our relation to the Other. As well as self-knowledge through recognition, there is also self-loss to contend with. Self-loss is not the same as surviving the other's fantasy of destroying you. The encounter with the other marks you, changes you. With self-loss, the self "never returns to itself free from the Other" (Butler, 2000, p. 286).

> Its ontology is precisely to be divided and spanned in irrecoverable ways. ... It is transformed through its encounter with alterity, not in order to return to itself, but to become a self it never was [Butler, 2000, p. 286].

To become a self, in Butler's account, is to be outside oneself, or "other" than oneself and to have always already lost oneself through a relation to the Other that returns one to oneself as different–as other. What Butler identifies is that this is only really possible in Hegel when the two self-consciousnesses recognize each other at a point of extreme vulnerability–precisely a life-and-death struggle. When true destruction is imminent, when the self truly stands to lose itself, then recognition can emerge to keep destruction in check. As a result, the self is "not its own" (Butler, 2000, p. 287). The relationship with the Other is aligned as ethical–we are reciprocally "given over" to each other.

What is most useful here is Butler's reinstallment of destruction as destruction, the fundamental risk the self takes in its encounter with the Other to become a self. Through Butler's reassertion of destruction, maternal subjectivity could be understood as a new subjectivity that emerges out of the encounter with the child. From the mother's perspective, we could say that as the infant destroys her, she is marked by the other, contending with self-loss, through which, according to Butler, an altered self may also emerge. From the infant's perspective, omnipotence functions to protect the child from the fantasy of maternal aggression–the baby is fearful that the devouring or powerful mother will really harm it and must protect itself. For the child to move beyond this, the child must experience the mother as having survived destruction rather than be marked by destruction itself: The mother and analyst, on the other hand, are relied on to risk being psychically destroyed and to retain the capacity to think, that is, to bear and contain the awareness that they have not "survived." The mother may destroy the infant in fantasy (the destruction may be notionally reciprocal in this sense), but her primary task is to survive the destructive attacks that the infant makes in a nonretaliatory manner. The continual and relentless attacks on the mother's psyche that the infant and toddler perform are described by Kraemer (1996) as putting mothers "in a losing battle to retain her center of gravity and solid sense of subjective choice or desire" (p. 771). In her view, mothers struggle with feelings of "enormous shame, confusion, self-reproach and anger" (p. 771), as, with difficulty, she maintains herself in the face of such attacks. In other words, she may well not bear it. The mother truly risks something in the encounter with this other, but, following Butler's argument, she also stands to gain something through "giving herself over" to the other. It is in this sense that I understand Butler's notion of the self that "never returns to itself free of the Other" (Butler, 2000, p. 286). The self is "transformed through its encounter with alterity, not in order to return to itself, but to become a self it never was" (Butler, 2000, p. 286). This, then, goes some way toward an account of maternal subjectivity in which subjectivity is understood as the remainder or what is returned to the self through the encounter with the Other, a self necessarily different from before.

LEVINAS

This leads us directly into a discussion of Levinas' work, as it is at the core of his philosophy that the subject emerges through an encounter with alterity. C. Fred Alford (2002) rather damningly talks of how Levinas has become everything to everyone. "We pretend we get it, writing in much the same style, so as to say whatever we wanted to say in the first place" (p. 1). Given the difficulty and complexity of reading Levinas for those of us outside of academic philosophy, it may be worth asking what it is about his work that seems so enticing. To be for another, first and foremost, seems a grand thing indeed. Perhaps Levinas appeals to the part of us that wants to show ourselves in our best altruistic light. But the question is how to achieve this. One reads on in the hope of finding out, but reading Levinas is like trying to read water. In Tina Chanter's words,

> There is a drive to continue reading despite the diminishing returns it seems to yield: the more one reads, the less one understands. ... The effect is to induce more reading [2001, p. 1].

She goes on to link this with the very structure of Levinas's ethics:

> The more I do, the more responsible I become. This infinite call, which deepens as I try to fulfil it, draws me in, captivating me. There is no escape. I am responsible despite myself and prior to any debt I incur [Chanter, 2001, p. 1].

Levinas' philosophy revolves around the relation between the Other and me. Crucially, this is a relation that constitutes these terms rather than describing a mode of relating that occurs between preestablished entities. This original form of subjectivity (this me-ness) cannot really be understood as ontological and is therefore barely understood as a subjectivity at all. What Levinas alludes to is a sphere that is neither being nor nonbeing but what he describes as "otherwise than Being" (Levinas, 1974). Before and beyond meaning, consciousness, or any notion we could term "I," there is the response to the call of the Other.

> I speak of responsibility as the essential, primary and fundamental structure of subjectivity. For I describe subjectivity in ethical terms. Ethics, here, does not supplement a preceding existential base; the very node of the subjective is knotted in ethics understood as responsibility. ... Responsibility in fact is not a simple attribute of subjectivity, as if the latter already existed in itself, before the ethical relationship. Subjectivity is not for itself; it is, once again, initially for another ...[Levinas, 1985, pp. 95-97].

Levinas is attempting to exit from the inevitability of colonizing the Other through knowing. As soon as we know the Other, the Other is returned to the "Same" and remains within what Levinas terms "totality." In contrast, if the Other is "infinity" to the extent that it exceeds or overflows the idea or representation we have of the Other (it goes beyond what we know of it), then the distance between the Same and the Other, between totality and infinity, is itself infinite. Radically alterity can be maintained, preventing collapse of otherness back into the realm of the Same.

Levinas's argument is in a different register from that of sameness and difference, recognition and reciprocity. Recognition, as discussed earlier, is not identical with responsibility. Self-recognition that relies on recognition by another subject will perhaps always run into difficulties with how to prevent a collapse of alterity due to the colonizing impulse that is inherent not only in "knowing" another but in recognizing too. In contrast, describing the relationship with the Other as an ethical relationship prior to self, a relationship that establishes the subject as a responsible subject before being a subject at all, Levinas redefines both the notion of the subject and the Other as well as the nature of their relationship and that of recognition itself. As Lingis (1978) states,

> If responsibility is a form of recognition, it is not recognition as cognitive act, that is an identifying, re-presenting, re-cognising act. It is effected in expressive acts by which one expresses oneself, expresses one's own being, exposes oneself, to the other [p. Xix].

Responsibility redefines recognition as an exposure of the self to the Other for whom one is responsible.

The psychoanalytic understanding of recognition that we explored through Benjamin's work relied on the presence of a nonretaliatory maternal figure who bears destruction so that the infant can develop the capacity for intersubjective space. This is a long way from the notion of the mother who recognizes her infant through her exposure to her infant's otherness. It is closer to Butler's critique, which gave us the notion of the self marked by the other, the self returning from an encounter with the other, changed, thereby opening the possibility of a maternal subjectivity arising out of an encounter with alterity rather than through the processes of surviving destruction. Here, in Levinas, we find responsibility redefining recognition. The issue becomes one of ethics—how do we take responsibility for the other through exposure to the other before the possibility of recognition by that other? This shift into an ethical domain has particular implications for the mother, given her skewed relations with her child. Here I am suggesting we rethink the maternal position from the perspective of the mother's exposure to the other who is her child, an exposure that entails beginning with responsibility for that other but one that gives rise to maternal subjectivity in the process. In order to pursue this further, we need to look at what Levinas himself does with mothers.

MATERNITY AND PATERNITY IN LEVINAS

In *Otherwise Than Being, or, Beyond Essence* (1974), we find Levinas' most extreme formulation of subjectivity, in which the subject gives herself over entirely to the other in an act of substitution. Levinas uses maternity to figure this ultimate substitution, with the pregnant body being drawn on to describe responsibility as the point at which one gives over one's own substance or flesh for the other:

> Maternity in the complete being "for the other" which characterizes it, which is the very signifyingness of signification, is the ultimate sense of this vulnerability [Levinas, 1974, p. 108].

Levinas' language, as Donna Brody (2001) has pointed out, becomes seeped in bodily sensation at this moment in the text, and it is through this invocation that Levinas wants to describe responsibility as "contact" or exposure to the Other, an order of experience in which the Other is now thought of as "the-other-in-the-same" (Brody, 2001, p. 55), or the other within. It is the maternal body that is used to invoke this "within-ness." Sonia Sikka (2001) notes that Levinas invokes the maternal body as

> a condition in which one is responsible for the Other with the very substance of her being, prior to any acquaintance with him or her, prior to any knowledge of his or her characteristics, and prior to any choice, but a subjection that is election rather than enslavement [p. 106].

On this reading, the maternal body is thus elevated to the site of an ultimate ethical gesture while simultaneously disappearing as it is given over completely to the Other.

Paternity has a very different function from that of maternity in Levinas' work. It is here that we begin to see Levinas develop a notion of the self returned to oneself as strange, thereby begetting subjectivity. The terms "paternity" and "fecundity" are used interchangeably and the adult-child relationship is exclusively discussed in terms of fathers and sons. However, Levinas (1985) wriggles out of a biological referent:

> Biological filiality is only the first shape filiality takes; but one can very well conceive filiality as a relationship between human beings without the tie of biological kinship. One can have a paternal attitude with regard to the Other. To consider the Other as a son is precisely to establish with him those relations I call "beyond the possible" [pp. 70-71].

What does Levinas mean when he talks of paternity as to do with a set of relations "beyond the possible"? Paternity is a particular set of relations with what is both same and other, yours and not yours. Unlike maternity, the relation is not one of substitution. Paternity establishes a particular ontological category in that the I is both singular and multiple simultaneously. The I transcends itself in paternity but is also returned to itself, as the son both is and is not the father.

> The son is not only my work, like a poem or an object, nor is he my property. Neither the categories of power nor those of knowledge describe my relation with the child. The fecundity of the I is neither a cause nor a domination. I do not have my child; I am my child. Paternity is a relation with a stranger who while being Other ("And you shall say to yourself, 'who can have borne me these? I was bereaved and barren ...'" *Isaiah, 49*) *is* me, a relation of the I with a self which yet is not me [Levinas, 1961, p. 277, original emphases].

So, multiplicity here has not to do with multiplying oneself in the sense of having many children. It has to do with facing what is beyond one's own possibilities but recognizing this beyondness (the son's possibilities) as also part of one's own possibilities. This can be done with anyone whom you elect as your "son." In this sense the paternal relationship is the relation with what is beyond the possible taken into the self.

> The fact of seeing the possibilities of the other as your own possibilities, of being able to escape the closure of your identity and what is bestowed on you, toward something which is not bestowed on you and which nevertheless is yours—this is paternity. This future beyond my own being, this dimension constitutive of time, takes on a concrete content in paternity [Levinas, 1985, p. 70].

Paternity, then, gives rise to a special kind of identity of the I, allowing the self to go beyond itself in "trans-substantiation" (Levinas, 1961, p. 266) without losing itself—otherwise logically the I dissolves as it transcends itself. Its uniqueness is that the "I breaks free of itself" (Levinas, 1961, p. 278) without ceasing to be I. As Kelly Oliver puts it, it is "the only relation in which the self becomes other and survives" (2001, p. 229). In Levinas' words, "The I is, in the child, an other" (1961, p. 267).

What we have here is a notion of subjectivity that does not rely on the idea that the Other must be recognized as a subject in order that recognition ensue. It is the very strangeness of the son that allows the subject to recognize himself, through which the subject's own strangeness or distinctness can come into being. As we have seen earlier, this gives rise to a relation with infinity that again engenders an ethical subject. In Levinas it is not that the father recognizes himself in the son, but he discovers himself there for the first time, engendering the father as much as it does the son. In relation to his son, who is both himself and not himself, the father discovers his own subjectivity, his distinctness and his strangeness to himself. Again, you return different.

Oliver (2001) asks the important question about how Levinas' "father" may relate to a daughter who represents a more radical "otherness" than a son. But perhaps another question we might ask is what happens if we think through Levinas' paternal figure from the perspective of the mother. Perhaps Levinas' paternal could be read as parental and therefore a figure who could include the mother's relation to the child (both son and daughter) as well as the father's. After all, Levinas has already told us that the biological relation is not necessary for constituting filial relations. We can elect anyone as our "child." Although perhaps deliberately risking collapsing the empirical and theoretical, I would suggest that on this reading, a mother too, discovering her child as a stranger, discovers her own distinctness, her own subjectivity, herself as ethical, not in the sense of her ability to give herself up for the child but in the sense that the relationship to her own infinity gives rise to an ethical subjectivity. This would be a very different ethical mother from the mother of either Ruddick's "maternal thinking" (Ruddick, 1989) or the maternal subject described, for example, in Kristeva's concept of herethics (Kristeva, 1977, p. 185).

I'm aware that there are many difficulties with simply co-opting Levinas' notion of the paternal in order to think about maternity and that issues of materiality and representation have been conveniently skirted. I am, nevertheless, intrigued by the implications of Levinas' filial relation. In characterizing the relationship between parent and child only in terms of fathers and sons, Levinas cannot be referring to empirical referents–without engendering any daughters, there are no more sons. In the same way he reminds us that paternity is not about the biological condition of having children, I would say that he forgets to remind us that it is also not about the biological condition of being sexed male. Paternity and fecundity are used much more clearly as tropes than the way maternity functions in his work, perhaps due to the difficulty of reading gestation unhooked from the female body. In this sense I think it is possible to construct a reading of the paternal in Levinas as a figure for parenthood and hence to reclaim this notion to think about aspects of maternal subjectivity.

MATERNAL SUBJECTIVITY

Let us then briefly look again at fecundity. Parenthood, it would be more accurate to say, could be thought of as a new subjective category, the condition of being both singular and multiple simultaneously. It is the recognition of the child as radically Other, as fundamentally a stranger, as well as being the same that establishes this relationship as ethical and hence as one in which we can begin to talk of the emergence of subjectivity. In recognizing the child as a stranger, as distinct, a mother as well as a father may also recognize what is distinct about herself. Motherhood (let us call it the female form of parenting) can then be thought of as a particular form of female subjectivity, one in which we transcend our own possibilities while recognizing this beyondness as also our own. Something comes back from the experience that is the self taken as other, similar perhaps to Butler's notion that the subject's encounter with the other is always transformative. It is this excess, an excess that is nevertheless returned to the subject, that Levinas evinces and that distinguishes his notion of ethics from that of reciprocity or recognition. I suggest that this ethical turn may go some way toward deepening our understanding of the developmental trajectory of motherhood.

IMPROPER NAMES

Something of this movement in which what is traditionally thought of as paternal can be widened to describe the maternal seems to show up in my anecdote about naming. Naming is surely the paternal function par excellence. Lacan's "Nom-du-Père" (Lacan, 1956) is perhaps the prime example of the link between the paternal name and the conferring of identity. It is the father's name that positions the child in the symbolic as well as signifying the Oedipal "no." Foreclosing the Nom-du-Père leads to psychosis. Yet the passing on or generation of new "given" and "family" names is culturally specific and continually in flux. Names can be proper (the ones that adhere or "stick" to people or things) or improper (the ones that just won't stick). In my anecdote, conferring a name was taken up by me, the mother, and accepted by my partner's nod. Did my discomfort around using my son's name stem from my unfamiliarity with the very process of naming anything? But then, how often do any of us get a chance to name the unnamed? Naming the unnamed is in fact a thing of childhood. We name our dolls or stuffed animals, our transitional objects, our imaginary friends. We name places and things that do not exist or whose existence we can manipulate and change. It is only perhaps our pets whom we name in such a way as the name sticks. Some animals come to recognize their names in the way a stuffed toy cannot, and then it feels unfair to keep changing it. To give something a proper name is precisely to confer a fixed point within the symbolic. Proper names are supposed to be for keeps.

So when the child (the one named Joel) calls his mother "Lisa," she is called into a peculiar awareness of herself. Mum, after all, is a command to silence. "To mum" is to mime, to act without words. The actors in such silent plays were called mummers. This is why to "keep mum" means to keep silent, usually about a secret. Mum is then a sounded word that signifies a command to silence. When my child renamed me "Lisa" he performed, for a second time, my original positioning in the symbolic by calling me out of my silence. For a few weeks I notice that I am no longer mum (silent) but Lisa (worded). I sense other people's discomfort–why does your son call you by your name? Did you ask him to, did you teach him that? I am truly as bewildered as they are, but I am also made aware of myself made-strange, with my distinctness that is a particular kind of indeterminacy, with, might we say, my maternal subjectivity.

REFERENCES

Alford, C. F. (2002), *Levinas, the Frankfurt School and Psychoanalysis.* London: Continuum.

Aron, L. (1996), *Meeting of Minds.* Hillsdale, NJ: The Analytic Press.

Baraitser, L. (2006), Oi mother, keep 'ye hair on!: Impossible transformations of maternal subjectivity. *Studies Gender & Sexuality,* 7(3):217-238.

Benjamin, J. (1990), *The Bonds of Love: Psychoanalysis, Feminism, and the Problem of Domination.* London: Virago.

_____ (1995), *Like Subjects, Love Objects: Essays on Recognition and Difference.* Cambridge, MA: Harvard University Press.

_____ (1998), *Shadow of the Other: Intersubjectivity and Gender in Psychoanalysis.* New York: Routledge.

_____ (2000), Response to commentaries by Mitchell and by Butler: Roundtable on the work of Jessica Benjamin. *Studies Gender & Sexuality,* 1(3):291-308.

_____ (2004), Beyond doer and done to: An intersubjective view of thirdness. *Psychoanal. Quart.,* 73:5-46.

Brody, D. (2001), Levinas' maternal method from *Time and the Other* through *Otherwise Than Being:* No woman's land? In: *Feminist Interpretations of Emmanuel Levinas,* ed. T. Chanter. University Park: Pennsylvania State University Press, pp. 53–77.

Butler, J. (2000), Longing for recognition: Commentary on the work of Jessica Benjamin. Roundtable on the work of Jessica Benjamin. *Studies Gender & Sexuality,* 1(3):271-290.

Chanter, T. (2001), Introduction to *Feminist Interpretations of Emmanuel Levinas,* ed. T. Chanter. University Park: Pennsylvania State University Press, pp. 1–28.

Deleuze, G. (1977), I have nothing to admit, trans. J Forman. *Semiotext(e),* 2(3):111-116.

De Marneffe, D. (2004), *Maternal Desire: On Children, Love and the Inner Life.* New York: Little Brown.

Frosh, S. (1997), Father's ambivalence (too). In: *Mothering and Ambivalence,* ed. W. Hollway & B. Featherstone. London: Routledge, pp. 37-52.

Gilligan, C. (1982), *In a Different Voice: Psychological Theory and Women's Development.* Cambridge, MA: Harvard University Press.

Hegel, G. W. F. (1807), *The Phenomenology of Spirit,* trans. A. V. Miller. Oxford, UK: Oxford University Press, 1977.

Hollway, W. (2006), *The Capacity to Care: Gender and Ethical Subjectivity.* London and New York: Routledge.

Juhasz, S. (2003), Mother-writing and the narrative of maternal subjectivity. *Studies Gender & Sexuality,* 4(4):395-425.

Kraemer, S. B. (1996), Betwixt the dark and the daylight of maternal subjectivity: Meditations on the threshold. *Psychoanal. Dial.,* 6:765-791.

Kristeva, J. (1977), Stabat Mater. In: *The Kristeva Reader,* ed. T. Moi. Oxford, UK: Blackwell, 1986, pp. 160-185.

_____ (1987), Freud and love: Treatment and its discontents. In: *Tales of Love,* trans. L. Roudiez. New York: Columbia University Press, pp. 21-56.

Lacan, J. (1956), *The Seminar of Jacques Lacan, Book III: The Psychoses,* trans. R. Grigg. London: Routledge, 1993.

Levinas, E. (1961), *Totality and Infinity: An essay on Exteriority,* trans. A. Lingis. Pittsburgh, PA: Duquesne University Press, 1969.

_____ (1974), *Otherwise Than Being, or, Beyond Essence,* trans. A. Lingis. Pittsburgh, PA: Duquesne University Press, 1998.

_____ (1985), *Ethics and Infinity: Conversations with Philippe Nemo,* trans. R. A. Cohen. Pittsburgh, PA: Duquesne University Press.

Lingis, A. (1978), Translator's introduction to E. Levinas, *Otherwise Than Being, or, Beyond Essence,* trans. A. Lingis. Pittsburgh, PA: Duquesne University Press, 1998, pp. xviii-xlv.

Lombardi, K. L. (1998), Mother as object, mother as subject. *Gender and Psychoanalysis,* 3(1):33-45.

Mitchell, S. A. (1988), *Relational Concepts in Psychoanalysis: An Integration.* Cambridge, MA: Harvard University Press.

_____ (2000), *Relationality: From Attachment to Intersubjectivity.* Hillsdale, NJ: The Analytic Press.

Noddings, N. (1984), *Caring: A Feminine Approach to Ethics and Moral Education.* Berkeley: University of California Press.

Oliver, K. (2001), Paternal election and the absent father. In: *Feminist Interpretations of Emmanuel Levinas,* ed. T. Chanter. University Park: Pennsylvania State University Press, pp. 224–240.

Parker, R. (2005), *Torn in Two: The Experience of Maternal Ambivalence.* London: Virago Press.

Raphael-Leff, J. (1996), Pregnancy–Procreative process, the "placental paradigm," and perinatal therapy. *J. Amer. Psychoanal. Assn.,* 44:373-399.

_____ ed. (2003), *Parent-Infant Psychodynamics: Wild Things, Mirrors and Ghosts.* London: Whurr.

Roseneil, S. (2004), Why we should care about friends: An argument for queering the care imaginary in social policy. *Social Policy and Society,* 3(4):409-419.

Ruddick, S. (1980), Maternal thinking. *Feminist Studies,* 6(2):342-367.

_____ (1989), *Maternal Thinking: Towards a Politics of Peace.* London: Women's Press.

Sevenhuijsen, S. (1998), *Citizenship and the Ethics of Care.* London: Routledge.

Sikka, S. (2001), The delightful other: Portraits of the feminine in Kierkegaard, Nietzsche, and Levinas. In: *Feminist Interpretations of Emmanuel Levinas,* ed. T. Chanter. University Park: Pennsylvania State University Press, pp. 96–118.

Tronto, J. (1993), *Moral Boundaries: A Political Argument for an Ethic of Care.* New York: Routledge.

Williams, F. (2001), In and beyond New Labour: Towards a new political ethic of care. *Critical Social Policy,* 21(4):467-493.

Winnicott, D. W. (1969), The use of an object. *Internat. J. Psycho-Anal.,* 50:711-716.

Maternal Silence

Miri Rozmarin, Ph.D.
Tel-Aviv University

In this article I argue that the project of figuring maternal subjectivity necessitates a reevaluation of the modalities of language that can bare the unique relations between subjectivity and Otherness that underlie maternal subjectivity. The first 2 sections of the essay discuss 2 alternative accounts of the relations between the child's Otherness and the mother's subjectivity, those of Simone de Beauvoir and Luce Irigaray. In the third and concluding section, I offer an account of maternal subjectivity in terms of witnessing that is committed to the child as an open future. I then argue that, as such, maternal subjectivity cannot be fully narrated.

One of the few things my mother repeatedly advised me, after I became a mother myself, was to keep a diary in which I would document the day-to-day development of my children, the little things they do, the smart and cute things they say. I remember these diaries from my own childhood. My mother had one for me and one for my brother. She addressed them to us, and so I used to read them without feeling I was invading her privacy. The entries in her diaries were more frequent when we were babies and became rare around our 3rd year. As a child, these diaries were for me an affirmation of my mother's clear voice, a voice I did not hear with such clarity in our relationship. When I became a mother, whenever I told my mother about something great one of my kids had done, she would say to me, "Write it down. You will forget it." So I tried to keep a diary like my mother. But I couldn't. I felt I was faking something, doing it for some kind of a future trial. Especially, I was bothered about addressing my experience of my children to their future selves. I felt bad about deciding what's important enough, smart, or sweet enough to document, as if I would be editing their past and by that narrowing their future. I felt obliged to remember, as if I hold a unique epistemological position, to provide my children access to their past. Not writing, I will most likely forget many small details and good stories, which could have held authoritative knowledge about "how you were." And yet it seemed to me that the overdetermination of documentation is unethical. Trying to figure out what would be foreclosed by my attempt to catch present events for the sake of the future, I realized it was the possibility of the future itself that I would be foreclosing here, a future that would not be a continuation of the present as I chose to remember and narrate it.

Since the 1980s, groundbreaking work—for example, Adrienne Rich's *Of Woman Born* (1986), Nancy Chodorow's *The Reproduction of Mothering* (1978), Sara Ruddick's *Maternal Thinking* (1989), and Jessica Benjamin's *The Bonds of Love* (1988)—has evinced a strong link between the project of figuring maternal subjectivity and mothers' ability to narrate their own experience in ways that affirm motherhood as a pole of epistemological, ethical, and social relations.

In what follows, I argue that the association of maternal subjectivity with the ability to narrate motherhood as an aspect of one's life does not take into account the way in which the Otherness of a child presents a unique temporality—a futurity—that cannot be a part of the maternal narrative. In order to rethink how the commitment to the child's singularity and indetermination shapes maternal subjectivity, I explore two options for viewing the relation between maternal subjectivity and responsibility, as presented by Simone de Beauvoir and Luce Irigaray. Through these discussions, I then offer an account of the triumph and limitation in associating maternal subjectivity with a mother's ability to narrate her account of her own motherhood, her relations with the child, and her view of the child's life.

MOTHER: THE SILENT SUBSTRATUM OF CULTURE

Simone de Beauvoir was the first to present a philosophical account of the contradiction between the subject position and motherhood. She argues that motherhood is an extreme manifestation of women's Otherness. Motherhood in Western culture *is* being-for-an-other, determined by the needs and expressions of another. The mother is the ultimate Other, the negation of whose subjectivity enables the existence of another as subject. As such, woman's maternal realization is her undoing as subject (de Beauvoir, 1989, p. 516).

De Beauvoir (1989) stresses the illusionary aspect of pregnancy and motherhood:

> She is no longer an object subservient to a subject; she is no longer a subject afflicted with the anxiety that accompanies liberty, she is one with that equivocal reality: life. Her body is at last her own, since it exists for the child who belongs to her. Society recognizes her right of possession and invests it, moreover, with a sacred character. Her bosom, which was previously an erotic feature, can now be freely shown, for it is a source of life . . . with her ego surrendered, alienated in her body and in her social dignity, the mother enjoys the comforting illusion of feeling that she is a human being in herself, a value. But this is only an illusion. . . . Creative acts originating in liberty establish the object as value and give it the duality of the essential; whereas the child in the maternal body is not thus justified; it is still only a gratuitous cellular growth, a brute fact of nature as contingent on circumstances as death and corresponding philosophically with it [p. 496].

According to de Beauvoir (1989), the mother who inhabits woman's consciousness as Other momentarily feels *like a subject*, creating and signifying, and experiences the legitimacy of wanting, of desiring, and of expressing this desire. However, this desire, which supposedly manifests her free self-determined consciousness, is an illusion.

In order to create a critical distance from this position of mother-as-Other, de Beauvoir (1989) chooses to depict motherhood from the viewpoint of the mother herself, who aspires to become a subject but fails. The text narrates the mother's experience and thus locates it as the first step toward being a subject whose consciousness tells the story of its own freedom and commitment.

De Beauvoir (1989) applies an image of a subject who is associated with freedom to negate a given factuality of reality and who, through his or her actions, determines the meaning of his or her universe. For de Beauvoir, the mother's capacity to become a subject is contingent on motherhood being an embodiment of freedom. The mother may become free through her ability speak up. These questions balance the authoritative voice of the text and stress that the daughter's account is radically open to be validated by the mother.

Irigaray assumes that the mother's silence is a symptom of her Otherness, both as a woman and as she who embodies the presymbolic. Thus this silence cannot be transformative; nor can it figure in a productive subjectivity (Irigaray, 1991, p. 52). It is for this reason that the I in the text calls her mother to articulate her position in language, and by that, to break the heritage of silenced femininity and to constitute her own subjectivity.

This account of maternal subjectivity dismisses the antagonism between responsibility and subjectivity found in both de Beauvoir and contemporary popular discourse. It provides instead a way to understand motherhood as a resource for subjectivity. By posing questions and narrating her own sense of losing her embodied subjectivity, the daughter summons the mother to answer and to reappear through this exchange. The appeal turns the mother into an *addressee.* This transformation positions her as a subject required to account for her motherhood. And her motherhood in turn is a locus of agency, freedom, will, and, as well, responsibility for the painful inheritance of femininity she passes to her daughter (Irigaray, 1981, p. 51). The daughter's appeal to the mother is meant to establish the mother as she who *can* respond, as a subject who can and must create herself as an enunciating-position. The daughter places the mother in a position of *response-ability*, which is at once a position of *responsibility* and subjectivity. Thus, Irigaray links the constitution of an accountable subject to participation in dialogue. This dialogic subject is first and foremost a coherent source of meaning and actions. In a sense, in order to fulfill the deep commitment to her daughter's life, the mother must break the silence forced by the image of the phallocentric subject and voice her own unique subjectivity.

I believe that the great contribution of Irigaray's thought to the project of refiguring maternal subjectivity lies in Irigaray's account of the relation between subjectivity and Otherness. For Irigaray, the relation with the Other is not one of complete negation. As Kelly Oliver (2001) stresses, ''for Irigaray limits or limitations do not have *negative* connotations, because the negative itself is reworked as a positive labor, a giving birth'' (p. 209). Irigaray argues for a unique aspect of Otherness, which she calls ''love of same,'' that is, love of the archaic undifferentiated Other who nurtures one's life (Irigaray, 1993, p. 83). Acknowledging this dimension of ''love of same'' is, according to Irigaray, necessary in order to be able to relate to the Other without reducing her or him to either an aspect of the I's world or to a complete and horrifying negativity: ''The Other can exist only if it can draw on the well of sameness as its matter, for the texture of its horizon, the emergence of its beyond-world'' (Irigaray, 1993, p. 83).

In these relations, the validation of one's being rests on a sense of closeness and intimacy with the Other. The Other becomes available to the I as who, in her difference, provides the resource of life itself. The I recognizes herself only in deep proximity to this enabling Other (Irigaray, 1996, p. 108).

''Love of same'' is an ontological openness toward the concrete embodied Other, which for Irigaray, following Levinas, is the unique feature of subjectivity as emerging from the corporeal generosity of the maternal body. The inability of mothers in phallocentric culture to integrate this scene of unique human relations into their subjectivity is the wound that is marked by maternal silence.

Irigaray's account provides a theoretical scheme in which the child's Otherness should not essentially be experienced as a negation of the mother's freedom and self-expression. The child's Otherness is a concrete and embodied singularity that cannot and should not be consumed.

However, it is not the Hegelian Other, that is, the total limit of the subject's self-attainment. The relations with the child offer the mother a chance to find, in her own embodied experience, the traces of the love of the maternal body disavowed by phallocentric culture. This love having been found, the Otherness of the child becomes an affirmative pole—an open horizon of difference toward which the mother reveals herself as a transformative dynamic—a becoming rather than an enclosed repetition.

In these relations the child-Other is a horizon of the future. She or he opens the world of the mother to a relationship in which neither the one nor the other is determined because each facilitates for the other a horizon of creative becoming. The mother, whom Irigaray tries to bring to life, is transformed through a continual movement toward the horizon of the Other, never to be unified, mapped, or exhausted by any description. The child's indetermination does not entail a failure on the part of the mother to constitute a sense of subjectivity. Instead, it is the principle of maternal subjectivity as a creative becoming—the responsibility for a future unforeseeable. The responsibility for the Other is also the condition for the mother's transformative desire.

Oliver argues that Irigaray's notion of love differs from the Hegelian notion of recognition. In acknowledging the limitation of one's subjective perspective to fully represent the Other, Oliver (2007) argues that, for Irigaray, ''recognition is a form of love that requires bearing witness to that which is beyond recognition, bearing witness to what cannot be seen. For Irigaray, love is witnessing that which is between us, the invisible bond created through the labor of the negative, which is not nothing'' (p. 132).

However, the rhetoric of Irigaray's text implies a demand that does not respect the sense of maternal subjectivity as witnessing. Irigaray's relational text assumes that in order for women to live their motherhood as a site of subjectivity, they must narrate their knowledge, sensations, and losses as mothers. This image, although to some extent necessary, still assumes the necessity of subjectivity as a core of coherent voice and presence. In this sense, experiences of extreme disorientation, disintegration, incoherency, and transformation, which are part of motherhood, still pose an immanent risk to the mother's subjectivity.

There remains, however, a crucial question that lies at the heart of the different visions of maternal subjectivity: to what extent is the need to ''be normal''—to reassemble the experiences of motherhood into some sort of coherent narrative—a demand posed by phallocentric culture that still acknowledges and worships only one ideal of subjectivity, that of the autonomous, self-determined subject? Or rather is motherhood intrinsically an abstraction that one can bare and work with while in itself being a challenge to one's subjectivity? Irigaray's theoretical framework provides a way to go beyond the identification of motherhood with intrinsic interruption, or at least show how this interruption is a productive resource for maternal subjectivity. However, I believe that in presupposing that the mother becomes a subject, first and foremost, as self-enunciating, Irigaray still echoes an image of subjectivity entrenched in a culture that rejects the notion of maternal subjectivity. I believe that, in order to provide a cultural and theoretical space in which maternal subjectivity can be thought in its unique relations with the Other, we have to go further, rethinking how we can communicate that unique position of being with the child's Otherness.

What I argue is that, in order to safeguard the child's Otherness as an open future, and in order for mothers to find in the relations with the child-as-Otherness their own way to embrace transformation and disruption as a path of becoming toward an open future, one ought to give up the wish to posit oneself as the authoritative narrator of this transformation. The meaning of the

AUTHOR BIO

Miri Rozmarin, Ph.D., is a lecturer in Philosophy and Women's and Gender Studies at Tel-Aviv University. She is the author of *Creating Oneself: Agency, Desire, and Feminist Transformations* (Peter Lang, 2011).

Part III: Maternality and Writing, Creativity

I'm in the Milk and the Milk Is in Me[1]
Writing from the Night Kitchen

Donna Bassin, Ph.D.

Although psychoanalysts have used psychoanalytic concepts to understand issues of writer's block as it affects the work of artists and writers, we have largely neglected the process of psychoanalytic writing per se. The author's personal relationship between self, text, and community is used as an initial contribution to the development of clinically near imaginative theory as well as to facilitate the generative authorship of others. The difficulty inherent in the arrogance of a creative thought–embodies one's envy, competitiveness, and destructiveness with her forebears and contemporaries–is considered.

As an analyst I have been taught to pay attention to the meaning and impact of my clinical interpretations, but I was never encouraged to examine the meaning and compelling press of my need to write, the seemingly disparate themes of my writings, or my inner life as I write. This kind of inner exploration seems an overlooked responsibility for all of us who write or want to write, especially in view of the current attention to the analyst's use of herself in the therapeutic encounter.

I am at my desk, in my own night kitchen, trying to combat my own anxiety of authorship.[2] I do know that I write about what I fear, what I don't understand, and what I desire. I also know not only that my writing is about the content of the text—the subjects that I write about—but also that the very activity of writing contains some attempt to fulfill some desire as yet unknown. The "what" I write about and the "why" of my press to write are inextricably bound. And in the service of this latter motivation, the actual product or finished text is often beside the point.

Speaking about my experience of writing has become an ironic task as I find myself having to move from the comfort of the already known—the already theorized—to the exciting anguish of the unfamiliar. The challenge, the hope, and, I suppose, the fear is to write something not already known by me and, in the most grandiose of worlds, not already known by others: to make the gift that makes the other grateful and I the writer indispensable and irresistible.

Writing, for the public, like the manifest content of a dream, is often only the surface manifestation of an array of wishes, questions, fears, hopes, and explorations subject to a long process of working through, synthesizing, hiding, illuminating, revising, and fretting. I experience my published papers as ultimately more certain and clear, but in exchange they seem more stagnant and suffocating than the original drafts. Writing for the public, like waking thoughts, tries to make thought conform to an intelligible world by plugging it up with shreds and patches and sanding it all together. But it also revises—what Freud (1900) referred to as the dream work or secondary revision—to get rid of the forbidden and objectionable. In this way, every piece of public writing becomes the petrified remains or death mask of this underlying vital and disorderly process.

[2] See Bassin (1983) for a detailed elaboration of this transformation.

undoing, weaving and unraveling, making presence and finding absence, having and losing, and putting together and taking apart that I have always understood as the necessary rituals, warmup, and entry to my writing, like fear and anxiety—tells me something essential about the allure and real desire of writing. What originally seemed like resistance, distraction, and avoidance moves usefully into inspiration and insight. The more I understand the meaning of the attendant rituals or rites of writing, the more I can transform enactments and repetitions into strategy and ideas for new writing. Writing rituals are transitional spaces but also can be transformational experiences.

Some writers would say that they write to manage anxiety and others that they manage anxiety in order to write. Freud was a prodigious writer and, by his own account, suffered the anxiety of authorship (see Grubrich-Simitis, 1996). He had very clear requirements in order to drop himself into his work-reflection and writing. He needed oversized paper, certain heavy fountain pens and wax crayons, a special desk chair, a room of his own away from family, the collection of statues he had on his desk, a fog of cigar smoke, and freedom from distractions from nuances (which included writing letters, chairing meetings, reading books, attending congresses, and even treating patients). In a letter to Ferenczi, December 6, 1915 (cited by Grubrich-Simitis 1996, p. 80) Freud wrote, in reference to his writing, "And once more, for me it has almost always been an agonizing struggle, Why should it be any better for you?" Freud said he needed the tension of that "modicum of misery" as an optimal condition for his mental activities.

I am a rather sloppy writer. I usually write without knowing exactly what I am writing about. In fact, writing is the only way for me to gain clarity on my usual formless and disorganized thinking. I have to write until I find those sentences which recognize my thoughts. More often than not, I write as if I were throwing words over some invisible sentence. The correct words seem to stick to the experience. The words drape over the experience, catch the edges, and create an initial contour. Then, during a process of successive approximation, I pull other words out. Sometimes I find a better fit, and most often I accept the limits of my own language. These idea fragments are now mated with other idea fragments that seem to illuminate each other, and, if a spark seems possible, I allow it to exist in a larger chunk of thought. All this is tentatively pieced together like a collage—my writing is under construction. The next phase is to remove the unnecessary; like a sculptor, I find myself chipping away the excess that has encased and burdened the sentence. I allow myself to see what is missing. Theoretically I know that it is during these writing moments, when anxiety wipes out calm and confidence and the illusory curtain of certainty is pulled away, that the opportunity for something new to come into existence arises.

Although brought about in a solitary situation, writing is a collaborative social process. Each text memorializes the contributions of many others, some recognized and cited; others, when our identifications are so complete as to negate the difference and influence, are imperceptible. I seek out these other writers in texts they have written when I am suffering from ontological anxiety or uncertainty about an idea. For me, writing is not possible without reading. Reading and writing are in a continuous loop. I write to be read by my own thoughts—to be comprehended and made intelligible to myself. If we allow it, our writing can look back at us and provide that connection between the inside out and the outside in, between public and private, body and mind, self and other.

I almost cannot read without a pencil in my hand or write without an array of books around me. In the margins of my more useful books are records of ongoing conversations with these author-partners who have had similar questions. I note a transformation in these conversations in the margins as I have noted a change in the way I use other theorists. Increased confidence in the legitimacy of my own thought and opportunities to manage conflict and difference without any apparent overwhelming destruction have allowed me to disagree, at least in the margins. This encounter with my books is one with a personal collection of useful others who survive no matter how much ranting, raving, and revising I do in their margins. The book remains for a new reading. Winnicott was right.

Our relationship to a professional literature is multilayered. A review of the literature provides a context and a historical perspective, but I believe our use of that literature in our writing serves other necessary psychological tasks.[4] Citations and acknowledgments can serve as reparation to ward off fears of retaliation. In a reparative act, we remember and cite our predecessors, our intellectual parents. Thus we temporarily restore the past and purify these ambivalent relationships of hate, competition, and envy. One can hide in one's literature, find oneself in it, and have a relationship with it.

It has been a psychoanalytic observation, now almost a tradition, to connect the dots between the making of a baby and creating something. Thus writing evokes all the anxiety attendant to the creation of a baby—imperfection, damage, separation, envy, oedipal transgression. And while this phenomenon has been clinically observed and spoken about by creators of all kinds—even Freud (cited in Grubrich-Smithis, 1986, p. 75) discussed the birth pangs surrounding his own writing—it seems to be a limited package. It seems to me that writing is an attempt not only to create a baby, as a mother does, but also to create and refind an object relationship, a recognizing other, a dynamic holding environment, a transformational muse. We write then not just a "baby," but a variety of our own personal partnerships—mother-daughter, father-daughter, lover-lover.

What is most compelling (and here I think is one of the sources of my own compulsion to write) is that writing is like the very beginning of a new romantic encounter. One is elated, excited by the possibilities until the inevitable disillusionment sets in

---

[4] Sandra Gilbert and Susan Gubar's (1979) groundbreaking book of essays is an effort to give sound and voice to the invisible history of literary production by women. They maintain that Harold's Bloom's model of the "anxiety of influence"—the anxiety of literary successors overthrowing their precursors is a model of literary paternity and as such is not a useful metaphor for women. If the history of literary transmission and inheritance is, as Bloom, suggests, a history of sons who must symbolically destroy their literary fathers, where are women in this oedipal tale? Gilbert and Gubar maintain that women writers do not battle at the crossroad but, rather, struggle with an anxiety of authorship. This anxiety of authorship has to do with the fear of isolation or personal destruction should the woman attempt to be a successor.

and the process/product is deemed inadequate. The unknown factor is what allows some of us to accept, or at least manage, the limitations—the gaps—without too much depression in which hopelessness and despair set in. Albrecht Dürer's etching of *Melancholia* illustrates this state of a disconnected and disabled mind, where the metaphoric utensils of everyday life lie on the ground, like our thoughts and relationships, unusable. I believe that the ability to mourn the loss, rather than identify with it, as occurs in melancholia, allows natural desire once again to emerge and instigate a process of refinding something once experienced as present, or at least imagined, and now absent. Desire drives the search, whereas intellectual discipline or external demands on the writing shape the specificity of the particular content.

I long for recognition in a reading, but, in the more exciting engagements, I experience the text as wanting me to complete it. I often rewrite others' texts; I find my own words to say what has already been said—I need to do that for memory—to make it my own. Years of being taught to put it into your own words now have different meaning. In conversations with my collaborative silent authors, I get, certainly not the true word, but at least the last word. Their texts are the initial structure, which contain and mediate my associative flow. Mingling in a counion allows me to try on their thoughts from the inside and rework them my own language and through my own experience. Eventually comes the anxiety. I must take my leave.

It is relatively easy to rattle off the conscious reasons that I write, which paradoxically seem to be the same reasons that I don't want to write. I write because I have an idea that I believe is useful and want others to benefit from it. I fear writing it because I don't want to be seen as aggressive, intrusive, or wrong. I don't write because I don't want to expose my egoism, envy, competition, and narcissism. I write to make order and meaning out of chaos and ontological insecurity—to calm or delude myself with some transient truth. I don't write for fear of not finding anything useful. I write for the pleasure of the aesthetic experience of crafting myself into something elegant and harmoniously patterned and desirable. I don't write for fear of or to make a space just to tolerate absence. I find myself working hard and long on my writing until the language itself opens to the rhythms and shapes of the emotions that are associated with the maternal and my indescribable something.

Women, we clinically observe, struggle with finding accessible and effective pathways for detaching themselves from mother, or, rather, the maternal "thing." And if the true acceptance of her absence is necessary for a real use of language in authorship and not merely word use, what hope do we have of really writing? Perhaps there is a clue in the process of writing itself, which is, paradoxically, a separation from one's inner world and objects and a pathway to keeping things all together. The pleasure of desire is in the perpetual tension between longing and futility. Writing is never finished, and there is always hope that next time one will get closer to that idea which is wished for. Writing involves a search for the maternal other and me, whose loss is the wellspring of origin. Hence my frequent occupation in the all-night kitchen.

REFERENCES

Arendt, H. (1970), Introduction. In: *Illuminations*, ed. H. Arendt (tran. H. Zohn). New York: Schocken Books.

Bassin, D. (1982), Women's images of inner space: Data toward expanding interpretative categories. *Internat. Rev. Psycho.-Anal.,* 9:191–203.

———, ed. (1999), *Female Sexuality: Contemporary Engagement.* Northvale, NJ: Aronson.

——— (2001), History: A biodegradable. *Psychoanal. & Psychother.,* 18:33–38.

Benjamin, W. (1931), Unpacking my library: A talk about book collecting. In: *Illuminations*, ed. H. Arendt (trans. H. Zohn). New York: Schocken Books, 1970.

Ellis, J. (1983), *One Fairy Story Too Many: The Brothers Grimm and Their Tales.* Chicago, IL: University of Chicago Press.

Freud, S. (1900), *The Interpretation of Dreams. Standard Edition,* 4. London: Hogarth Press, 1963.

——— (1919), A child is being beaten. *Standard Edition,* 17:175-204. London: Hogarth Press, 1961.

——— (1933), Femininity. *Standard Edition,* 22:112-135. London: Hogarth Press, 1961.

Gilbert, S. M. & Gubar, S. (1979), *The Madwoman in the Attic: The Woman Writer and the Nineteenth-Century Literary Imagination.* New Haven, CT: Yale University Press.

Grubrich-Simitis, I. (1996), *Back To Freud's Texts: Making Silent Documents Speak* (trans. P. Slotkin). New Haven, CT: Yale University Press.

Lear, J. (1996), The introduction of Eros. *J. Amer. Psychoanal. Assn.,* 44:673–698.

Sendak, M. (1995), *In the Night Kitchen.* New York: HarperCollins.

Mother-Writing and the Narrative of Maternal Subjectivity

Suzanne Juhasz, Ph.D.

This essay discusses how writing from a maternal perspective can construct maternal subjectivity in a linguistic form. Maternal subjectivity is understood as the aggregate of subject positions, or "representations," experienced by a woman who is a mother. Writing can form connections between subject positions, including those which have been split off or denied because of culturally induced ambivalence, to establish a subjectivity that is multiple rather than split. Through a reading of Mary Gordon's novel, *Men and Angels,* I show how the text's narrative structure, as it represents a mother's discourse with her own mother, her discourse with herself, and her discourse with her child, incarnates the plurality of self positions that mothers possess and constructs a relationship or "grammar" between them. By evoking this complex maternal subjectivity, mother-writing can be understood as a gesture toward recognition—both within the text, for its characters, and outside the text, for the mother/writer.

Psychological theory, with its "developmental tilt" (Mitchell, 1988), generally talks about identity, subjectivity, recognition, and maturation from the perspective of the child. The daughter needs and demands recognition, to paraphrase Jessica Benjamin (1988, 1995); the daughter's adult writing may be viewed as another facet of her search to get recognition; that is, writing can become a site, and a process, for negotiating this originary relationship. The many modern American and British novels, stories, poems, and autobiographies written from the daughterly perspective are testimony to the power of the need and the relentlessness of the search. Frequently, by way of this writing, the daughter/author is able to recognize the separate subjectivity of the mother, and this achievement helps to bring her own identity into being—even as her own vantage point or subjectivity is what permits her to recognize her mother. This is one way to understand Benjamin's (1988, 1995) concept of mutual recognition: the mother recognizes the daughter as subject; the daughter recognizes the mother as subject; and, in the process, the daughter is recognized. The writing daughter's creation of the mother's subjectivity is at once a self-serving and a generous act.

This conception of the role of writing in cultural experience is predicated on a view (advanced by Winnicott, 1971, and Ogden (1986), for example) that language and symbolization are themselves a product of the original mother–infant dyad; further, the transitional space of mother–infant interrelating, which requires the mother's position as object mother as well as environment mother, enables the processes of confronting difference and similarity. It is a space of play, creativity, and symbol formation; it is "the root of symbolism in time" (Winnicott, 1971, p. 6). Language-learning itself is a matter of relationality, establishing new modes of interaction between child and mother (Trevarthan, 1979; Dore, 1983; Stern, 1985). Rather than attributing symbolization to the oedipal moment, as does Lacanian theory, this Winicottian line of reasoning sees the negotiation of the space between self and other (or object) as very much an aspect of the ongoing process of recognition that Benjamin (2000) so powerfully takes up in her work.[1] When

[1] Benjamin (2000, pp. 304–305) has discussed "the third" that exists in the mother–infant dyad as a mental function or capacity that is a foundation for symbolic representation. See also Ogden (1986, p. 72) on the triangularization

experience as mother. There are works about which we have trouble saying for certain, "This is a mother-text," or "This is a daughter-text," because the two subject positions interrelate, get mixed up, even confused. In fact, many of the daughter-texts that crowd our bookshelves are written by women who are also mothers. You might say that their experience as daughters remains so important to them, when they are 30, or 40, or 50, or 60, because it is unfinished business: unfinished because they have not yet gotten their quota of recognition. The daughter-book is the one they have to write if they are to come into identity at last. Is there, then, no distinction between mother-writing and daughter-writing?

I think that there is. I propose that, when a mother-writer writes from all these subject positions, she demonstrates, first of all, that, contrary to popular opinion, they all exist. If so much maternal ambivalence derives from the external and internalized pressure to disavow one or the other of these identities–indeed, to disavow subjectivity itself–then their very linguistic embodiment brings them into being and into the same textual space. Second, writing can potentially create a *connection* between maternal identities, so that each can be related to and even enhance the other. This is a goal described by Suleiman (1985), who proposes hopefully that, rather than being an obstacle or source of conflict, motherhood might be a "source of connection to work and world" (p. 22) and that maternal tenderness and the urge for self-expression might support, not hinder, each other (p, 26). Writing can make sense of the parts and the relationship between them, can construct or create that relationship even or especially when it is *not* the lived experience of the writer.

Yet my discussion reminds us dramatically that mothers are daughters. Winnicott (1965, p. 39) said that there is no mother without a baby. As a corollary, there is no baby without a mother (alive or dead, absent or present). Not only is the daughter who becomes a mother still the daughter of her mother, but her daughterhood is part of her motherhood. Mothers of all kinds mother as they do because of the daughtering they have done. Yet the significance of daughterhood changes importantly with the advent of motherhood, so that the daughter who is a mother is not the same kind of daughter as one who is not a mother.

Therefore, although mothers may be daughters, mother-writing is not the same as daughter-writing, if only because mothers are *more than* daughters. The multiplicity that defines and organizes maternal subjectivity is composed of a series of relational positions: a mother-who-is-a-daughter in relation to her own mother; a mother-who-is-a-daughter in relation to her child; a mother-who-is-a-woman in relation to the social world, where she functions as lover, worker, political being; a person of a certain gender, sexuality, class, and race: a mother-as-her-child's Fantasy of Motherhood (the capital M Mother) in relation to herself as lowercase mother, the everyday woman who mothers; a mother-as-her-own-Fantasy of Motherhood, in relation to her lowercase self; a mother in relation to her child. I am proposing that mother-writing can work to construct, or even create, maternal subjectivity by bringing together in the same textual space the aggregate of identities that mothers possess and establishing a viable relationship, or "grammar," among them. Though frequently difficult to achieve in lived experience, this process is enabled by locating a connecting point in the woman herself, for all these identities are hers. Such writing demands the willingness, ability, and sheer need of the author to utilize her complex feelings and experience in behalf of the creation of such a text.

These uneasily associated subject-positions are discussed by Stern (1995), who presents a different but related assessment of maternal self-representations, as he terms them.

> With the birth of her first baby, the mother's basic status and identity in life are changed overnight. A sweeping reappraisal of the organization and priority of most of her self-representations begins. . . . the mother's self as woman, mother, wife, career-person, friend, daughter, granddaughter; her role in society; her place in her family of origin; her legal status; herself as the person with cardinal responsibility for the life and growth of someone else; as the possessor of a different body; as a person "on call" 24 hours a day; an adventurer in life, a creator, a player in

> evolution's grand scheme, and so on—in short, almost every aspect of her life. [p. 24].

The relationality of maternal positions is unique, because biological motherhood originates in the act of giving birth to another person. Birth engenders a split (literally) that underrides the attachment to the new person who has thereby been created. From the physical fact that what makes a woman into a mother is that she was one, then two, then one again, comes a psychological identity that is multi- and contradictorily-valenced: close/distanced; expanded/depleted, finding/losing. Tenderness, fear, anger, joy, grief jostle for pride of place. Maternal desire is paradoxical at its root: both wanting to have and wanting to be (possession/identification), a passion that both expands and contracts one's sense of self-identity. Recognition of such a complex subjectivity would go a long way towards enabling such a person to feel that she is real.

MOTHER LOVE

A woman gives birth to a baby, *her* baby. Oh, it's you! You who are so beautiful, so special, so delicate, so needing, so giving. You who give me a sense of who I am, for I am (now) your mother. You are mine. I am the one responsible for you, for your life and your growing. And I am yours. From this moment until I die I will be in thrall to you, even though you will no doubt see it as the other way around. My passion for you is composed of powerful and sometimes conflicting emotions, including fear and anger: fear that I cannot give you all that you need, fear that I will fail as my mother before me, in one fashion or another, failed; anger that you can (must) ask and I can (should) not. You take me from myself as much as you give me a new self, and it is this tension with which I must struggle every day of my life so that I can be for you what you need most: a mother.

Here is maternal desire, in the words of Shirley Abbot (1998):

> I gazed into her eyes and she into mine, as hopelessly infatuated as two creatures have ever been on earth. I managed to wait out the time until I could lay my hands on

> her, giving myself over to pure lust, look at her hands and feet, inspect every inch of her, tell her I would love her until I died and then some. . . .
>
> Never had I fallen for a man in such a manner. I could understand why breast-feeding had for many years been frowned on, out of fashion. After all, could such pleasure—the comic smacking noises of a baby at the breast, her impatient need, her helpless satisfaction afterward, the brazen intimacy—really be legitimate, could it truly have medical sanction, provide needed calories and nutrients and immune factors? . . . Every other love I'd ever experienced, between the covers of a bed or a book, now seemed a triviality [pp. 201–202].

To give birth to another person, to produce that person out of one's own body and self, frequently engenders an overwhelming love that is bound up with an "euphoric sense of possession": "Mine," I cried, "mine!" (p. 200). The baby is more than beautiful, exquisite, adorable: she is your own. Made by you, made for you—needing you alone. For along with the love, complementing, enhancing it, even, is a fierce sense of responsibility for the baby that translates into, "I am the one who must give her exactly what she needs."

Both emotional states may create the perception of the mother as all-loving, or all-controlling, but within her they can be the cause of deep conflict. For to love someone that much is to feel a unique and wonderful sense of self: "I am surging with energy toward you. I am enlarged and enhanced." At the same time, to feel so much responsibility—"You are dependent on me, and I must care for you, keep you alive at all costs"—can mean a depletion of self: "I am here only for *you*. I am *only* here for you. I am no longer 'I.'"

> As he drew the milk out of me, my inner self seemed to shrink into a very small knot, gathering intensity under a protective shell, moving away, moving further and further away, from the changes being wrought by this child who was at once separate and a part of me. Frightened that he would change my life completely, I desperately tried to cling

> to my boundaries. Yet I held him very close, stroked his skin, imagined that we were still one person [Lazarre, 1976, p. 28].

That is Jane Lazarre in *her* testimony to the maternal experience. Hailed as a feminist classic, her book documents resentment and desperation as well as joy—and, most important, as its dust jacket proclaims, "the struggle to reclaim a sense of self."

I myself do not think that way of nursing a child. For me nursing, in its sensuality, intimacy, and beauty was joy; but maybe I have selectively forgotten the 3:00 a.m. feedings. I do, however, know the feeling of which she speaks, although for me it was more often associated with other moments during early infancy. Trying to do something else during a naptime that was cut short for some reason known only to the baby; understanding over and over again that I was needed to the exclusion of any attention I might pay to needs of my own—that is, other than this need, a real one, to care for my child. What "other" needs? I had been taught that none existed, and, even if they did, they were wrong, or bad. I had been taught not to register any other need if I ever felt it stirring. My baby was my need, or, rather, her needs were mine.

But despite pages of theory attesting to the inevitability and primacy of symbiotic merger, it is actually impossible to achieve. Many a mother has been impaled on this dilemma's horns—not only because the contradictory and usually complementary feelings that the baby is (1) yourself and (2) something causing you to lose yourself are common, but also because you continue to inhabit other identities besides this baby, this birth. And because the baby herself in so many ways does not really want such merger. The part of you that may even desire it is sure to be thwarted. Abbott (1998) puts it this way:

> For inevitably the baby smiled, sat up alone, drummed upon the high-chair tray with a spoon, expressed her unalterable preference for peanut butter over string beans, toddled fearlessly across the floor, climbed out of her crib alone at an early hour and woke me by patting my face and

> demanding pancakes, outgrew May's summer sandals by July 1, broke out of my protecting grasp in the playground, climbed recklessly to the top of the jungle gym, laughed at me from above as I stretched my arms, entreated her to climb down, and pleaded with her not to take such chances with her precious little bones: evidence enough that one day the child would follow her own will and test her strength in other ways and gradually vanish altogether [p. 204].

Separation and connection orchestrate the trajectory of motherhood.

Rozsika Parker (1995), in a passage that balances Abbott's words, describes how the child may go but the mother stays:

> While children move with more or less difficulty towards an ever-increasing sense of themselves as individuals separate from their mothers, women evolve from one maternal identity to another. Thus they move from being a mother supporting a head, to a mother pushing a buggy, to a mother holding a hand, to a mother waving a hand, to a mother waiting for a hand to hold. *But always a mother.* Theirs is a "vertical" development compared to their children's "horizontal" growth away from them [p. 103].

How complicated a state is motherhood, an identity that may begin with the child's birth but that lasts a lifetime.

MATERNAL NARRATIVE

Why does a mother write? To document and even try to achieve maternal subjectivity. Writing becomes a potent agent for reconfiguring not the multiplicity of maternal subjectivity (indeed, in this postmodern age contemporary psychoanalysts advise that multiplicity is the normative experience for subjectivity), but the ambivalence and splitting that often result from it. Maternal writing, like daughter-writing, is a gesture toward recognition.

Mitchell (1993) described postclassical psychoanalytic views of the self as based in "a plural or manifold organization of

how an interaction is perceived and understood through the many lenses (fantasies, hopes, fears, family traditions and myths, important personal experiences, current pressures, and other factors) particular to the participant of the interaction (p. 12). I would stress a similar significance to literary narrative.

If the writing mother can construct a narrative that presents this multiple subjectivity, it can then be recognized in various ways. Within the text the mother *character* can find recognition from other characters–her daughter, or her own mother, or other mothers. The mother-*writer* can find recognition from her readers and even by way of the text that she has created. Because of the social construction of motherhood as an idealized selflessness, mothers are often wary of revealing to others the range, complexity, and contradictions of their subjectivity–a major reason, I believe, why so little mother-writing is done. Readers, too, who come to the text as daughters, or as mothers, or as sons or fathers, have their own vested interests for not wanting to encounter the multiplicity of maternal subjectivity. The writing process may be as fraught as it is necessary for the mother-writer.

Representation of maternal subjectivity is of great importance, for not only has it been culturally denied in Western history, but even now, despite frequent references to its existence, there is no fully developed theory of maternal subjectivity in psychoanalytic discourse.[4] The taboo against

[4] There seem to be several reasons for this difficulty. First, the perspective of the daughter tends to take over theory as well as fiction and poetry about the mother–daughter relationship. For example, despite being included in a section promisingly called "Motherhood," Bergman and Fahey (1996) focus entirely on the *daughter's* experience of this relationship. Even when mothers are studied, as in Mary Main's (2000) work on maternal narrative (in interviews) and attachment dynamics, the purpose is to understand the attachment responses of their children. For example, when the mother presents a coherent, collaborative discourse while maintaining objectivity, her child seems to be more secure (p. 1091). Second, as Kraemer (1996) observes, the insidious romanticization of the maternal, even in contemporary feminist writing that calls for the mother's right to a subjectivity of her own, stops short of exploring the "grimmer" experiences of ordinary hate, aggression, and failure; at contending with "the ways motherhood strains the ability of all mothers to tolerate ambivalence" (p. 766).

acknowledging its existence creates barriers for researchers against knowing how to look, how to develop a methodology. This is why Stern's (1995) recent work is of such value. He and his colleagues in infant research have focused carefully on mothers, and in particular, on their representations, in order to study the mother–infant relationship and to do therapy with mothers and babies. In his portrait of the relationship he includes as well the representations of infants, fathers or partners, and therapists, yet his emphasis is forcefully on mothers. Stern's interest in representations is particularly helpful to me in my concern for writing. In literary expressions of maternal subjectivity the formal and structural arrangements of the text, as well as its narrative content, are clues to the nature of maternal subjectivity. The processes of representation and discourse as Stern describes them can serve as a lens through which to examine literary maternal narrative, its structures and its preoccupations, because such writing is one means not only of documenting such representations but also of experiencing, organizing, and revealing them—seeking, in the process, recognition.

MEN AND ANGELS

In this essay I focus on narrative structure itself by reading Mary Gordon's (1985) *Men and Angels* through its patterns of narrative organization: the forms it creates for embodying and organizing the multiplicity of maternal subjectivity. Gordon's well-known novel is a good example of a contemporary, white, middle-class text of mother-writing. As such, it has aspects in common with and differences from maternal work in other social groups within and outside the United States. My own research contrasts it with Toni Morrison's (1987) *Beloved* to show that, although race and class provide for salient distinctions, the concern for constructing maternal subjectivity as multiple remains constant. For Morrison's character Sethe, for example, who is an escaped slave, claiming the identity *of* mother, once she is in the North, is a critical step toward achieving subjectivity. Nonetheless, the novel shows that she has not achieved a full self-identity until she can also define herself as well as a social woman who lives in the world and in history.[5]

I am defining narrative structure here in several ways. First, it refers to who is narrating a text. The writer is, of course, doing the writing, but within the text, characters or an authorial voice speaks her words. In many texts of mother-writing the mother-character's own narration alternates with someone else's, and that someone is usually her daughter. The mother-writer's rendering of the daughter's point of view along with the mother's has several functions. It helps to establish maternal multiplicity, because the mother's subjectivity is constituted by her relationship to her child as well as by other factors. Also, by employing daughter-narration along with mother-narration, the mother-writer facilitates recognition of the daughter's subjectivity, an important piece of maternal work that helps her to understand and care for her daughter's needs. The format can be used as well to induce the daughter's recognition of the mother (as the mother-writer imagines it). *Men and Angels*'s third-person narrative alternates chapters focused in the consciousness of the main character–mother, daughter, and art historian Anne Foster–and her live-in babysitter Laura Post, a would-be daughter to Anne.[6]

Another way to look at narrative organization is in terms of Stern's (1995) idea of maternal discourses, "carried out internally and externally." Mother-writing is characteristically orchestrated by the mother's discourse with her mother (or mothers), with her daughter (or daughters), and with her self

[5] This essay is an earlier and abbreviated version of chapter 4 in Juhasz (2003). In chapters 4 and 5, on maternal subjectivity, I discuss *Men and Angels,* Morrison (1987) and Lisa Nelson (2000).

[6] *Men and Angels* is less typical than many other mother-novels and daughter-novels in this respect, because Laura is neither Anne's biological nor surrogate daughter. *Beloved* , for example, alternates the discourse of the mother, Sethe, and her two daughters, Denver and Beloved, along with her surrogate mother, Baby Suggs, and her lover, Paul D. Liza Nelson's (2000) *Playing Botticelli* alternates the narrative voices of the mother, Godiva Blue, and her daughter, Dylan. Many other recent novels, such as Elizabeth Strout's (1999) *Amy and Isabelle* and Marianne Fredricksson's (1998) *Hanna's Daughters* also employ this pattern.

(or selves). Discourse with the character's "mother-as-mother-to-her-as-a-child" significantly establish her sense of herself as daughter and as mother. Discourse with her child or children renders her evolving sense of motherhood. Discourse with her own several "selves" brings these subject positions into existence and relationship.

Often in contemporary novels sexuality and work exist in counterpoint with the mothering activities of the woman who is a mother. Particularly in middle-class white novels such as *Men and Angels* (Gordon, 1985) work emblematizes self-identity in a way that frequently comes into conflict with the cultural ideology of motherhood. In *Beloved* (Morrison, 1987), on the other hand, work is not a salient determinant of self-identity: a slave is objectified as the work that she does. Sethe works (it goes without saying) when she is an escaped slave as well as when she is a slave, and her quest for self-identity involves other factors: a revised concept of sexuality and, most significantly, a concept of self that allows for differentiation from as well as connection to her children.

The narrative of mother-writing is characterized as well by the tonal register of maternal desire. I see maternal desire as an aggregate of wanting to have and wanting to be. Wanting to have (attachment or object love) leads both to possessiveness and to responsibility–the urge to protect, even to control. Wanting to be (identification, or narcissistic love) at its best occasions an expanded sense of self and self-worth; yet, when accompanied by an overly strong sense of responsibility, it can also produce a feeling of depletion, of having been taken over or invaded by the child, which results in various forms of hostility. (It should be noted that I am using these Freudian categories of desire not from the perspective of the child, as originally conceived, but from the complementary perspective of the mother.)

Such urges find themselves in constant interplay with a different kind of wanting, which is to recognize the other as a separate subjectivity. Benjamin (2000), commenting on the construction of intersubjective (or internal) structures, sees the tension between recognition and omnipotence as "the inner conflict that shapes the interpersonal world. . . . The problem of whether or not we are able to recognize the other person as outside, not the sum of, our projections or the mere object of need, and still feel recognized by her or him, is defining for intersubjectivity" (p. 297). If the desire to identify can alter from omnipotence to a different form of idealization, in which recognition of the daughter's subjectivity affects the mother's ideas about her own present or potential subjectivity, then the fantasy element that is always present in desire changes to a different and less controlling mode. In narrative, such shifts are shown in plot as well as character development; but the inflections of desire are always there.

Men and Angels employs each of these modes of narration to meditate on maternal subjectivity, particularly as it is constituted by the relationship between motherhood and work. In an interview Gordon (Keyishian, 1988) comments on the difficulties in writing about motherhood: it is "threatening to people," she says. Motherhood is

> so overwhelming, and everybody knows that, and so they confine it to an inferior status simply because it's so frightening and so potent. That's one thing. The other thing is that there is so much literal drudgery about the care of children that people simply hate it. . . . And, of course, you know, you can get a little ridiculous if you do nothing but care for children all the time. I could no more stay home with my kids all day than I could be a neurosurgeon. You have to remember that there's a world out there [p. 720].

The conflict, or multiplicity (depending on how you look at it) between the three aspects of motherhood expressed in Gordon's comment (frightening and potent, drudgery, and isolating) is explored in *Men and Angels*. "Frightening and potent" calls up the fantasy element in motherhood: the capital M Mother. "Drudgery" is admittedly a part of its everyday manifestation. And "isolating" points to aspects of the mother's subjectivity that also exist: for example, the social woman, the woman who works at something other than maternity.

In her discourse with her own mother, with her self(ves), and with her children, Gordon's (1985) character Anne Foster, who declares at the outset, "It's my ruling passion, maternity" (p. 336), develops a subjectivity that changes from a place where she has both split off and denied aspects of her self to a more complex, multiple, and coherent sense of self. A series of other relationships, all of them versions of the mother–daughter or daughter–mother dyad, help define her activities and thinking. In the course of the novel, Anne moves from a belief that "mother" and "worker" are contradictory identities, threatening to one another, to a belief that some "maternal spirit" will make children and work a part of one another, to an understanding that the connection point she is seeking is the woman herself: a person who has a child and does work. These identities are necessarily related because all are hers.

That Anne is obsessed at the novel's beginning with "good mothers" and "bad mothers" alerts us to the fantasy elements organizing her thinking. Suleiman (1994), one of the first literary critics to connect psychoanalytic theory and maternal writing, explains the origins of maternal fantasy by using Klein's concept of splitting. A very young infant who experiences the mother's breast alternately as gratifying and pleasure-giving and, when it is delayed or withheld, as hateful and frustrating, says Klein, splits off the object world around her into "good" and "bad" mothers. The existence (creation) of a bad mother preserves the image of a good mother, necessary if only because the infant feels totally dependent on the mother. Suleiman refashions this notion into an idea about *maternal* splitting, whereby the child's myth of maternal omnipotence is transposed into an equally potent fantasy for mothers of absolute or ultimate maternal responsibility. Suleiman reads the pattern of relationships in *Men and Angels* between an assortment of mother-figures and child-figures as examples of maternal splitting, so that good mothers can be split off from bad mothers, with good and bad referring specifically to the conflict posed by the novel between the ability to protect a child and the need to do work (pp. 47–50).

Maternal splitting seems to me, however, to be an extension of the infant's splitting, in that both fantasy projections see the mother as only one component of her multiple self-positions: the capital M Mother. Anne's negotiations of the "good" and "bad" dichotomy with which she begins the novel leads her to some surprising places, which ultimately cause her to reevaluate this schema itself as a paradigm for the meaning of motherhood. As the novel begins, Anne sees herself as the unloved (good) child of her own (bad) mother, and as the loving (good) mother to her own two children, except for her fear that her work as art historian will make her a *bad* mother. After years of part-time positions, she has been asked to write the catalogue essay for the first major retrospective exhibition of an American expatriate painter, Caroline Watson. Accepting the position initiates her relationship with the au pair Laura, to whom she feels like a bad mother; but it also produces her intense and intimate relationship, by way of her paintings and journals, with Caroline herself, and with Caroline's daughter-in-law, Jane.

Caroline seems to have been a good artist *and* a bad mother to her only son, Stephen. Now, Caroline serves as a mother-figure for Anne. Before his early death Stephen married Jane, to whom Caroline was a loving mother-figure, even as Jane was the unloved daughter of her own mother. Jane, very much alive at 78, also mothers Anne. Gordon develops this complex pattern of mother–daughter, daughter–mother relationships to question what "good" and "bad" mean in the ethics of motherhood and how these fantasies might be adjusted in service of maternal identity.

Discourse with her own mother—a lifelong interpretation of her childhood—has set Anne's maternal practices in motion. Anne's memories of her mother "covering her ears and begging her children not to fight, crying when her youngest daughter refused, for the fiftieth time, to drink her milk" (p. 31) have symbolized her own abiding sense of failure. She was not lovable enough, she felt, or her mother would not have been unhappy. We learn later that her mother's coldness and hostility had a great deal to do with depression—which, however, ceased when she later went back to school and got a degree. Her mother's antagonistic feelings were also occasioned by the favoritism shown to Anne by her father. Her mother's complete distaste for home life (along with her father's seductive behavior) generated Anne's early belief that "she had to be the mother of the house" (p. 31). Anne's fantasy of a good mother, as opposed to her own bad mother, is of someone for whom being a mother—being Anne's mother, in particular—would be wonderful. Fathers are romantic and distant—they go to work (p. 72); but mothers ought not to need anything but their children.

Attempting to redress the wrongs of her own childhood, "this shame, this failure" (p. 31), Anne as a young wife and mother placed motherhood first and denied her own need to work. Her early marriage to Michael, who also had to behave maternally toward a single mother who adored him but could not handle the responsibility of the home, had everything to do with their shared attempt to "reinvent" domestic life. Another lesson might have been learned from her mother's experience—that is, that repression of all her identities ("Anne's mother" was as well "Susan Holliwell, Mount Holyoke, class of `41") can make a mother depressed. But Anne's perspective as she entered into her own maternity was that of the child, the daughter. This rooted-in-childhood discourse with her mother initially frames all Anne's attempts to be a wonderful mother and her conflicts with herself when her maternal attention is diverted from the children by her own desires for something else. It is true that Anne's mother is rejecting: Anne's adult experience of her mother's lifelong coldness occurs twice in the present tense of the novel, once during a family visit and again at the conclusion, when her mother cannot begin to comfort her after Laura's suicide. But the novel creates a shift in which Anne's interpretation of her mother's effects on her can change.

Anne's discourse with her own children, nine-year-old Peter and six-year-old Sarah, is a constant aspect of her consciousness. She admires Peter's fastidiousness and Sarah's irony; she is vitalized by their presence, when the air becomes more vivid and heated, every object in the house growing more alive (pp. 22–23). Passion and responsibility organize her motherhood. Desire for her children, she had discovered, was surprising and all-powerful. "No one had told her what it would be like, the way she loved her children. What a thing of the body it was, as physically rooted as sexual desire, but without its edge of danger

. . . it was savage, lively, volatile . . . she was lifted up and down by waves of passion: of fear, of longing, of delight" (pp. 22, 24). The attention born of this passion manifests itself in an urgent need to protect them, a need heightened surely because she felt herself so emotionally unprotected by her own mother. "There was . . . not much that you could do to influence the course of things determined so much by their natures and their fates. All you could do was, while they were still children, keep them safe" (p. 26). Iterated again and again is the mantra, "You did not hurt your children. You kept your children safe" (p. 114).

By means of this focus on her children, Anne has repressed another component of her identity, which, however, manifests itself when she is asked to write the catalogue for Caroline Watson. "Seeing those paintings, something grew in Anne, something she'd lived with . . . but hadn't known before, a push or a desire. . . . The paintings made her greedy to be with them, to speak of them" (p. 35). This is the urge to do work. It surfaces at a difficult time, because Anne's professor husband, Michael, who, no matter how loving, has always had the *right* to work, has accepted a grant to be in France for the year. This is why Anne needs help in caring for the children and how Laura comes into the novel. A surrogate mother is needed. Anne thinks this is a bad thing, but the novel is created to show the contrary: it all depends on who the surrogate mother is, and why.

Discourse with herself in her various subject-positions comprises the bulk of the novel. The majority of its chapters are narrated through the consciousness of Anne, as she both engages with and reflects on her experience. New experience is largely about her increased professionalism, which, in turn, is manifested in a series of relationships with women. Her husband, Michael, whom she loves, is, however, largely out of the picture, both in the story and in the play of her thoughts. Gordon sends him to France, so that Anne is freed from his influence as helpmeet or sexual partner. Even when he returns for a Christmas visit, Anne feels at a distance from him because she suspects him of having an affair in France. In response, she talks herself into attempting an affair with her electrician, a "motherly" sort of man who is thoroughly engaged with caring for his young son and invalid wife. He (predictably) repels Anne's advances, and we understand that in this novel heterosexuality is less important than maternal care in all its various forms, forms that often include an erotic component.

Almost all the mother–daughter pairs are in love: Caroline enters Anne's life "like a lover," and Jane married Caroline's son, Stephen, a man she did not love, so that she might have a formal relationship to Caroline—that is, have his mother for her own (p. 279). Gordon is thereby emphasizing both the absolute centrality of the mother–daughter relationship and its basis in powerful desire, which can be seen as homoerotic for mothers and daughters in the sense that the mother–infant relationship, the paradigm for all love relationships, contains elements of romance and eroticism along with such functions as nurture, protection, and education. Freud noted this, and later commentators have been both intrigued and repelled by the idea.[7]

Anne's research on Caroline Watson is articulated through her entry into relationships with Caroline herself and with Jane, who has hired her. Each becomes a new or surrogate mother to her, in different yet complementary ways. Caroline enters her life, "intrusive, overwhelming, siphoning attention" (p. 38). Anne sees how relentless Caroline was in her devotion to her work and is drawn to the "hard shining thing in the center of Caroline Watson that had never lodged in Anne" (p. 38). Her work on Caroline seems to her an act of daring paralleling Caroline's own: defying her father to study abroad and leaving her child 10 months of the year: "Unwomanly, they would have called her, but was that what people meant, had always meant, by womanliness—mere submission?" (p. 39). Gordon's imagery for Caroline as lover and artist—"intrusive" and "hard"—is not

[7] For example, Freud (1914) says that "the persons who are concerned with a child's feeding, care, and protection become his earliest sexual objects; that is to say, in the first instance his mother or a substitute for her" (p. 87). Irigaray (1981) observes that "given that the first body they have any dealings with is a woman's body, that the first love they share is mother love . . . women always stand in an archaic and primal relationship with what is known as homosexuality" (p. 44).

womanly but manly or "phallic," in the same way that the preoedipal mother—active and agential—is described in psychoanalytic parlance as phallic, even though she never was a man. She is called phallic because there has historically been no language for an "unfeminine" woman other than that of masculinity. And yet Caroline was an unloving mother. Anne thinks this is a profound barrier between them: "'You have done wrong,' she wanted to tell her" (pp. 113–114). However, this combination, good artist/bad mother, is, I believe, the source of Anne's passion for Caroline, at once unsettling and exciting. Exciting because it rattles the cage of her own ideas about motherhood; exciting, too, in that it releases Anne's well-defended love for her own mother, another bad mother.

Jane, who has never born a child, crustily dismisses Anne's attempts to connect Caroline's personal history with her art: "Marriage, childbirth, menstrual cycles, hysterectomies: they have nothing to do with the work. Give no more attention to them in the career of Caroline Watson than you would do in the career of Matisse" (p. 81). But to Anne it is central: "No one would have pored through a male artist's letters to his children as she had through Caroline's to Stephen. It was that Caroline was a woman and had a child and had created art; *because the three could be connected in some grammar*" (p. 114, italics added). How can it be, she wonders, that Caroline, who has created art, "beauty that would endure" (p. 156), has created as well a child she could not love?

Caroline, the mother-lover, teaches Anne about their connection by way of difference. For as *this* novel starts, Anne is neither as good at mothering nor as bad at doing work as she thinks. Her love for Caroline forces her to privilege her own work in behalf of Caroline and (therefore) to love Caroline wholly despite her wrongdoing. "Only if she lived with Caroline as a beloved presence could she come close to her in understanding," she thinks. "To do justice to the dead required an intimacy in which justice had no part . . . you needed to embrace them with the unquestioned love with which you embraced an infant" (p. 114).

Indeed, Anne needs to *recognize* Caroline, both literally (she achieved only a modest reputation in her lifetime) and psychodynamically. In this way she is less a mother to Caroline than a daughter who creates her own identity by seeing the mother's separate subjectivity. Using Caroline as a surrogate mother who is not unlike her biological mother, Anne comes to see her own mother's separate subjectivity in the novel's final pages. Even as she longs for comfort from her mother, she understands her mother's fear of her—because of her looks, good fortune, and ability to please her father, her mother's husband (p. 384). She understands as well that she is now an adult because, though she wants her parents, she knows they will not come (p. 386).

It takes Jane's outright nurture, however, to give Anne the trust and the sense of psychological freedom to do this work. Jane's no-nonsense confidence in Anne's ability to do the job well, her generosity and unsentimental appreciation—her *recognition*—elicit Anne's love. When Jane says, "I see you almost as a member of the family," Anne embraces her, enjoying Jane's large bones and firm flesh, and thinks how her own mother had always seemed too delicate, too vulnerable. She is delighted because Jane "had taken her in" (pp. 173–174). She need *not* mother Jane. It is Jane, in the end, who offers gruffly to care for Anne's children after Laura has committed suicide.

In these ways Gordon's narrative structure suggests that mothering, daughtering, and doing work are all distinct yet associated aspects of maternal subjectivity. Each is a different self-representation, but all generate and are generated by interpersonal relationships, for subjectivity is an organization of relational positions. As Anne renegotiates both her experience and understanding of these crucial positions, subjectivity itself changes.

Why, then, is Laura necessary to the novel, and why are chapters told from her point of view? Laura is not Anne's daughter, although she would like to be, choosing Anne in the stead of a mother who has entirely rejected her. Laura's world is based in a bizarre and obsessive religiosity concocted to show that mothers are not necessary: "a mother and her children, all that famous love, was nothing more than flesh to flesh, would drown them all, would keep them from the Spirit" (p. 57). Laura is a disaster as a "mother" to Anne's children. Some have suggested that she is there to prove Anne's (and many mothers') worst—and contradictory—fears: if you leave your kids with someone else, she will (1) try to murder them and (2) reveal your own incompetence. Not so. Laura's mishandling of the children—its culmination in ignoring them at the lakeside, where they might have drowned if Anne had not come to their rescue; Anne's firing her; and her subsequent suicide in Anne's own bathtub, her body to be found by Anne's son—are in the novel to prove something more profound. Anne's basic tenet for being a good mother—you must protect your children at all costs—is an impossible goal and an inadequate articulation of maternal desire.

To believe that protecting your child is the primary form of expressing maternal love is to deny the child her or his subjectivity through omnipotent overidentification—a process that at the same time negates the mother's subjectivity. The mother's loosening of protective identification releases her to accept and act with other aspects of herself, such as doing work. Desire, although unconditional by nature, must become conditional in expression, inflected by recognition in forms that can change. Anne learns this first by way of her new daughter-mother and mother-daughter relationships and then dramatically through her association with Laura.

Such a belief negates as well the existence of the outside world, composed of forces well beyond the mother's control. Laura represents that outside world. She lacks the ability to be either a surrogate daughter or a surrogate mother; she remains a stranger, and she is dangerous. As she turns to Anne needily for mothering, Anne finds herself "unaccountably" disliking Laura—she, who has always prided herself on being such a good person, such a mother, at heart. After all, she can see that Laura "seems so unloved, so unmothered." "Listen, you're not her mother," replies Jane. "You're her employer. Your responsibility is to pay her a fair wage and not to overwork her. You don't have to save her life" (p. 188).

Anne cannot and does not save Laura's life: not because she cannot love her but because Laura is responsible for her own life, her own death. I do not think that Laura, as Suleiman (1985) suggests, is Anne's split-off bad-mother self but, rather, is Anne's split-off, badly mothered child self, representing the lost child in all of us–lost and unwilling to be found. That Laura's menace leads not to the death of Anne's children, which is what we fear, but to her own suicide is at once a relief, a horror, and a cautionary tale. What Anne understands in the end is that children can*not* be protected. Laura does not kill them, but she does die in their home; they witness death. From subsequent encounters with Laura's unyielding parents and her own unyielding parents, as well as from her interactions with Caroline and Jane, Anne also sees that mother love can never be perfect and that it cannot be everything.

Thus the novel concludes with Anne's meditation on mother love and maternal subjectivity, which starts with a shocking list of ways in which mother love transpires: mothers who loved their children in a way that cut the children's breath and stopped their hearts; mothers for whom the sight of their children meant nothing; mothers who hated their children from the moment of their birth; mothers who bent to kiss the children's flesh and felt the flesh stop up their mouths and make them fear for their next breath. From this comes a second revelation: "It was not all of life. And that was wonderful; it was a tremendous mercy" (p. 399). Because "there wasn't much that you could do. You gave them life, you loved them, then you opened them out to the world. . . . That was the mercy, that you could turn from them to something else, something they couldn't touch or be a part of" (p. 400). For example, her work. She will "take her mind, sharpen it, make it single," so as to write the words for Caroline. And then, refreshed, "dive back down to the dense underworld, to her children, and say, 'This is life. What shall we make of it? For it is terrible, and shining, and our hearts are sore'" (p. 400).

The structure of *Men and Angels*–the protagonist's interweaving discourse with her original mother and her other mother, with her children, and with her self as mother, daughter, friend, wife, worker, and sexual woman, in counterpoint with Laura's narrative–creates a maternal subjectivity that is multiple rather than split. Anne's perspective as she entered into her own maternity was that of the child, the daughter. The novel turns her into a mother who is, among other things, a daughter. Her adult relationships, as surrogate daughter and surrogate mother, are what enable her to move beyond that bifurcating split. When she thinks of Caroline as a woman who had a child and who created art "because the three could be connected in some grammar" (p. 114), we surmise that the novel is an attempt to write that grammar. Anne learns that Caroline made wonderful paintings of Stephen but could not help him flourish. Yet even in Caroline a connection exists: it resides in the consciousness or subjectivity of the woman who is a mother, who has a child and creates art. À la Stern (1995), Anne comes to understand that her maternal self-identity involves more than caring for her children, even as all her experiences are defined by relationality. Her representations, in other words, create a grammar of maternality, so that her many subject positions, no matter that they are differentiated, make sense in relation to one another: make for a multiple subjectivity.

In its construction of maternal narrative, *Men and Angels* does not, as do many other texts of mother-writing, create an internality or subjectivity for any of the characters other than Anne, except for Laura. Especially, Anne's biological children are not given their own narratives. Although Anne learns of their separateness from herself, Peter and Sarah are viewed through Anne's consciousness and are therefore *textually* her creations. When she cannot understand them–"What was this doing to them? What should she do to help them?" (p. 367)–we can't, either. This format tells us, I believe, something about the particular kind of recognition that Gordon, a mother who makes art, seeks for her heroine. From whom does Anne need recognition? Not from children but from a mother. Anne's maternal subjectivity is recognized in the text by Jane and obliquely by Caroline, although never by her own mother. Daughters and mothers alike, it seems, need recognition by mothers. And even as Gordon's character seeks and finds recognition from other characters who function as surrogate mothers, so her text seeks recognition for its construction of maternal subjectivity from readers who, in maternal fashion, will likewise see and accept this kind of mother self.

RECOGNIZING MOTHERS

I am proposing that writing can serve as an agent for constructing maternal subjectivity, because the transitional space of language allows for representation that is inventive as well as mimetic. Art is not exactly like life because it can transform as well as describe. When Anne characterizes Caroline's art as "taking experience and making this of it, that of it: beauty that would endure, that would say to life, stop here, now; that would hold life, thicken it and make it valuable, enduring, hard" (p. 156), she is referring, I think, to its ability to mold experience into shapes that facilitate meaning.[8] In the mother's lived experience, as I have discussed, the elements of maternal subjectivity can be disparate and contradictory. Mothers struggle with and often silence (split off, repress) such multiplicity because it is threatening to their own sense of motherhood and that of others. Writing offers to the mother-writer the opportunity for form, so that complex relationship, if not easy coherence, can be shown. The aggregate of multiple maternal subject-positions can make sense.

To whom might it make sense? Who, in other words, can recognize the mother's subjectivity? For writing must be read to come alive. Sources for recognition exist inside and outside the text. The mother-character achieves recognition within the story. The mother-writer looks for recognition from outside, by way of her writing–from the reader, who might serve as yet another surrogate mother. *Men and Angels*, like many mother-

[8] Gordon is surely echoing Virginia Woolf (1927) when the painter Lily Briscoe remembers the mother-figure, Mrs. Ramsay, as "making of the moment something permanent (as in another sphere Lily herself tried to make of the moment something permanent)–this was of the nature of a revelation. In the midst of chaos there was shape; this eternal passing and flowing, . . . was struck into stability. Life stands still here, Mrs. Ramsay said" (p. 61). Lily, who has rejected marriage and maternity so she can paint, and who yearns for Mrs. Ramsay as a mother/lover, learns that Mrs. Ramsay's maternal art form, the dinner party (or community), functions in ways akin to Lily's painting to create the moment that endures. At the same time Mrs. Ramsay's *procreation* leaves children, including Lily, whose re-creation of the mother in art helps her to construct her own identity.

texts, emphasizes the possibility of other mothering figures beyond the biological mother. Other mothers mean other sources of recognition, sources possessing assets as well as liabilities derived from not having been there at the beginning. What is critical is that there be recognition for maternal subjectivity. Mothers establishing maternal subjectivity are "daughters" not only because they never cease being the biological daughter of a mother but because maternal subjectivity is a new version of the self. In *Men and Angels,* for example, the mother/protagonist does not get this recognition from her biological mother. New sources for recognition are created for her: they tell us that mothers, and recognition, can come in many forms.

As well as the reader there is the writing itself. In *Beloved,* Morrison (1987) describes language as being like a mother, for it provides recognition to those who speak and those who listen. Telling stories becomes "a way to feed her," thinks Sethe (p. 58). The text that the mother-author writes can be seen not so much as a child to her as a mother. Linguistically embodying all the multiple aspects of maternal subjectivity in the same textual space, it creates a connection or "grammar" between maternal identities. Making sense of the many parts and the relationship between them, it demonstrates that there must be a relationship, that the parts are there in a particular configuration. Language can offer, in a word, recognition.

REFERENCES

Abbott, S. (1998), *Love's Apprentice: The Romantic Education of a Modern Woman.* Boston: Houghton Mifflin.

Aron, L. (1996), *A Meeting of Minds: Mutuality in Psychoanalysis.* Hillsdale, NJ: The Analytic Press.

Bach, S. (1994), *The Language of Perversion and the Language of Love.* Northvale, NJ: Aronson.

Bassin, D. (1994), Introduction. In: *Representations of Motherhood,* ed. D. Bassin, M. Honey & M. M. Kaplan. New Haven, CT: Yale University Press.

Benjamin, J. (1988), *The Bonds of Love: Feminism, Psychoanalysis, and the Problem of Domination.* New York: Pantheon.

——— (1995), *Like Subjects, Love Objects: Essays on Recognition and Sexual Difference.* New Haven, CT: Yale University Press.

——— (2000), Response to commentaries by Mitchell and Butler. *Stud. Gender & Sexual.,* 1:291–308.

Bergman, A. & Fahey, M. (1996), Two women and their mothers: On the internalization and development of mother-daughter relationships. *J. Amer. Psychoanal. Assn.,* 44(Suppl):409–482.

de Kanter, R. (1993), Becoming a situated daughter. In: *Daughtering and Mothering: Female Subjectivity Reanalyzed,* ed. J. van Mens-Verhulst, K. Schreurs & L. Woertman. London: Routledge, pp. 26–34.

Dore, J. (1983), Feeling, form and intention in the baby's transition to language. In: *The Women and Language Debate: A Sourcebook,* ed. C. Roman, S. Juhasz & C. Miller. New Brunswick, NJ: Rutgers University Press, 1994, 234–253.

Flax, J. (1990), *Thinking Fragments: Psychoanalysis, Feminism, and Postmodernism in the Contemporary West.* Berkeley: University of California Press.

Fredriksson, M. (1998), *Hanna's Daughters.* New York: Ballantine Books.

Freud, S. (1914), On narcissism: An introduction. *Standard Edition,* 14:67–104. London: Hogarth Press, 1957.

Gordon, M. (1985), *Men and Angels.* New York: Ballantine Books.

Hirsch, M. (1989), *The Mother-Daughter-Plot: Narrative, Psychoanalysis, Feminism.* Bloomington: Indiana University Press.

Irigaray, L. (1981), The bodily encounter with the mother. In: *The Irigaray Reader,* ed. M. Whitford. London: Basil Blackwell, 1991.

Juhasz, S. (2003), *A Desire for Women: Relational Psychoanalysis, Writing, and Relationships Between Women.* New Brunswick, NJ: Rutgers University Press.

Keyishian, M. D. (1988), Radical damage: An interview with Mary Gordon. *Liter. Rev.,* 32:69–83.

Kraemer, S. B. (1996), "Betwixt the dark and the daylight" of maternal subjectivity: Meditations on the threshold. *Psychoanal. Dial.,* 6:765–792.

Kvisteva, J. (1980), *Desire in Language: A Semiotic Approach to Literature and Art,* trans. T. Gora, A. Jardine, & L. S. Roudiez. New York: Columbia University Press.

Lazarre, J. (1976), *The Mother Knot.* Durham, NC: Duke University Press, 1997.

Main, M. (2000), The organized categories of infant, child, and adult attachment: Flexible vs. inflexible attention under attachment-related stress. *J. Amer. Psychoanal. Assn.,* 48:1055–1096.

Mitchell, S. (1988), *Relational Concepts in Psychoanalysis: An Integration.* Cambridge, MA: Harvard University Press.
——— (1993), *Hope and Dread in Psychoanalysis.* New York: Basic Books.
Morrison, T. (1987), *Beloved.* New York: New American Library.
Nelson, L. (2000), *Playing Botticelli.* New York: G. P. Putnam's Sons.
Ogden, T. (1986), *The Matrix of the Mind: Object Relations and the Psychoanalytic Dialogue.* Northvale, NJ: Aronson.
Parker, R. (1995), *Mother Love/Mother Hate: The Power of Maternal Ambivalence.* New York: Basic Books.
Stern, D. (1985), *The Interpersonal World of the Infant: A View from Psychoanalysis and Developmental Psychology.* New York: Basic Books.
——— (1995), *The Motherhood Constellation: A Unified View of Parent–Infant Psychology.* New York: Basic Books.
Strout, E. (1999), *Amy and Isabelle.* New York: Random House.
Suleiman, S. (1985), Writing and motherhood. In: *Risking Who One Is: Encounters with Contemporary Art and Literature.* Cambridge, MA: Harvard University Press, 1994, pp. 13–37.
——— (1988), Maternal splitting: "Good" and "bad" mothers and reality. In: *Risking Who One Is: Encounters with Contemporary Art and Literature.* Cambridge, MA: Harvard University Press, 1994, pp. 38–54.
Trevarthen, C. (1979), Communication and cooperation in early infancy. In: *The Women and Language Debate: A Sourcebook,* ed. C. Roman, S. Juhasz & C. Miller. New Brunswick, NJ: Rutgers University Press, 1994, 216–233.
Winnicott, D. W. (1965), *The Maturational Processes and the Facilitating Environment.* Madison, CT: International Universities Press.
——— (1971), *Playing and Reality,* London: Tavistock.
Woolf, V. (1927), *To the Lighthouse.* New York: Harcourt, Brace.

Part IV: Maternal Representation in Culture

"It Ain't Fittin'"
Cinematic and Fantasmatic Contours of Mammy in *Gone with the Wind* and Beyond

Maria St. John, M.F.T.

The racial stereotype of the mammy figure continues to proliferate in North American culture despite its blatantly offensive and seemingly archaic character. Mammy's continued popularity is evidenced by her numerous literary and film appearances, as well as by the consumer appeal she exercises in the form of Aunt Jemima. Mammy is here analyzed as a dominant cultural fantasy, and the Mammy in *Gone with the Wind* is closely examined. The mammy fantasy, it is argued, remains active today in the context of the cultural construction of whiteness. Elements of Kleinian and Lacanian theory are brought together to elucidate ways in which primitive defensive mechanisms are retroactively represented in racial terms.

RACIAL INTERPELLATION AND THE MAMMY STEREOTYPE

Psychoanalytic explorations of the operations of gender and sexuality have been revolutionary in such academic fields as literary criticism, visual cultural studies, gender studies, and queer studies. Race constitutes another primary social category–

in fact, one that Butler (1993a) and others have argued is inextricable from gender—that warrants, and has begun to receive, psychoanalytic attention across disciplines.

Race is here considered to be a social category and a field of subjective experience that is fraught, contested, and problematic, both psychically and politically, in many of the same ways that we currently accept gender to be. The confluence of social, critical, and psychoanalytic theories that has been so productive with respect to contemporary understandings of gender may be channeled similarly into the questions and problems of race. Althusser's concept of "interpellation," for example, offers a crucial conceptual link between individual psyches and the broader social orders from which they are inextricable and in relation to which both gender and race come to be embodied.[1]

Althusser (1971) elaborated his theory of interpellation as the process whereby ideology "'recruits' subjects among the individuals (it recruits them all) or 'transforms' the individuals into subjects (it transforms them all)" (p. 174). Althusser's example of a scene of interpellation consists of a police officer calling out to a man on the street: "Hey, you there!" Althusser contends that "the hailed individual will turn round. By this mere one-hundred-and-eighty-degree physical conversion, he becomes a subject" (p. 174). As Lacan (1953) suggested, subjects are in effect interpellated even before they are born, insofar as they are "expected"—anticipated by the family into which they are born and the broader social order that will circumscribe the places they may come to occupy. Specifically, subjects are interpellated as either masculine or feminine. Summarizing Lacan's (1957) theory, Rose (1982) wrote, "Sexual difference is a legislative divide which creates and reproduces its own categories. . . . 'Any speaking being whatever' must line up on

[1] Althusser (1971) made unique use of the word interpellation, suggesting that it might designate the process whereby individuals hypothetically adrift with respect to social structures inevitably become moored—defined, beholden, and accountable—in relation to them. As Butler (1997) writes, "Althusser's doctrine of interpellation continues to structure contemporary debate on subject formation, offering a way to account for a subject who comes into being as a consequence of language, yet always within its terms" (p. 106).

one or other side of the divide" (p. 42). I argue that, just as social subjects are hailed and thus defined as either masculine or feminine, so are subjects granted cultural recognition only insofar as they take up designated racial identities.

Consider the workings of racial interpellation in Fanon's (1967) frequently cited autobiographical essay. Fanon described a brutal scene in which he was walking down a street and was subjected to a racializing hail. He recounted, "'Look, a Negro!' The circle was drawing a bit tighter . . . 'Mama, see the Negro! I'm frightened!'" (p. 112). The stifling effects of this interpellation are evoked in Fanon's reflection on his experience on the street. He wrote, "I tell you, I was walled in: No exception was made for my refined manners, or my knowledge of literature, or my understanding of the quantum theory" (p. 117).[2]

Clearly, the effects of such an instance of racial interpellation would be devastating for many black people in some of the ways Fanon reported it was for him. The psychological causes and effects of this toxic process for the frightened white child, his mother, and the social cluster of which *they* are a part, however, may be less obvious. If we are to understand the psychic and cultural consequences of these phenomena for people of any designated racial category, psychoanalysis must continue to cultivate ears and eyes for race.

Toward that end, this essay examines, by the light of certain concepts developed by Klein and Lacan, a particular racialized cultural icon: mammy. Mammy is one among countless stereotypes that organize conceptions of race. Mammy is the fantasied jolly, fat, black woman who works as a nanny, cook, or housekeeper (or in any of those roles) for a white family to whom she is devoted. This fantasied figure accepts her condition of servitude absolutely. The Kleinian and Lacanian constructs taken up here suggest that this fantasy is central to the psychosocial project of constructing whiteness.

The black-white racial opposition is taken to define the prevailing Western myth of racial difference. The prolific reproduction of the mammy stereotype is considered in the

[2] For a more extended analysis, see Kaja Silverman's (1988) discussion of Fanon's depictions of racial interpellation (pp. 27–31).

context of the general interplay between intrapsychic and cultural processes of representation of race. Klein's (1946) elaborations of paranoid-schizoid phenomena, when brought together with Lacan's (1948, 1949, 1953, 1958) distinction between symbolic and imaginary identifications, clarify the functions that a collective representation such as the racist stereotype mammy can serve for an individual psyche as it works to come to terms with cultural categories of race.

Because the Mammy character in *Gone with the Wind* (*GWTW*), in both Margaret Mitchell's 1936 novel and David O. Selznick's 1939 film, may be seen as the quintessential mammy figure, I focus on and return to her throughout this essay, moving promiscuously between references to Mammy the specific character in the book and film and mammy the generalized stereotype. References to actual African American women occur rarely in this essay, because my project is primarily devoted to understanding the psychic processes involved in fantasizing mammy in the service of the construction of whiteness.

CULTURAL CONTOURS OF MAMMY

The following description by the white writer Margaret Mitchell (1936) of the imaginary black character Mammy enacts in two sentences the representation of blackness in the service of the construction of whiteness. Mitchell (1936) wrote:

> Mammy emerged from the hall, a huge old woman with the small, shrewd eyes of an elephant. She was shining black, pure African, devoted to her last drop of blood to the O'Haras, Ellen's mainstay, the despair of her three daughters, the terror of the other house servants [p. 25].

Although she is syntactically firmly rooted as the subject of both sentences and is overtly offered as a "pure" sample of blackness, Mammy is stretched "huge" right away and is made to stand variably for a jungle animal and the essence of an entire continent. The clue to her lability seems to lie in the fact that what starts out as an introduction of Mammy as an individual swiftly gives way to a list of her functions in relation to numerous other people. Mammy is "devoted" to the white family she serves not only in the sense that, at the level of the narrative, this character never questions her servitude, but also in the sense that, when *GWTW* is read symptomatically, the figure of Mammy is a figment of white imagination that allows whiteness to escape the perils of representation altogether–to remain an invisible, impregnable, naturalized source of power.

Here, and wherever she appears, Mammy is big. Visually identifiable by her girth right along with her blackness, she is big on screen. In the very first scene of Selznick's *GWTW* she fills up–indeed, extends beyond–the window frame, suggesting that perhaps the filmic frame itself will prove too narrow to contain her. She is big throughout Mitchell's book as well (floorboards are forever moaning) and big in the culture at large "then" and "now." She is big across time as well as space because, within and beyond the supertext[3] of *GWTW* as nostalgia machine, Mammy's is the face of timelessness. This quality of temporal sprawling serves a very specific purpose.

GWTW participates in a well-established American tradition of producing ostensibly historical works that actually obscure historical contradictions and obfuscate national responsibility for real atrocities through their deployment of conventions of nostalgia. Christian (1997), for example, has noted that,

> for reasons having as much to do with the inability of America to acknowledge that it is capable of having generated a holocaust, as well as the horror that such a memory calls up for African Americans themselves, the Middle Passage[4] has practically disappeared from American cultural memory [p. 364].

Berlant (1996) argues that this kind of disappearing is an act, the passivity-inducing action of amnesiac cultural production: "We live in a modernity that appropriates in a kind of aversive blur the now mythified archaic authenticity of slave affliction"

---

[3] In her discussion of *ShowBoat*, Berlant (1996) introduced the term supertext to refer to "the novel and its adaptations" (p. 403).

[4] The Middle Passage refers to the trans-Atlantic voyages made over four centuries institutionalizing the abduction of tens of millions of African people into chattel slavery.

(p. 400). Inducing amnesia is, Berlant argues, the business of the culture industry, which

> makes erotic, normal and personal the risks and failures, the violences, deferrals, and impossible promises of democracy under capitalism. It does this first by referring the life-sustaining longing that people have to particular forms of intimacy–for example, the romantic couple, the conjugal family–and then by creating conventions of amnesia in which the costs of depending on these forms appear merely ordinary, necessary, or profitable [p. 404].

In her study of racial melodrama, Williams (2001) analyzes the particular iconography of the amnesia-inducing substitution of the "plantation legend" for the historical realities of the institution of slavery in America. Williams demonstrates the ways in which the idealized image of the rural Southern home is posited in racial melodrama as the lost "space of innocence" that Brooks (1976) argued is a key element in melodrama (p. 29). As Williams demonstrates, Tara, the plantation propelled by the labor of devoted "field hands," functions in this way in *GWTW*.

Like Mammy, *GWTW* is famous for its bigness alone. Big across time, the novel was "an instant best-seller when it was first published in 1936, it sold a million copies in the first six months; 25 million more have been sold since then" (Taylor, 1989, pp. 1–2). There have been 155 editions, it has been translated into 27 languages and has been published in 37 countries. As Goings (1994) notes, "total sales have rivaled only the Bible" (p. 51). It appears that 90% of the North American population saw the original *GWTW* film, and a television airing drew 110 million viewers (Pyron, 1983, pp. ix–1). In the summer of 1998, the film was digitally remastered(!) and rereleased in Technicolor, and "in the year 6939 a time capsule containing the book, sealed by fans at the 1939 N.Y. World's Fair, may be opened" (Taylor, 1989, p. 2).

Mammy is an icon that pervades countless cultural forms. As Rogin (1996) and Lott (1993) have documented, mammy was performed on the minstrel stage before she appeared on screen. And she was in films that long preceded *GWTW*. Bogle (1997) notes that mammy is one of five basic character types introduced during the early silent cinema era that "dominated black characters for the next half century. . . ." (p. 14). Bogle wrote, "She is big, fat, and cantankerous" (p. 14).

In a review of mammy's literary appearances, Manring (1998) discusses the work of dozens of writers, including Thomas Dixon, Mark Twain, and Fannie Hurst, as well as Margaret Mitchell. Edwards (1993), editor of *Essence* magazine, establishes that mammy is one of "the most persistent images of black women in the media" (p. 216) and suggests that the mammy stereotype is perpetuated in "four of the most powerful media in the last half of the 20th century–television, advertising, music videos and the press" (p. 216). One of Edwards's most compelling pieces of cultural criticism is her suggestion that "even Oprah Winfrey's media success may be in large measure a reflection of America's love for the quintessential maid or mammy figure–the big, warm-hearted black woman is a natural in a medium as intimate as the television talk show" (p. 216).

Mammy has been fashioned out of almost every imaginable substance. Taylor (1989) begins her discussion of the reactions to Mammy of fans of *GWTW* with a description of Mammy's Cupboard, the 30-foot-high concrete drive-through figure of a "vast, grinning, turbaned, ear-ringed, tray-carrying Mammy" that stands on Highway 61, near Natchez, Mississippi (p. 168). In the same vein, but on a contrasting scale, Goings (1994) describes and analyzes images of mammy in the form of ashtrays, cookie jars (see Figure 1), and doorstops. Goings's examination of the production and consumption of black collectibles and memorabilia finds Mammy frequently taking the form of Aunt Jemima, a commercial figure whose history has been traced in a fascinating treatise by Manring (1998). Manring describes a trip to a contemporary supermarket and a promenade down the aisle containing breakfast items:

> Looking out at us, at about eye level, is one of those seemingly unexplained relics, something that has been around so long, put to so much ordinary use, that it seems not to require much explanation anyway. The black woman on the box of Aunt Jemima pancake mix still smiles at us in much the same way she did in 1920. She has changed her hair, added some jewelry, and lost some weight, but she has not gone anywhere since the turn of the century. Maybe

Figure 1 McCoy cookie jar modeled after Hattie McDaniel. Ca. 1940s. Kenneth W. Goings collection.

> she keeps sticking around because she is more successful than ever, with her face on about forty products, accounting for an overwhelming lead in market share in the ready-to-prepare breakfast category, with sales of more than $300 million annually. But that is not much of an explanation for why she is there. It tells us she still works for Quaker Oats, her owner, in some way, but it does not explain how she works and why people decided originally to put her there [p. 7].

Or, I would add, why she is still there. The question is simply, why is Mammy still so big? (Figure 2).

THE DOMINANT FICTION OF RACE

In Mitchell's (1936) *GWTW*, Scarlett O'Hara demands, "Is Mammy here, Pork? Tell her I want her" (p. 399). We would not want Mammy so persistently, would not seek her in so many places (film screen, television screen, page, and pantry), if her functions were few or her effects incidental. Indeed, we would

Figure 2 Betye Saar, *The Liberation of Aunt Jemima* (1972). Mixed media 11-3/4 × 8 × 2-3/4 inches. University of California, Berkeley Art Museum; purchased with the aid of funds from the National Endowment for the Arts (Selected by the Committee for the Acquisition of Afro-American Art) 1972.84.

not risk the alienation-effect[5] that her image threatens (Mammy all but hails consumers as "Master") if we did not sorely need her bulk just there, obscuring the very contradictions she embodies. Specifically, Mammy's cheerful width covers over the

[5] Brecht (1957) theorized the purposeful, political use of alienation effects in epic theater in order to "make the incidents represented appear strange to the public" so that "the audience was hindered from simply identifying itself with the characters in the play" (p. 91). I suggest here that, as conventions of realism shift over time, representations that at one time seem natural strike viewers of another era as archaic and therefore strange or alien. Such alien representations expose contradictions that they managed to conceal at the moment of their original reception, and introduce a new critical distance between the viewer and the text.

fact that people who identify as white have no essential claim to the privilege that the assumption of this identity affords. When mammy appears to broadcast her natural blackness, she is shoring up the category "white." In *GWTW*, Mammy, energetically policing racial boundaries, dictates what and how white and black people should do and be, respectively, and complains bitterly, "It ain't fittin'," whenever she perceives a transgression.

Mammy is a dominant cultural fantasy, reenacted with each new production of her image. This fantasy may be understood in relation to what Silverman (1992) calls the dominant fiction. Silverman argues that "ideological belief . . . occurs at the moment when an image which the subject consciously knows to be culturally fabricated nevertheless succeeds in being recognized or acknowledged as a 'pure, naked perception of reality'" (p. 17). She suggests that belief, the arbiter of reality, is granted at the level of fantasy, rather than of consciousness. She asserts further that,

> within every society, hegemony is keyed to certain privileged terms, around which there is a kind of doubling up of belief. Since everything that successfully passes for "reality" within a given social formation is articulated in relation to these terms, they represent ideological stress points [p. 16].

I suggest that the social system of race represents such a stress point and that mammy is erected to soothe the strain.

Lacan's theory of subjectivity offers a compelling account of the kind of strain that an image like the mammy stereotype serves to ease. Lacan articulated his reading of psychoanalytic theory in opposition to contemporaneous developments within ego psychology, and the founding premise of Lacanian theory holds that there is a radical noncoincidence between identity (the purview of the ego) and subjectivity. This noncoincidence is, according to Lacan, irresolvable; it is a basic condition of human life. For the ego, however, this disjuncture represents an irritation if not an insufferable source of anxiety. The ego, therefore, seeks reflections in the external world that provide the illusion of coherence.

Social categories of race cohere not by virtue of any "natural" law but as a result of the cultural production and regulation of racial distinctions. Mullen (1994) discusses the personal and collective representational labor involved in perpetuating myths of racial purity in the United States, where the reality of mixed-race ancestry (not only African–Anglo, but also Native–Spanish and countless other ethnic and racial crossings) is ubiquitously denied.

At the level of the family and broader social groupings, then, the coherence of the image of racial purity depends on denial of ancestral mixings. Many scholars have noted that the mammy stereotype represents desexualized black femininity as a way of denying the historical reality of interracial relationships and the rape of black women by white men. Countless other representational strategies are deployed at the cultural level to reinforce dominant racial categorizations. Family television situation comedies, for example, are as a rule easily classifiable in terms of race.

At the level of cultural representation, then, mammy is one among the number of images that "reflect" (or produce) the dominant fiction of race, or the impression of racial coherence. But if Lacan's assertion of the disjuncture between subjectivity and identity holds, then the ego's sense of coherence is threatened from within the psyche, and even the proliferation of categorizable racial images produced by the media cannot provide an enduring sense of stabilization.

PSYCHIC MULTIRACIALITY

A number of psychoanalytic theorists have addressed the instability of the meanings of race at the intrapsychic level. In an essay on psychoanalysis and race that has informed my discussion of the dominant fiction of race, Spillers (1997) suggests that "race may be not fact, but our deadliest fiction":

> "[R]ace" alone bears no meaning, even though it reifies in personality; it gains its power from what it signifies by point, in what it allows to come to meaning. . . . "[R]ace" is not simply a metaphor. It is the outcome of a politics, and for one to mistake it is to be politically stupid and endangered.

> But it is also a complicated figure or metaphoricity that demonstrates the power and danger of difference, that signs and assigns difference as a way to situate social subjects [p. 137].

Spillers suggests that a socioethical analysis involves thinking in terms of the problematics of culture rather than of race, because to reiterate "race" is often to reify it. (In fact, Spillers puts the word "race" in quotation marks throughout her essay as a way of continually denaturalizing it while discussing it.)

Spillers's assertions suggest that race functions as an assignation in much the same way that many feminist theorists have argued that gender does. In other words, such characteristics as skin pigmentation, facial features, and hair texture are conscripted into underwriting the elaborate cultural construction of race just as male and female genitalia and secondary sexual characteristics are called on to substantiate what Rubin (1975) termed the sex-gender system. With respect to the organizing opposition of blackness and whiteness, for example, the culturally and historically specific presence or absence of the category mulatto exposes the forces of construction at work. Black and white are terms that are defined by their opposition and that encompass, or exclude, different groups of actual people at different historical and geographical points on the basis of the political/ideological requisites in operation at the time and place in question.

What is the intrapsychic correlate of the historical and cultural contingency and variability of racial categories? It is the notion that a subject's assumption of a singular racial identity, rather than occurring as a matter of course, is an ideologically laden psychic achievement. I suggest that we may think of psychic multiraciality in much the same way that many feminist psychoanalytic theorists (Mitchell, 1974; Chodorow, 1978, 1989, 1994; Mitchell and Rose, 1982; Benjamin, 1988; Silverman, 1988; Butler, 1990, 1993b) have urged us to read the psychic hermaphrodism or bisexuality postulated by Freud. Doing so would mean seeing lived racial identities as compromise formations, just as lived gender identities must be understood in part as compromise formations if the notion of psychic hermaphrodism is accepted. The stakes, dangers, pleasures, costs, and possibilities involved in the discrepancy between psychic multiraciality and hegemonic cultural reproduction of race vary monumentally from one subject to another, depending on the racial position each of us is asked to occupy and the intrapsychic, interpersonal, institutional, and discursive routes by which we take up or refuse our spots.

When I posit the term psychic multiraciality, I am referring to the psychic conditions that pertain once a child has attained language. Lacan (1953, 1957, 1958) postulated that, in the process of acquiring language, a child also assumes the sexually differentiated subject position assigned to him or her. I am suggesting that a child must assume a racially differentiated position as well.

Lacan distinguished between identifications that occur in pure form before a child learns to speak–and thereby becomes fully subjected to the social or "symbolic" laws inherent in speech and other symbolic systems–and those that occur afterward. He referred to the former alternately as primary or imaginary identifications and to the latter as secondary, symbolic, or structural identifications. Although primary identifications occur throughout life, they are modeled on and follow the logic of identifications formed during the preverbal years; that is, they are formed in ignorance of or indifference to symbolic laws.

The identifications that occur before speech, with its attendant incorporation of the speaking subject into various systems of social classification, would have to be described as nonracial, just as primary identifications before sexual difference have to be thought in nongendered terms. Raced and gendered meanings are, it seems to me, assigned retroactively to these rudimentary identifications from the subsequent vantage point of a child for whom race and gender stratifications have begun to register as such.

These rudimentary representations would take the form, if language could be put to them, of such qualitative experiences as tones of voice, firmness of touch, gradations of size, senses of texture and smell, quality of light, and degrees of hunger, comfort, pleasure, distress. The affectively rich visual/kinesthetic representations imbued with a sense of "withness" that have been observed and theorized by such infant researchers as Stern (1985) and Beebe and her colleagues (Beebe and Lachmann, 1994; Beebe, Lachmann, and Jaffe, 1997) long precede the recognition of the symbolic otherness inscribed in distinct structural positions. By the time there is, in the symbolic and structural sense, a mother for an infant, he has been making himself up in relation to her for a long while.[6]

These mutually constructed (primary/imaginary) identifications might go something like we-lift-up, we-warm-up, we-fill-up-with-music, we-fill-up-the-mirror. Again, these primary identifications are, I claim, reshuffled and retroactively defined in gendered and raced terms based on the dictates of secondary (symbolic/structural) identifications. Secondary identifications are organized in terms like "I am a boy like Daddy," or "Our family belongs to the same group as the family next door, and not to the group of families across the tracks." Once one is fully within language, sexual difference, and race, identifications of both orders are formed and dispensed with perpetually.

Although they are never totally reconcilable to each other's terms because they have different psychic textures, primary identifications become grist for the mill of secondary identifications. For example, imagine a white 18-month-old and a black 18-month-old who are well matched temperamentally and energetically so that they enjoy circular games of chase that end in euphoric tumbles in the sandbox. These children's imaginary identifications with each other might be theorized as being nonracial. Indeed, race has not congealed as a category for these preverbal children; but racialization presses in on them in the form of their caregivers' racially inflected different levels of comfort with sandy hair, highly physical play, the very fact of their interracial friendship, and so forth. Furthermore, these early identifications with each other will come to take on racialized meaning retroactively for the children once it becomes clear to them that they will be asked to stand on one or the other side of a monumental racial divide. In older childhood and adulthood, cross-racial imaginary identifications, and even many within-a-single-race-that-is-defined-in-opposition-to-other-races imaginary identifications, are inflected with racialized meaning no matter how purely formal, affective, or sensation based they may seem to be.

[6] Winnicott's (1963, pp. 182–183) distinction between the "environment-mother," who is "human" for the infant, and the "object-mother," who is "a thing," is pertinent here.

A number of contemporary relational theorists (Harris, 1996, 1998; Aron, 1998; Dimen, 1998; Layton, 1999) are articulating what might be thought of as the perpetual imbrication of primary and secondary identifications as bodily, fantasy, and social experiences unfold in concert. Consider, for example, Harris's (1998) call to relational theory to "commit itself . . . to a view of body states and processes as inseparable from fantasy, interaction, and meaning." Harris suggests that "the child's body is densely textured in meaning and affect for the parents; the child's material life offers itself profoundly to parental battle, parental excitement and to the family's—and probably also the culture's—conscious and unconscious fantasies" (p. 43). Surely the "complex imaginary construction" described by Harris defies the binary logic of the myth of black–white racial opposition and muddies the myth of racial purity. In the context of such rich and nuanced understandings of the interconnectedness of various registers of experience, how are we to account for the ego's achievement of a singular racial identity and the subject's accommodation to the dominant fiction of race?

I suggest that imaginary identifications on the part of a subject who is supposed to be white with whatever is taken to be blackness, or with qualities of individual African American people, become dangerous liabilities in the face of racial interpellation or the call to assume secondary identifications. Theorizing the mutual implication of the various orders of experience (intrapsychic, interpersonal, social, cultural) means conceptualizing instances not only of resonance across these fields but also of constitutive exclusion. Some imaginary identifications are inadmissible at the level of the symbolic except at extremely high psychosocial prices. Benjamin (1988) has illustrated, for example, the way an oedipal boy musters his masculinity in part by a repudiation of his primary identifications with his mother, which, now that he finds himself gendered, have become a liability. In a similar way, I suggest that whiteness is derived in large measure through the repudiation of primary identifications with blackness as emblematic of racial otherness. And this is where I think mammy comes in.

In the dominant cultural imagination, and in response to the dominant investment in consolidating and maintaining whiteness, mammy officiates at certain scenes of racial interpellation. She is erected as a testament to the cultural insistence on, egoic investment in, and simultaneous psychic impossibility of absolute interracial disidentification in the face of the cultural construction of racial difference. Mammy both is not and is the black mother of the white child she tends. That is, she is taken for the mother at the level of fantasy and primary identification (where racial barriers do not hold sway) at the same time that she assumes a role distinct from that of mother at the level of cultural representation and secondary identification (where race is regulated and reproduced). The instability and contradiction inherent in the simultaneous cultural requirement for and psychic impossibility of absolute racial disidentification produce a dilemma so urgent and vexing that mammy is retained full time, "never beyond the reach of a summons day or night" (White, 1985, p. 47).

RACE RELATIONS/OBJECT RELATIONS

Butler (1993b) has described the "white racist imaginary" in terms of the "[complete] . . . circuit of paranoia: the projection of . . . aggression, and the subsequent regarding of that projection as an external threat" (p. 19). Although she did not here refer to Klein directly, Butler's definition of the white racist imaginary invokes psychoanalytic constructs central to the work of Klein. And Klein's is indeed an apt theoretical world for anyone in search of a psychoanalytic account of racism or even, following Spillers's (1997) intervention, race relations (as opposed, in Spillers's terms, to the "problematics of culture").

In his lecture "The Topic of the Imaginary," Lacan (1954b) repeatedly cited and insulted the work of Klein.[7] He said, for example, "Melanie Klein has neither a theory of the imaginary nor a theory of the ego" (p. 82). Lacan's belligerence notwithstanding, a great deal of his own work unfolds in explicit or implicit dialogue with that of Klein and her colleagues. It is clearly beyond the scope of this essay to delineate the many

[7] See Jacobus's (1998) "'Tea Daddy': Poor Mrs. Klein and the Pencil Shavings" for an analysis of the defensive functions Lacan's devaluation of Klein served for him.

permutations of the productive challenge the Kleinian approach represented for Lacan. Still, a field of communication between the Kleinian and Lacanian paradigms can be sketched, and it will enable a more vivid account of the intrapsychic and cultural representations of race than either theory can offer alone.

It is at the level of the Lacanian Imaginary that experiences of psychic multiraciality represent a threat (although it is here that they occur, and are registered as well), because multiplicity cannot be tolerated within this order. The moment that is emblematic of the Imaginary is the "mirror stage," the hypothetical instance in which the ego of the human infant is constituted on the basis of its identification with an image, specifically its reflection in a mirror (Lacan, 1949).[8] Beginning with this early instance of formative identification, in which the subject fantasmatically[9] takes the place of his or her image, the Imaginary is characterized by primary identification, duality, and the "relation of exclusion" (Lacan, 1955b, p. 138). As Lacan (1955a) described, "every imaginary relation comes about via a kind of *you or me* between the subject and the object. That is to say–*If it's you, I'm not. If it's me, it's you who isn't*" (p. 169). Corporeal representations and intersubjective relations alike are registered in the mirrors of the Imaginary, where pleasurable

---

[8] Silverman (1996, p. 10) suggested that the mirror stage may be read as an elaboration of Freud's (1923) famous assertion that "the ego is first and foremost a bodily ego; it is not merely a surface entity but is itself the projection of a surface" (p. 26).

[9] Laplanche and Pontalis (1973) proposed the term "phantasmatic" to account for the totality of an individual's fantasies, both conscious and unconscious. They write, "the Freudian problematic of phantasy, far from justifying a distinction in kind between unconscious and conscious phantasies, is much more concerned with bringing forward the analogies between them, the close relationship which they share and the transitions which take place between one and the other. . . . [It] is the subject's life as a whole which is seen to be shaped and ordered by what might be called, in order to stress this structuring action, 'a phantasmatic'" (p. 317). Silverman (1992) introduced the spelling of the word used here (fantasmatic) in her elaboration of the relationship between two psychic cateogires. She writes, "The first of these categories–the ego–provides the support for 'identity' or the 'self'. The second–the fantasmatic–organizes and regulates desire" (p. 3). I trace in this paper the contours of the collective cultural fantasmatic that produces the mammy stereotype.

impressions of coherence are achieved at the expense of another and are in perpetual danger of giving way to fragmentation. The Imaginary investment in the myth of racial purity derives from this definitional short-circuitry.

The Symbolic refers to the preestablished order of signifying networks that "envelop the life of man" (Lacan, 1953, p. 68). These networks include language, institutions, traditions, kinship structures, and cultural codes. Symbolic systems that interpellate subjects into race include racist rhetoric, discriminatory employment practices, miscegenation laws, and census polls, as well as community-specific dialects, dress codes, literatures, musical forms, and countless other cultural practices. The Symbolic is a register internal to the psyche as well as an order that precedes and inscribes it, as was claimed most famously by Lacan (1964) in his assertion that "The unconscious is structured like a language" (p. 20). The Real is "what resists symbolization absolutely" (Lacan, 1954a, p. 66) not just in the sense that it is not named, or that it is material as opposed to symbol, but rather in the sense that it represents the vanishing point of the representable, "the impossible" (Lacan, 1964a, p. 167) of the Symbolic order.

Klein also described psychic registers, or "positions," that differ from each other and adhere to distinct logics–the paranoid-schizoid (1946) and the depressive (1935, 1940). Klein's depressive position represents the psychic achievement of ambivalence that allows for whole-object relatedness. It is hard won and precariously sustained. The paranoid-schizoid, by contrast, is described as a primitive order that manages the challenges of existence by way of the crudest of psychic tools–omnipotence; the fantasies of splitting, projection, and introjection; and the attendant elaborations of persecution and idealization.

Klein described in brilliant detail the dirty psychic work Lacan indicated from a distance. Jacobus (1998) suggests that, "for Lacan . . . Klein's interest lies primarily in the account she gives of . . . 'the domain of the imaginary'" (p. 93). Indeed, Klein's descriptions of what she called the paranoid-schizoid conform to the dictates of the order Lacan designated the Imaginary, but she went much further than he in spelling out the mechanisms whereby the ego attempts to rid itself of the threatening specter of instability and impurity. Mammy is herself intimately bound up with dirty work. (From this point forward, I adopt the Kleinian terminology in this analysis of mammy, with the understanding that, as I see it, this does not lead outside of but rather enriches understanding of the Lacanian Imaginary.)

Although Lacan insisted on the irreconcilability of the Imaginary and Symbolic orders, Kleinian theory represents a challenge to any facile opposition between internal and external worlds. Within the paranoid-schizoid, there is no such thing as equilibrium. Every impulse ricochets wildly about, so that the distinction between that which arises within the subject and that which emanates from outside is a precarious one at best. "Internal" instances of hatred and impressions of badness are instantly exiled lest they destroy the lovely feelings of goodness that they are defined over and against. But, by virtue of the fact that they are disavowed, these forces take on in fantasy a life of their own, a life dedicated to the persecution of the ego that expelled them. (With respect to the vulnerability of the ego to fragmentation, Klein and Lacan seem to agree.) The sense of danger proliferates endlessly.

These paranoid-schizoid mechanisms are exhibited in the case of racial paranoia. The paranoid-schizoid is a psychic register operant in everyone to a greater or lesser degree and under certain conditions. When the paranoid-schizoid governs, the dizzying and terrifying processes of division (i.e., the proliferation of splitting and projection) are only with great difficulty contained from within. Attributing the danger to an external object offers apparent relief when internal containment is, for whatever reason, not achieved. Described in this manner, the system goes a long way toward accounting not only for private paranoid moments in relation to others, but also for public strategies of racial paranoia. Institutionalized racism and the prolific production of racist images and discourses conspire to recruit racially marked others as convenient targets for the outward attribution of white aggression.[10]

It seems that the busy attribution of badness to the other in the form of splitting and projection described by the Kleinian

[10] Butler's (1993) essay "Endangered/Endangering: Schematic Racism and White Paranoia" offers a vivid account of the stunning racist reversal of aggressor/aggressed in the instance of the beating of Rodney King.

(1946, 1955) paradigm provides an apt account of this regime of regulation at the intrapsychic level. A conscious acknowledgment of psychic multiraciality would come at the price for the white-identified subject of forfeiting this particular route to the alleviation of the problems of internal aggression. Instead, the social system of race remains intact and works in the service of the consolidation of whiteness. The dominant fiction of race holds sway to the extent that we live our lives as though we "belong" to one race or another, and we take it for granted that those we encounter are, in a complementary fashion, proper to our own or to another race. This fiction both feeds on and fuels the regulation of mutually exclusive racial categories. As Klein (1946) wrote, "it is in phantasy" that splitting and projection occur, "but the effect of this phantasy is a very real one" (p. 181).

GOOD BREAST, BAD BREAST, MAMMY, AND MOTHER

It is something of a feat to have gotten even this far inside Kleinian theory without encountering "the breast." In Klein's view, splitting is deployed initially and perennially in an attempt to preserve a positive relation to the maternal breast and its derivative representations. Klein (1955) put it this way: "The observation that in the infant's mind the mother primarily appears as good and bad breast split off from each other . . . helped me to understand the importance of the processes of splitting and keeping apart good and bad figures" (p. 52). The Kleinian paradigm accommodates mammy especially well, in my view, not only because, as I argued in the previous section, race relations, with their definitional basis in aggressivity and mutual exclusion, seem best accounted for in terms of primitive object relations, but also because of the resonance between the all-important doubleness of the maternal breast constellation for Klein and the maternal doubleness in relation to breasts that mammy signifies.

As many commentators on the mammy phenomenon have observed, Mammy's significance is derived in large part from her relation to the white mistress (see, e.g., Dagle and Kalinak, 1994, p. 19; hooks, 1996, p. 201; Manring, 1998, p. 23; Roberts, 1994, p. 108). Whether she is paired with Ellen-angel-in-the-house, as she is in *GWTW,* with the don't-keep-me-in-the-house New Woman of *Imitation of Life,*[11] or with the dwelling-in-God's-house-now dead mother of *Corrina Corrina,*[12] Mammy is always the other mother. And whether Mammy is "good" and mistress is "bad" or vice versa depends on the demands of the moment, but in either case the pair suggests a split. Mammy's meaning is inextricably linked to that of the white mistress through a series of binary oppositions that flesh out the psychic splits deployed in the vicinity of infantile need and primitive fantasy—the psychic terrain in relation to which the mammy-mother pair derives its resonance.

Whether or not she serves literally as a wet nurse, mammy is etymologically tied to the breast in a way that her white counterpart is not. To utter the word mammy is literally to say "mam-," or to call out (for a) "breast." This linguistic concreteness, as well as her bigness and her blackness, ties mammy to the materiality of maternity in contrast to her white counterpart, who is frequently and significantly referred to as "the absent mistress" (see, e.g., Manring, 1998, p. 139). Mammy is then associated with the bodily realm, whereas the absent mistress governs the ethereal. (In *GWTW,* Ellen frequently ministers to the spiritual needs of her family and neighbors; Mammy tends to their bodily needs.) Mammy's association with darkness, earthiness, and fleshiness—in contrast to the white mistress's lightness, heavenliness, and absence—naturalize a peculiar division of domestic labor in the antebellum South (with contemporary extensions nationwide) and psychic labor currently. The mistress is able to remain prim and proper to the extent that mammy does the dirty work. Conversely, Mammy

---

[11] *Imitation of Life* is the title of three different versions of the story of an alliance between a white woman and the black woman who (among other things) acts as nanny to her daughter. Fanny Hurst's novel was published in 1933; John Stahl's adaptation was released in 1934, and in 1959 Douglas Sirk directed a re-make. These three versions provide an interesting history of their own of what might be called the shifting conventions of mammy-ism. See, for example, Berlant's (1991) comparative study of the three versions with respect to the varying strategies of commodification each represents.

[12] Whoopie Goldberg plays a mammy/nanny in this 1994 film. See Rogin's (1996, p. 116) discussion of the role.

represents bodily contact and nurture as long as the white maternal figure remains aloof from such messy business.

These oppositions are played out in a series of passages in the novel version of *GWTW*. As soon as Scarlett misses her mother, she misses Mammy. She thinks it is Mammy's arms to which she wishes so much to return. She "longed for Ellen's sweet face, for Mammy's strong arms around her" (Mitchell, 1936, p. 358). But, when she finally sees Mammy, Scarlett "[runs] to her" and "lays her head on the broad, sagging breasts which had held so many heads, black and white" (p. 409).

Scarlett, it seems, splits furiously. First, she is unhappy; she "misses." But, as soon as there is an object ("her mother"), there is another ("Mammy"). Moreover, it is not images of whole objects that Scarlett uses to comfort herself. Rather, she calls to mind pieces of both bodies: the face of one, the breasts-then-arms of the other. Now the proliferation of splits is exponential, because arms and breasts come in pairs; and then there have been so many other heads at those breasts–heads that are, in turn, divided into black and white ones. It appears that, for Scarlett O'Hara, the problem of missing mother gives rise to a dizzying series of splits and images of composite, mixed-race bodies.

Nested within this and countless other series of splits surrounding and constituting the mammy figure is, I believe, the kernel of the dearly held dominant fantasy that is mammy—the scene of the white child suckling at the black woman's breast. In Mitchell's (1936) book, this fantasy is elaborated most fully through the figure of Dilcey:

> Her faded calico dress was open to the waist and her large bronze breast exposed. Held close against her, Melanie's baby pressed his pale, rosebud mouth greedily to the dark nipple, sucking, gripping tiny fists against the soft flesh like a kitten in the warm fur of its mother's belly [pp. 407–408].

The key elements of the fantasy are these: The greedy child is pale, the dark breast is perennially available and inexhaustible, the embrace is mutual (she holds tightly, he presses and grips), and the mammy is fantasmatically mother.

That only a small percentage of white children may ever have been nursed literally by black women, or that wet nursing per se has fallen out of fashion, diminishes in no way the psychic power of the image of black–white suckling. People do not have to live or have any literal access to the particular ingredients of a fantasy in order to harbor it. Klein (1952, 1955, 1956) suggested that the symbolic importance of the maternal breast is powerfully operative regardless of whether or not a child has literally been breast-fed. Through "phantasying backwards" (Klein, 1952, p. 117) bottle-fed children proceed psychically as if they had been suckled, substitute the breast for the bottle fantasmatically, and relate to their objects through the same mammo-templates as their La Leche League counterparts. Klein (1952, p. 117) explained this phenomenon as an expectation of the nipple that takes the form of a primary fantasy. It seems useful to consider that these fantasmatic elaborations of psychic modes of relating may instead be installed discursively.[13]

But what exactly is enacted in the fantasmatic scene of black-white suckling, which, I argue, is disguised in the generic costume of mammy? I suggest that the operations of envy, as Klein conceived them, provide an answer. Specifically, the construction of whiteness comes at a cost—the installation of envy of what is posited as blackness in those who take themselves to be white. Rosenfeld (1971) reported that Klein

> thought that envy appears as a hostile, life-destroying force in the relation of the infant to its mother and is particularly directed against the good feeding mother because she is not only needed by the infant but envied for containing everything which the infant wants to possess himself [p. 244].

When mammy is fantasmatically embalmed, with her shirt open and her breast full, the irritating infantile problem of privation is temporarily staved off. But "dependence stimulates envy" (Rosenfeld, 1971, p. 246), and reliance on this fantasy stirs dependence doubly—at the level of the structure, the activity of

---

[13] It has amused me to contemplate the American Dairy Association's successful "Got Milk?" campaign in this light. In his account of the advertising strategy, Manning (1999) referred to the core concept proliferated by this multi-million dollar campaign as "milk deprivation" (p. 21). Hundreds of television and billboard images were dedicated to constructing milkless people as deprived, tortured, and utterly bereft.

fantasizing is being relied on, and at the level of content, as mammy is imagined as having the power to satisfy, or not. So, a new problem rears its head in the form of envy of mammy's nurturing/nourishing capacities (and complementary power to withhold). Rosenfeld (1971) said that envy is unbearable, because Kleinian envy is lethal. Klein (1956) wrote:

> It is the nature of envy that it spoils the primal good object and gives added impetus to sadistic attacks on the breast . . . excessive envy increases the intensity of such attacks and their duration, and thus makes it more difficult . . . to regain the lost good object [p. 214].

Klein was describing a self-escalating psychic problem. What does this problem imply for racial envy? As long as envy remains split off from the ego, the rift becomes ever wider, the stakes higher, and the possibility of reconciliation (fusion) more remote. How does the subject-that-would-be-white escape from the psychic bind in which his fantasmatic dependence on mammy and subsequent envy of her places him? Both Klein and Rosenfeld suggested the urgent necessity of assisting envious analysands in recognizing the painful fact of their envy so that it may be integrated into the ego and mitigated by hope and love. But how can a would-be white subject consciously entertain and thus work through envy of the black female figure when the cultural "fact" of her worthlessness is reinforced at every discursive and institutional turn? In what image can he recognize his love of her when her reproduction is synonymous with her debasement? How can he speak of her inestimable value to him when her devaluation constitutes the very basis on which the economy he was born into perpetuates itself?

Rosenfeld (1971) suggested that, when working through is not possible (as it is not, I assert, within the social system of racism and the paranoid-schizoid register that underwrites it), the psyche manages the problematic specter of the enviable other by fantasmatically incorporating it, so that all its imagined virtues are believed to accrue to the self, and the very separateness of the other is disavowed.

The processes Rosenfeld described may be neatly mapped onto the situation of the would-be white subject plagued by envy of the fantasied racialized other. Under such desperate psychic conditions, Rosenfeld suggested, indications of the separateness of the other can give rise to feelings of humiliation, despair, rage, hatred, and revenge. The other is therefore fantasmatically controlled–anticipated, appropriated, and regulated through omnipotent distortions so that the impression of coincidence with the subject can be maintained. The subject's condition of dependence on the object constitutes an indignation that cannot be borne, and so this dependence is denied at the same time that the other's separateness is disavowed.

When these arrangements are entrenched to an extreme, Rosenfeld (1971) claimed, the internal world is

> dominated by an extremely ruthless part of the self . . . [that pledges] freedom to indulge in any sadistic activity. The whole structure is committed to narcissistic self-sufficiency. . . . [And] the destructive impulses sometimes appear openly as overpoweringly cruel [p. 250].

The mammy stereotype may be read as a demonstration of these cruel strategies of construction of self-sufficient whiteness by way of projection and sadistic control of what is posited as "blackness." Seen in this way, the specter of mammy is a public display, thinly disguised, of a violent fantasmatic scene of consumption and punishment, an oral incorporation that accomplishes the defense against envy as articulated by Rosenfeld. Any number of scenes of racism could be fruitfully considered in the light of these mechanisms, but one recorded by White (1985) stands out as especially keyed to these terms of self-sufficiency and brutality. White recounts that the slave

> Henry Bibb reported a whipping where [his wife's] "naked quivering flesh" was "tied up and exposed to the public gaze of all. . . ." The [white] man who whipped Bibb's wife was often heard by Bibb to exclaim that he had rather "paddle a female than eat when he was hungry" [p. 33].

This scene of voyeurism and whipping[14] graphically illustrates the violence of fantasies of oral incorporation, the concreteness

[14] We might read this as a racially inflected version of the classic fantasy "A Child Is Being Beaten," analyzed by Freud (1919).

of the consumptive function they serve, and the way in which the publicness of such a scene can amplify its effects.

The same things happen in the contemporary supermarket, television show, and movie theater. When we obsessively proliferate the mammy image and avariciously consume it, we stave off our envy by repeatedly exposing this fantasied mammy to the public gaze; we force her to absorb the hateful impulses of the dominant cultural psyche and to respond with a smile and a pancake. An ashtray in mammy's image cheerfully welcomes the butts of the cigarettes of her collectors; another represents her as a washerwoman who, leaning over her work, has gotten her breast caught in the ringer. A toy fashioned in mammy's likeness encourages children to make her eyes roll by pulling on her whiskers. Perhaps most tellingly of all, her "pickaninny" children are perpetually portrayed in "darky memorabilia" in the jaws of alligators and in various other states of peril.[15] (See Figures 3 and 4.) It makes sense that, although the mammy image on which the dominant psyche in question is

Figure 3 Lake County (IL) Museum/Curt Teich Postcard Archives

[15] All examples of "darky memorabilia" are taken from Goings's (1994) study.

Figure 4 Lake County (IL) Museum/Curt Teich Postcard Archives

dependent must be preserved as endlessly as she is destroyed (i.e., represented in states of bountiful calm, in the form, for example, of a solid, welcoming cookie jar), her fantasied children would be prey to the unmitigated destructive forces of envy and would be represented in openly brutal configurations.

To return to the broader argument, I have suggested that psychic multiraciality poses a threat to the construction of white self-sufficiency, the illusion of whiteness that owes nothing to blackness. At the painful site of exclusive racial identification of the dominant cultural subject-to-be, a pleasurable unconscious fantasy of interracial mother–child union is installed. This fantasy sustains the dominant cultural subject in his unconscious experience of multiraciality at the same time that it answers the generic demand for immediate and uninterrupted gratification.

Ideally gratifying though this scene is at the level of fantasy, it presents two problems. The first is that, according to Rosenfeld (1971), the possibility of satiation (via the good breast) implies the threat of its being withheld, so this prospect of satisfaction is experienced as a state of dependence, and dependence stimulates envy. The second problem is that the fantasy celebrates a culturally despised other and exposes the fictional status of race. The fantasy is rarely, therefore, represented in its explicit form. The fantasmatic mammy must then be punished for her crime of stirring in the would-be self-sufficient subject awareness of his vulnerable state of dependence, and at the same time her significance must be diminished. Mammy is thus contorted and manipulated, displayed and consumed, ridiculed and demanded, exploited and obsessively proliferated at the level of cultural representation because, at the level of individual psychic representation, she evokes an unthinkable dependence. Because her reproduction is her punishment, mammy continues to haunt–and her conjurer continues to want.

"IT AIN'T FITTIN' "

The first Oscar ever to be bestowed on a black actor went to Hattie McDaniel for her performance as Mammy in Selznick's *GWTW.* Of the scenes devoted to her in the film, the most famous is the one in which Mammy helps Scarlett get dressed for the barbecue. As the scene opens, Mammy is lacing Scarlett's corset while Scarlett braces herself against a bedpost. A great deal is made of the narrowness of Scarlett's waist. An argument ensues about what Scarlett will wear and whether she will eat. The scene closes when Scarlett's father calls up to her window that it is time to depart. I suggest that the enduring success of this emblematic Mammy scene derives from the fact that it represents so fully, while concealing pleasurably, the suckling fantasy I have described.

This is ostensibly a scene about Scarlett's 18-inch waist. In fact, the scene is as much about her breasts; she and Mammy have a veritable tug-of-war over her bustline, and Mammy scoffs at the prospect of Scarlett's getting freckles after all the "cocoa butter" she administered to Scarlett's lily-white skin all winter. (Mammy is here the source of milk products as well as chocolate.) The scene is equally about Mammy's breasts, represented by the food she attempts to force-feed Scarlett. The details of this infantile feeding scene include the fact that Scarlett's first line is "Ooo," to which Mammy replies, "Just hold on and suck in." Later, Mammy puts a bib on Scarlett, and there is a good deal of concern about spitting up. (Mammy: "Now don't eat too fast. It ain't no need having it come right back up again." Not to mention the projectile parasol thrown across the room by a tantrumming Scarlett.) And, just like a good feed, the scene ends with a burp. (Scarlett: "Oh, dear. Fastened [the corset] so tight, I know I'll never be able to get through the day without belching.")

More generally, but equally Kleinian, this is a battle scene, and the battle is over the locus of control of Scarlett's insides. Mammy wants to dictate when and where Scarlett eats, but Scarlett wants her not to. Scarlett huffs and tromps around, pushes the tray away, clamps her mouth shut. Mammy's moment of victory consists in her sneakily revealing that not only are the contents of Scarlett's stomach Mammy's purview, but so are the thoughts inside Scarlett's head; Mammy reports that she knows what Scarlett is planning to do (eat later), whom she is thinking about (Ashley), and why (she is scheming for a marriage proposal). When Mammy thus demonstrates to Scarlett that her insides are not her own but are accessible to Mammy as well, Scarlett's ruse of self-sufficiency and autonomy is undone. Scarlett's defeat here is signaled by her sulkily shoving a biscuit into her mouth in compliance with Mammy's directive.

This moment of compliance notwithstanding, throughout the scene Scarlett performs her racially sanctioned, ruthless exploitation of Mammy. She alternately demands and dismisses, orders and ignores Mammy. Scarlett does not want to need what Mammy has to offer, but Mammy reminds her not only that she is subject to hunger, but that race—the currency of Scarlett's contempt for Mammy, the permission for her disregard of her—is meaningless in the face of hunger. Scarlett will, Mammy predicts, be "eatin' like a field hand" by the afternoon. ("Field worker" is the euphemism of choice for "slave" in *GWTW*.)

Mammy thus reminds Scarlett that they are united around Scarlett's hunger. This is true in two ways. First, no matter how self-sufficient a would-be white woman attempts to make herself, she is ultimately prone to hunger and is thus reminded of her subjective state of dependency. Second, Scarlett's very self-sufficiency and whiteness are constructed by way of splitting and projection, the evacuation from within Scarlett of her deep, dark need. Because Mammy has the milk Scarlett does not want to need but does need, Scarlett envies Mammy, and this envy is disavowed through Scarlett's devaluation of Mammy. But Scarlett can neither escape her nor conceal things from Mammy because

Scarlett's insides are Mammy's business, and this is what Mammy reminds her of when she predicts her hunger and when she lets on that she can read Scarlett's mind and knows the contents of her heart.

Ultimately, though, Mammy *is* Scarlett's insides. Mammy is rendered as a repository of Scarlett's unwanted parts, the perfect and necessary counterpart that guarantees Scarlett's whiteness. Mammy's "It ain't fittin', it just ain't fittin'," echoed throughout the film, betrays the fact that the projections with which Scarlett wants Mammy to be coincident will always fit her ill. "It," the projected image, does not fit together because "it," the mammy stereotype, embodies the contradictions that "it," the dominant cultural imaginary, disavows through secretly nursing the fantasy.

ACKNOWLEDGMENTS

I thank Muriel Dimen for her generous editorial assistance. Thanks also to Linda Williams, Kaja Silverman, Peter Goldberg, and Janet Adelman and the Townsend Center Object Relations Psychoanalysis Working Group for many rich and varied comments. Finally, thanks to Robin Silverman for her immeasurable editorial support and conceptual collaboration.

REFERENCES

Althusser, L. (1971). Ideology and ideological state apparatuses. In: *Lenin and Philosophy*, trans. B. Brewster. London: Monthly Review Press, pp. 127–186.

Aron, L. (1998), The clinical body and the reflexive mind. In: *Relational Perspectives on the Body*, ed. L. Aron & F. S. Anderson. Hillsdale, NJ: The Analytic Press, pp. 3–37.

Beebe, B. & Lachmann, F. (1994), Representation and internalization in infancy: Three principles of salience. *Psychoanal. Psychol.*, 11:127–165.

——— ——— & Jaffe, J. (1997), Mother–infant interaction structures and presymbolic self and object relations. *Psychoanal. Dial.*, 7:133–182.

Benjamin, J. (1988), *The Bonds of Love: Psychoanalysis, Feminism, and the Problem of Domination*. New York: Pantheon Books.

Berlant, L. (1991), National brands/national body: *Imitation of Life*. In: *The Phantom Public Sphere*, ed. B. Robbins. Minneapolis: University of Minnesota Press, 1993, pp. 173–208.

——— (1996), Pax Americana: The case of *Show Boat*. In: *Cultural Institution of the Novel,* ed. D. Lynch & W. Warner. Durham, NC: Duke University Press, pp. 398–421.

Bogle, D. (1997), Black beginnings: From *Uncle Tom's Cabin* to *The Birth of a Nation*. In: *Representing Blackness: Issues in Film and Video,* ed. V. Smith. New Brunswick, NJ: Rutgers University Press.

Brecht, B. (1957), Alienation effects in Chinese acting. In: *Brecht on Theatre,* trans. J. Willett. New York: Hill & Wang, 1964, pp. 91–99.

Brooks, P. (1976), *The Melodramatic Imagination: Balzac, Henry James, Melodrama, and the Mode of Excess*. New Haven, CT: Yale University Press.

Butler, J. (1990), *Gender Trouble*. New York: Routledge.

——— (1996), *The Psychic Life of Power*. Stanford, CA: Stanford University. Press.

——— (1993a), *Bodies that Matter: On the Discursive Limits of "Sex."* New York: Routledge, pp. 167–185.

——— (1993b), Endangered/endangering: Schematic racism and white paranoia, In: *Reading Rodney King: Reading Urban Uprising,* ed. R. Gooding-Williams. New York: Routledge, pp. 15–22.

Chodorow, N. (1978) *The Reproduction of Mothering: Psychoanalysis and the Sociology of Gender*. Berkeley: University of California Press.

——— (1989), *Feminism and Psychoanalytic Theory*. New Haven, CT: Yale University Press.

——— (1994), *Femininities, Masculinities, Sexualities: Freud and Beyond*. Lexington: University Press of Kentucky.

Christian, B. (1997), Fixing methodologies: *Beloved*. In: *Female Subjects in Black and White: Race, Psychoanalysis, Feminism,* ed. E. Abel, B. Christian & H. Moglen. Berkeley: University of California Press, pp. 363–370.

Dagle, J. & Kalinak, K. (1994), The representation of race and sexuality: Visual and musical construction in *Gone With the Wind. Post Script,* 13(2):14–27.

Dimen, M. (1998), Polyglot bodies: Thinking through the relational. In: *Relational Perspectives on the Body,* ed. L. Aron & F. S. Anderson. Hillsdale, NJ: The Analytic Press, pp. 65–93.

Edwards, A. (1993), From Aunt Jemima to Anita Hill. *Media Studies J.,* 7:216.

Fanon, F. (1967), *Black Skin, White Masks*. New York: Grove Weidenfeld.

Freud, S. 1919), "A child is being beaten": A contribution to the study of the origin of perversions. *Standard Edition,* 17:179–204. London: Hogarth Press, 1955.

——— (1923), The ego and the id. *Standard Edition,* 19:12–66. London: Hogarth Press, 1961.

Goings, K. W. (1994), *Mammy and Uncle Mose: Black Collectibles and American Stereotyping*. Bloomington: Indiana University Press.

Harris, A. (1996), Animated conversation: Embodying and engendering. *Gender & Psychoanal.,* 1:361–384.
——— (1998), Psychic envelopes and sonorous baths: Siting the body in relational theory and clinical practice. In: *Relational Perspectives on the Body*, ed. L. Aron & F. S. Anderson. Hillsdale, NJ: The Analytic Press, pp. 39–64.
hooks, b. (1990), *Reel to Real: Race, Sex, and Class at the Movies.* New York: Routledge.
Jacobus, M. (1998), "Tea daddy": Poor Mrs. Klein and the pencil shavings. In: *Reading Melanie Klein*, ed. J. Phillips & L. Stonebridge. London: Routledge.
Klein, M. (1935), A contribution to the psychogenesis of manic-depressive states. In: *The Selected Melanie Klein,* ed. J. Mitchell. New York: Free Press, 1986, pp. 115–145.
——— (1940), Mourning and its relation to manic-depressive states. In: *The Selected Melanie Klein,* ed. J. Mitchell. New York: Free Press, 1986, pp. 146–174.
——— (1946), Notes on some schizoid mechanisms. In: *The Selected Melanie Klein*, ed. J. Mitchell. New York: Free Press, 1986, pp. 175–200.
——— (1952), On observing the behavior of young infants. In: *The Writings of Melanie Klein, Vol. III: Envy and Gratitude and Other Works 1946–1963.* New York: Free Press, 1975, pp. 176–235.
——— (1955), The psychoanalytic play technique: Its history and significance. In: *The Selected Melanie Klein*, ed. J. Mitchell. New York: Free Press, 1986, pp. 35–54.
——— (1956), A study of envy and gratitude. In: *The Selected Melanie Klein*, ed. J. Mitchell. New York: Free Press, 1986, pp. 211–229.
——— (1957), Envy and gratitude. In: *The Writings of Melanie Klein, Vol. III: Envy and Gratitude and Other Works 1946–1963.* New York: Free Press, 1975, pp.176–235.
Lacan, J. (1948), Aggressivity in psychoanalysis. In: *Ecrits: A Selection,* trans. A. Sheridan. New York: Norton, 1977, pp. 8–29.
——— (1949), The mirror stage as formative of the function of the I as revealed in psychoanalytic experience. In: *Ecrits: A Selection*, trans. A. Sheridan. New York: Norton, 1977, pp. 1–7.
——— (1953), The function and field of speech and language in psychoanalysis. In: *Ecrits: A Selection*, trans. A. Sheridan. New York: Norton, 1977, pp. 30–113.
——— (1954a), Discourse analysis and ego analysis. In: *The Seminar of Jacques Lacan, Book I: Freud's Papers on Technique 1953–1954*, ed. J. Miller (trans. J. Forrester). New York: Norton, 1988, pp. 62–70.
——— (1954b), The topic of the imaginary. In: *The Seminar of Jacques Lacan, Book I: Freud's Papers on Technique 1953–1954,* ed. J. Miller (trans. J. Forrester). New York: Norton, 1988, pp. 73–88.

——— (1955a), The dream of Irma's injection. In: *The Seminar of Jacques Lacan, Book II: The Ego in Freud's Theory and in the Technique of Psychoanalysis 1954–1955,* ed. J. Miller (trans. S. Tomaselli). New York: Norton, 1988, pp. 146–171.
——— (1955b), The Freudian thing. In: *Ecrits: A Selection,* trans. A. Sheridan. New York: Norton, 1977, pp. 114–145.
——— (1957), The agency of the letter in the unconscious or reason since Freud. In: *Ecrits: A Selection,* trans. A. Sheridan. New York: Norton, 1977, pp. 146–178.
——— (1958), The signification of the phallus. In: *Ecrits: A Selection,* trans. A. Sheridan. New York: Norton, 1977, pp. 281–291.
——— (1964a), The deconstruction of the drive. In: *The Seminar of Jacques Lacan, Book XI: The Four Fundamental Concepts of Psychoanalysis,* ed. J. Miller (trans. A. Sheridan). New York: Norton, pp. 161–173.
——— (1964b), The Freudian unconscious and ours. In: *The Seminar of Jacques Lacan, Book XI: The Four Fundamental Concepts of Psychoanalysis,* ed. J. Miller (trans. A. Sheridan). New York: Norton, pp. 17–28.
Laplanche, J. & Pontalis, J.-B. (1973), *The Language of Psychoanalysis,* trans. D. Nicholson-Smith. New York: Norton.
Layton, L. (1999), *Who's That Boy? Who's That Girl? Clinical Practice Meets Postmodern Gender Theory.* Northvale, NJ: Aronson.
Lott, E. (1993), *Love and Theft: Blackface Minstrelsy and the American Working Class.* New York: Oxford University Press.
Manning, J. (1999), *Got Milk? The Book.* Rocklin, CA: Prima.
Manring, M. M. (1998), *Slave in a Box: The Strange Career of Aunt Jemima.* Charlottesville: University Press of Virginia.
Mitchell, J. (1974), *Psychoanalysis and Feminism.* London: Pelican Books.
——— & Rose, J., eds. (1982), *Feminine Sexuality: Jacques Lacan and the Ecole Freudienne,* trans. J. Rose. New York: Norton.
Mitchell, M. (1936), *Gone with the Wind.* New York: Warner Books.
Mullen, H. (1994, Optic whiteness: Blackness and the production of whiteness. *Diacritics,* 24:71–89.
Pyron, D., ed. (1983), *Recasting:* Gone With the Wind *in American Culture.* Miami: University Presses of Florida.
Roberts, D. (1994), *The Myth of Aunt Jemima: Representations of Race and Region.* New York: Routledge.
Rogin, M. (1996), *Blackface, White Noise: Jewish Immigrants in the Hollywood Melting Pot.* Berkeley: University of California Press.
Rose, J. (1982), Introduction II. In: *Feminine Sexuality: Jacques Lacan and the Ecole Freudienne,* ed. J. Mitchell & J. Rose (trans. J. Rose). New York: Norton, pp. 27–57.

Rosenfeld, H. (1971), A clinical approach to the psychoanalytic theory of the life and death instincts: An investigation into the aggressive aspects of narcissism. *Internat. J. Psychoanal.*, 52:169–178.
Rubin, G. (1975), The traffic in women: Notes on the "political economy" of sex. In: *Toward an Anthropology of Women*, ed. R. Raiter. New York: Monthly Review Press, pp. 157–210.
Silverman, K. (1988), *The Acoustic Mirror: The Female Voice in Psychoanalysis and Cinema*. Bloomington: University of Indiana Press.
——— (1992), *Male Subjectivity at the Margins*. New York: Routledge.
——— (1996), *The Threshold of the Visible World*. New York: Routledge.
Spillers, H. (1997), "All the things you could be by now, if Sigmund Freud's wife was your mother": Psychoanalysis and race. In: *Female Subjects in Black and White: Race, Psychoanalysis, Feminism*, ed. E. Abel, B. Christian & H. Moglen. Berkeley: University of California Press, pp. 135–158.
Stern, D. (1985), *The Interpersonal World of the Infant: A View from Psychoanalysis and Developmental Psychology*. New York: Basic Books.
Taylor, H. (1989), *Scarlett's Women:* Gone with the Wind *and Its Female Fans*. New Brunswick, NJ: Rutgers University Press.
White, D. G. (1985), *Aren't I a Woman? Female Slaves in the Plantation South*. New York: Norton.
Williams, L. (2001), *Playing the Race Card: Melodramas of Black and White from Uncle Tom to O. J. Simpson*. Princeton, NJ: Princeton University Press.
Winnicott, D. W. (1963), Communicating and not communicating leading to a study of certain opposites. In: *The Maturational Process and the Facilitating Environment: Studies in the Theory of Emotional Development*. New York: International Universities Press, 1965, pp. 179–192.

What About the Baby? The New Cult of Domesticity and Media Images of Pregnancy

Katie Gentile, Ph.D.

John Jay College of Criminal Justice

This article explores the explosion of images of pregnancy in the media since 9/11. Recent articles from *The New York Times* to academic journals have noted a marked increase in the representations of traditional gender roles since 2001, what the author here is comparing with the cult of domesticity that arose in the 19th century as an attempt at gaining cultural organization in a time of upheaval. According to Brown (2005), our culture is also facing the death of modernity—the promise of a better future. The author ties these seemingly disparate ideas together by quantitatively and qualitatively analyzing representations of pregnancy in the media. As the author details, the focus on pregnancy may be an attempt to instill faith in a future that has been rendered uncanny and unknowable by the recent awareness of our potential annihilation. The implications and dangers of this form of temporal linking are discussed.

> She won an Oscar and married a rock star, but Gwyneth Paltrow's life didn't truly have meaning until she became a parent. "I never feel like I don't know what my purpose is anymore. They [my children] have given me a real life. The mom has to be there and put time into every relationship in the house. Once you're a mother, you see everything in a different light [Interview with Gwyneth Paltrow, *In Touch* magazine, June 23, 2008].

It seems each time I pick up a magazine or newspaper I am faced with an image of, story about, or just a laudatory pull quote like this one about pregnancy or/and babies. I wish I could say that as an analyst and academic, I can transcend this explosion of cultural messages about the centrality of babies but I can't. Such quotes, whether real or accurate or manufactured, have the power to make me feel a failure. In the glow of the romanticization and glorification of pregnancy and babies it is easy to believe that the highest contribution, the most meaningful activity I could achieve, is having a baby.

I am not alone in thinking there has been a disturbing increase of media messages about pregnancy. Whenever I tell a woman I am writing this paper, the response has consistently been affirmative. They begin eagerly telling me how each magazine cover provokes anger, frustration, or/and self-critique about life choices. According to feminist historian Mary S. Hartman (2004), motherhood is the "enduring" defining behavior of the female gender role, so with the media functioning as a "pronatalist juggernaut" (Tietjens Meyers, 2001, p. 759) portraying motherhood as the defining credible avenue for women's fulfillment, it is difficult not to pay attention on some level of consciousness. Certainly I am not saying I or other women blindly follow the commands of the media, but subjects are constituted through power; we are both ''vehicles'' and ''targets'' of it (Brown, 2005), so although we may not blindly follow, we are nonetheless impacted by it. This inextricable nature of media and subjectivity makes critique and resistance complicated and necessary.

According to a report on National Public Radio (Smith, 2007), the number of children in upper class families has increased by 30% in the past few years so that for the first time in a century, upper class heterosexual couples are having more children than lower class couples. Women interviewed for the report claimed that this is due to a rechanneling of energy, where a generation of ''overachieving'' women are engaging in ''competitive birthing'' (see Kargman, 2007). If having two kids is good, four is better. *The New York Times* recently noted that nothing says opulence like multiple children (Haughney, 2007). (Of course, having multiple children is a status symbol only for those in the upper middle class. For others, multiple children can culturally signify a lack of control.)

In celebrity magazines it seems a baby or a pregnancy ''bump'' has become the hottest accessory. *US Magazine* even has a ''Bump Watch'' column. Magazines like *People* meticulously follow pregnant celebrities and endlessly speculate about those who might be pregnant (''bump patrols''). Coupled with these stories on pregnancy is what seems to be an obsession with postpartum weight control. Model Heidi Klum was celebrated for being able to walk on the Victoria's Secret lingerie runway just 6 weeks after giving birth. Then, Natalia Vodianovahas bettered this record by taking to the runway a mere 2 weeks after giving birth (see *Vogue*, December 2007). Jennifer Garner and Gwyneth Paltrow's respective postbaby dieting and workout tips were each *People* magazine cover stories. Not all celebrities comply but there is a price. A picture of Deborah Messing ran the caption that 2 years after the birth of her baby she ''finally'' shed her baby weight. Liv Tyler lamented that failing to lose her ''baby weight'' fast enough meant that for months the captions for magazine photos of her kept speculating that she must be pregnant again. Although such scrutiny of women's bodies is not new, and celebrity antics have long made for profitable media fodder, the preponderance of stories about pregnancy and critiques of postpartum bodies hints at something more important happening culturally of which the media may be symptomatic.

The events of September 11, 2001, and the United States government's response have ushered in a new awareness of cultural vulnerability. This awareness constitutes a specific threat to the social body involving annihilation anxiety (Lifton, 2003; Gentile and Gutwill, 2005; Strozier and Gentile, 2005). Since that year, I have become aware of an increased emphasis on pregnancy in newspaper and magazine stories. I am not alone in seeing a change. Negra (2008) described the reappearance of conservative gender roles in movies since 9/11. She writes that there has been a preoccupation with a stability and rigidity of gender organized around themes of female ''retreatism,'' the ''(re)masculinization'' of authority, and the reification of ''traditional'' family values. Scott (2008) and Dargis (2008), writing in *The New York Times*, both have noted a significant shift in gender roles in movies, particularly how in the most popular recent films, female characters have been limited to being either princesses or pregnant (Dargis, 2008).

But terrorism is not the only threat to the cultural body. The majority U.S. culture has finally come to acknowledge the damage humans are doing to the environment, the limits to the planet's resources, and the resulting unpredictable and violent weather patterns. Recent news articles note an increase in people seeking out artificial reproductive technologies to achieve pregnancy. Certain countries in Europe are facing what some consider a crisis of childlessness (Shorto, 2008). Realistic or not, the specter of infertility so frighteningly conveyed in the book and film versions of *The Children of Men* seem to be hanging over us.[1] Whether lower birthrates are due to environmental toxins, genetic problems, stress, or choice—including choosing to reproduce later in life when a woman may only be able or want to have one child whereas in the past she may have had multiples—the fears of humans becoming yet another extinct species are in the air. Indeed, the future is terrifying and uncertain on many different levels.

Feminist theorists have observed that cultural upheavals often coincide with changes in gender ideals, most often focusing on increased control of women's bodies and the installation of rigid female gender roles and expectations (Narayan, 1997; Mohanty, 2004).[2] In times of social chaos, change, war, and militarism, this control can increase in intensity and misogyny (Enloe, 2004). These changes need not only involve war and militarism but any sudden cultural shake-up. For example, during the industrial revolution of the 19th century the economic systems of family-based farming and home-based production were replaced by urban factory work (Amott and Matthieu, 1996). This shift required a change in the organization of society indicative in terms of labor distribution. Wage labor outside of the home became identified as masculine whereas unpaid labor in the home became exclusively feminine. As with any ideal, it was not available to all women. Lower class and immigrant women were employed within certain areas of manufacturing and homes whereas African American women were laboring inside and outside the home as slaves (see Amott and Matthieu, 1996), demonstrating the inextricability of gender, ethnicity, race, and class.

This cultural shift did not just happen. It was fostered in part by the proliferation of women's magazines and advice books that together created a unified ideal of femininity that has been termed the ''cult of true womanhood'' or ''domesticity'' (Welter, 1966). As discussed later, the cult of domesticity codified an ideal of femininity that emerged in the United States beginning around 1820, and despite the ethnic, race, and class divides supported by this ideal, it functioned to create within most women a desire for a home-based existence revolving around a family. Similarly, the changes brought by World War II and the use of the atomic bomb were also met with a flight to the cult of domesticity. The ideal 1950s woman was a suburban housewife supposedly fulfilled by her duties to care for children and her husband.

So I began wondering if the cultural shock of 9/11 was reverberating into a neo cult of domesticity focused on baby-making. Now, having framed the question I need to clarify some things. First, I know I can only conceptually link the events of 9/11 with an increase, should there be one, in representations of pregnancy, not prove causation. Also, as I noted earlier, I think 9/11 shook the U.S. culture into awareness of a number of threats to existence, all of which are impacting us. Second, although cultural patterns are reflected in media (and vice versa), I am

[1]Even this example is illustrative of the use of gender. Although based on the book, the film made one important plot change. In the book men became infertile and as a result their bodies were subject to constant medical surveillance. In the movie women are unable to conceive. This significant change may be indicative of the use of women's bodies to contain cultural anxieties about male vulnerability and cultural vulnerability in general. This is discussed further later.

[2]It is important to note that these gender changes certainly include changes in masculinity as well; however, these are beyond the scope of this paper, where I focus primarily on women.

not seeking to examine the relationships between media and individuals; I am analyzing the media representations. Welter (1966) took the leap to describe individual intentionality when she wrote that the cult of domesticity served to instill in women a particular desire for home life. Attributing desire or intention is not my goal here. I am not implying that women are blindly following the commands of the media; nor am I speculating whether or why women are or are not reproducing or potentially leaving the public sphere. After all, power and resistance are much more complicated. But as we learned quite clearly in the reports leading up to the invasion of Iraq, the media need not reflect any sense of ''truth'' or ''reality'' to garner power and influence. Media matters because we are altered when we take it in even when we reject it. It does change the environment (see culture and media studies writings such as *Culture, Media, Language* by Hall, Hobson, Lowe, and Willis, 1992). Still this paper does not discuss individual choice making; nor does it claim to theorize how people take in these media discourses. In this paper I focus exclusively on the media to explore the particular story about pregnancy that is being created and some potential functions this particular story may have for the organization of the culture as a whole.

Third, I know it is a leap to assume that the cultural mind/body can be analyzed through the theoretical lens we use for individuals and that it responds to trauma and uncertainty similar to how we theorize individuals respond. Given this last issue in particular, I decided to use an integration of cultural/political theory (primarily Brown, 2005) and psychoanalytic theory (Loewald, 1980; Gentile, 2007) to explore how we culturally and psychologically (knowing these distinctions themselves to be artificial) construct time and space in the face of trauma. I then searched two different kinds of print media—*The New York Times* and *People* magazine—before (1996–2000) and after (2002–2006) 9/11 for images and stories about pregnancy. I wanted to assess both the potential quantitative (was there an increase in the number of articles?) and qualitative (was there a difference in the way in which the stories and pictures appeared and the language that was used?) differences in coverage.

In this paper I first discuss the theoretical basis for the analysis of the texts. Then I contextualize this analysis historically, describing what I think has been a pattern of how the U.S. culture has responded to uncertainly, namely, the creation and proliferation of what has been termed the ''cult of domesticity'' (Welter, 1966). Then I discuss how I collected the data and what patterns I did and did not find. As with all research, we look at what strikes our attention, but the analysis in this paper emerged from the data; the data was not selected or organized around my preconceived notions of what I believed was going on. In fact, I did not exactly find what I expected.

CULTURAL AND PSYCHOLOGICAL THEORIES OF TIME AND SPACE

According to Brown (2005), Western culture has functioned on the belief that the future will be better than the past or present. As she writes, ''If modernity was always only a promise, then fruition is not its telos; rather, modernity's achievement *was* this promise'' (p. 104). Modernity organizes the culture through the belief that the future will automatically unfold as positive progress. As such, the promise of a future provides meaning for the present. This is a complex process. As Bourdieu (1977) observes, the future orientation functions to deny or disavow links to the past, where the idea of the future emerges. Here the past is denigrated in relation to the progressive future. These temporal delineations are also culturally gendered and raced such that the past is marked as "other": feminine, brown-skinned, backward, unindustrialized, and/or not modern whereas the future is full of potential, White and male (Kristeva, 1981; Freeman, 2005). The past is something to be disavowed; the links to it are to be severed. But when the future is in question due to increasing and unpredictable forms of potential annihilation, the cultural orientation toward a better future becomes imperiled. Brown describes this as the equivalent of an epistemological earthquake that is shaking up the very structure upon which our culture makes its meaning.

Brown (2005) contends that this shift requires a form of cultural mourning. Mourning this expectation of a better future means mourning the very process of creating anticipation, and as Brown notes, we are not prepared to live without this. We are not prepared because anticipatory temporality is not just cultural; it is the foundation of psychological development (Gentile, 2007) and subjectivity (Boellstorff, 2007). Indeed, the institutionalized force of temporality feels like "somatic facts" (Freeman, 2007, p. 160), creating our embodied experience such that we come into being through this particular shape of time (Gentile, 2007). Loewald (1980) describes this developmental process occurring through temporal linking, emerging from the "mother's" rhythms and patterns of satisfaction and frustration. Held within a bubble of predictability, the infant creates the initial patterns of expectation and anticipation, a projected future from a held collection of past experiences. So in a time of discomfort children are taught to use their accumulated history of positive (ideally) interactions with a caretaker to project themselves into a more comfortable and satisfying future state of calm. From this capacity to create time a regulating relational self emerges (Gentile, 2007). As Loewald notes, this creation of temporal linking enables the differentiation of self and other and is the basis for secondary process and symbolization. Indeed, the capacity to link in this particular future-oriented pattern is the state of being required for entry into the Western temporal world. Here within this world, words become symbolizations only as they contain the temporal link between primary and secondary process. They are meaningful to the extent that they are embedded within a space of timed interaction, conjuring up the past experience. So the word *hungry* becomes meaningful only as we are able to temporally link a past experience of what is labeled "hungry" with the experience of being fed and then satiated. Temporality emerges from these links between hunger, food, and satisfaction, the creation of one's experiences of a past, present, and future. Here we learn early to create subjectivity in the present moment by linking experiences of the past to the future, expectation (past) to anticipation (future). Thus, to lose the promise of modernity is to lose our reliance on the pattern of temporal movement through which we create subjectivity.

Brown (2005) writes that mourning this temporal pattern of modernity is also difficult due to the fact that we are losing an idea, a future promise not a corporeal body. Here I disagree. First, as I have described of the development of temporal linking, the promise exists only through its impact on the corporeal; thus the process of generating a particular future is distinctly an embodied one as it emerges from the embodied experiences of the past (Gentile, 2007). Additionally, *GLQ: Journal of Lesbian Gay Studies* dedicated an entire issue (*GLQ*, Vol. 13, Nos. 2–3, 2007) to exploring temporality, in particular how the future orientation of culture is embodied and reinforced by a cultural emphasis on reproduction, labeled reprofuturity (see Dinshaw et al., 2007). So the cultural organization of reproduction may further function to embody this future orientation. Second, it is not the promise of a future itself that is being lost but the capacity to make meaning of the present by linking anticipation and expectation, using the past and future to create the experience of going on being in the moment. What is lost is not an idea or a particular future but the process of being able to generate faith in a particular pattern of temporal linking. When Brown describes the impossibility of living outside of modernity, she is talking about living outside of this particular pattern of temporal linking process.

If we are in a future-oriented culture with a tenuous future, then pregnancy could be seen as the embodied manufacturing of the future, which would be a perfect focus for cultural anxiety. As Bourdieu (1977) wrote,

> The whole trick of pedagogic reason lies precisely in the way it extorts the essential while seeming to demand the insignificant: in obtaining the respect for form and forms of respect which constitute the most visible and at the same time the best-hidden (because most ''natural'') manifestation of submission to the established order [pp. 94–95].

In a heterocentric culture, what pedagogical trick could be more invisibly manipulated than cultural constructions of pregnancy? The processes of reproduction appear to be the most *natural* of behaviors yet the ways in which we construct them are decidedly ideological. Take, for instance, fertility treatments. Here, regardless of the identified problem (i.e., the woman's hormones or the low quality of her male partner's sperm), the site of fertility treatment is the woman's body. Intervening to increase the quality of sperm is not an option in the Western cultural model of fertility medicine (see Franklin and Ragoné, 1998; Finhorn and Van Balen, 2002) even though it is in other non-Western medicines (A. Vitolo, personal communication, July 7, 2006). So the ''natural'' process of conception is culturally constructed. One could describe the cult of domesticity functioning as a pedagogical trick to cloak rigid gender ideology in the ''*natural*'' at a time of immense cultural anxiety and change. So regulating pregnancy can function as a defense against anxiety and as an attempt to reestablish anticipation and expectation as the organizational structure of cultural meaning making. This is imperative in the face of the realization that the future is now uncanny—beyond our expectations.

Hesford and Diedrich (2008) have described Western culture since 9/11 as being framed by a ''tyranny of emergency,'' where forward-looking thoughtfulness is erased in favor of immediate gratification and an inability to reflect (Bindé as quoted by Hesford and Diedrich, p. 6). Here ''the future is only imagined in terms of the repetition of an (idealized) past, a compensatory move that attempts to deny the passage of time itself'' (p. 7). ''Emergency time'' creates a false sense of mastery through impulsive action that is a displacement. So, as Hesford (2008) notes, global warming, economic instability, and health care threats take a backseat to the war on terror, where ''action, myth and amnesia become the drugs of certainty'' (p. 181). Here the present can secure its future only by ''reordering the past'' (p. 174), creating a myth that is empty of historicity (a reflective, thoughtful past) and full of a ''mythical future'' (p. 175). The resurgence of the cult of domesticity with a focus on pregnancy may function to create a future based on a past mythology of gender arrangements.

Another way of approaching the needs of mourning modernity and its temporal pattern is to look at psychoanalytic literature that outlines what happens when we as individuals are left bereft of time. This literature focuses on the impact of trauma as the destroyer of time, when self-destructive violence can often be the only way to link internal intentional states with external events (Fonagy and Target, 1998), expectation with anticipation. This self-destructive violence is often focused on the body. As has been written (Davies and Frawley, 1992, 1994), the embodied collection of abusive experience is often contained within the body and split off from awareness in favor of a Western fantasy of disembodied, minded existence (Gentile, 2007). Here experiences of trauma are kept out of awareness as long as the body is kept out of awareness. Given that Western culture typically genders mind-psyche as male and the body as female, this means that in our psychological theories of trauma, we take it as a given that survival requires splitting off and containing uncontrollable past memories of abuse in the (female) body in order to save the forward-moving (male) psyche-mind (Gentile, 2007). Thus the loss of the capacity to create, anticipate, and expect a future might also be experienced as a wound to the (male) order of progression.

Ehrenreich (1995) contends we are experiencing a decline of patriarchy. This is not to be confused with the end of men's domination of women but a decline of men's monopoly in the public sphere and the end of the ''mutuality'' of the arrangements of the cult of domesticity. This is reflected in current films where heterosexual men are often portrayed as choosing (vs. having fewer options due to economics) to no longer be responsible breadwinners for the family but instead are ''committed to a brazen and unyielding refusal of maturity . . . nudged toward responsibility, . . . by a woman who represents an ideal amalgam of supermodel and mom'' (Scott, 2008, p. 33). If, as noted, the future is male and progressive whereas the past is female and regressive, then destruction of temporal linking as future oriented is also a destruction of the patriarchy and what it is founded upon, including the destruction of the fantasy of male invulnerability and transcendence of embodiment. If this is the case, then mourning modernity may also be so difficult because it necessitates mourning our current organization of patriarchy. So a flight to pregnancy may be a focus on Bourdieu's (1977) *natural* that is multiply determined with multiple advantages and costs to the organization of the culture.

Although Welter (1966) in her assessment of the cult of domesticity searched women's magazines for ideals of womanhood in general, I focused only on constructions of pregnancy. I did this because as Scott (2008), Dargis (2008), and Negra (2008) have already noted, gender ideals as a whole have become rigidified and bifurcated in the past 7 years. As Scott observed, the ideal woman is now not only a supermodel but also a mother to men and children. An unrealistic standard of beauty for women is not new, but a return to an emphasis on being a mother is. I was initially struck not by the proliferation of supermodel pictures—I grew up with these—but the explosion of articles on and images of pregnant women. So I wanted to know, was my experience accurate, just overly sensitive due to my own circumstances, or are we witnessing an important shift in ideals of femininity around pregnancy?

A HISTORICAL CONTEXT OF THE CULT OF TRUE WOMANHOOD

As noted, the cult of domesticity emerged during a time of great flux in the United States. Manufacturing was moving into factories shifting the culture from a home-based economy and creating a significant increase in the middle class. This destabilization of society coincided with the cult of domesticity that developed, in part, to teach newly middle-class women the (upper class) ideals of femininity, that is, the cultural meanings of race, class, and gender. These ideals were proliferated through advice books and women's magazines. Welter (1966) studied those published between 1820 and 1860 and identified four cardinal virtues of femininity: piety, purity, submissiveness, and domesticity. Pious women were the handmaidens of God. Purity required sexual abstinence and vacating oneself of any sexual desire. Domesticity and submissiveness meant complete obedience to a husband's will while creating a home that would be a haven from the evils of the public world. As Welter noted, without these virtues, ''no matter whether there was fame, achievement or wealth, all was ashes. With them she was promised happiness and power'' (p. 152). And with motherhood, a woman takes a ''higher place in the scale of being'' (p. 171). These ideals were reinforced by pat statements, for instance, that religion was a ''tranquilizer'' for undefined physical or psychological and intellectual longings as ''it was better to pray than to think'' (p. 153). A physician of the time stated that a woman ''has a head almost too small for intellect but just big enough for love'' (p. 160). But not just any love. ''Proper women have no sexual feelings at all and are animated by maternal instincts alone'' (Hartman, 2004, p. 264). Thus, women were to work only for ''pure affection, without thought of money or ambition'' (p. 160). These were her ''natural'' born talents.

In the face of rising industrialization, a new middle class, economic uncertainty, a shift from a home-based economy to a factory-based one, the public world took on real and imagined ideas of ungodliness: greed, wanton behaviors, temptations, and violence. In relation, ''the domestic fireside [was] the great guardian of society against the excesses of human passions'' (*The Young Ladies' Class Book* as quoted by Welter, 1966, p. 162). Indeed, the woman was to bring a ''restorative power'' to men that money could not possibly purchase. Staying home and holding a religious, calming, and civilizing influence over their men was the best form of patriotism a woman could exercise. This, of course, was an argument not only for the cult of true womanhood but also against women's suffrage (Welter, 1966). Women who refused to conform, who wrote and pursued intellectual studies, were considered only ''semiwomen'' and ''mental hermaphrodites'' (p. 175), demonstrating how spaces, times, psychological qualities, and intellect were gendered. Here, cultural stability was built around these ideals; any form of social change was considered tantamount to an attack on women's virtue, and any proposed change in gender relations (i.e., suffragettes) was seen as unpatriotic and a threat to the universal order.

One can see how the cult of domesticity would function to organize society in the face of industrialization. It also organized a racially and ethnically integrating society with a growing suffrage movement. But as historian Hartman (2004) contends, although it kept women within the home not competing for wage jobs or for the stature of the public sphere, it also served to define and reify women's work. So even though the public world was identified as men's (and men were granted all the authorities that go along with the public world), women were given the mandate to save men's souls, to do God's work, and to have and nurture their children. Thus, it was not that women were blind followers of some cultural ideal designed to keep them from power. As Hartman notes, throughout the history of Western culture women's presumed ''nature'' has been identified as uncontrollable and dangerous (and nature, the ultimate uncontrollable force, is still feminized). It has been the excuse for witch hunts and other forms of collective and individualized violence against women. The cult of domesticity, while confining women to the home, also created/identified and elevated their previously negative ''natural'' talents to being godly. Their supposed irrationality was suddenly valuable in terms of emotional nurturing. Yes, they did not get the rewards and security of wage work, but they were constructed as having a very important role. As Welter (1966) writes, women gained power and stature from embodying the ideals, even though these gains were primarily confined to the home.

Additionally, as Hartman (2004) notes, confining women in the home was culturally fruitful. Social movements such as abolition, women's suffrage, first- and second-wave feminism, and much of the Civil Rights movement were born from/of women's segregation. Segregation created the conditions for consciousness-raising and social change. As noted earlier, power and resistance are complicated.

A CULT OF DOMESTICITY FOR THE 21ST CENTURY

These religious-based ideals may seem a far cry from our current cultural landscape of badly behaving female celebrities and their drunken, drug-addled sex tapes and ''girls gone wild'' videos. Piety and purity are still relevant, but they are wielded from different altars. Dieting; exercising; living cleanly with no fat, or no carbs, or no sugar, depending on the accepted ''religion,'' that is, diet, is the new purity. Piety is being ''good'' and staying on a diet. Women can have sex and advertise it. Pregnant bodies, once hidden under tentlike asexual smocks, can now burst out in Lycra formfitting clothes and walk proudly down award show carpets. However, both states of women's bodies need to be pure and pious according to the new definition: they must be thin. Even pregnant, the only parts of the body that can swell and be displayed are the belly (the pregnancy bump) and the breasts. Dieting is the tranquilizer.

Finding the modern version of domesticity and submission is easy, especially if you are in an upper middle-class neighborhood. As Belkin (2003) observed in *The New York Times Magazine,*

> Wander into any Starbucks in any Starbucks kind of neighborhood in the hours after the commuters are gone. See all those mothers drinking coffee and watching over toddlers at play? If you look past the Lycra gym clothes and the Internet-access cellphones, the scene could be the 50's, but for the fact that the coffee is more expensive and the mothers have M.B.A.'s

Now, it is important to note that this ideal that was covered prominently in *The New York Times Magazine* is purely that, an ideal. According to census data, more women than ever are working while raising a family. It is women in the top 5% of the income spectrum and women with high school degrees who are most apt to ''opt out,'' and for the latter group, this is not a choice but a result of the rigid, nonflexible labor conditions of most lower income jobs (Coontz, 2006). Yet, despite the statistics, the ideal of the mother opting out, finding meaning primarily in raising a family, is still popularized in the media in many ways. Take any advertisement for cleaning products, diapers, or baby food. None of these commercials in television or print media feature men doing the domestic duties. (Indeed, the only man in these commercials is typically Mr. Clean, who does not have to unfold his arms.) Although this is nothing new, with the increase of women's participation in the public sphere and the corresponding (although not equal) increase of men's participation in the private sphere, these representations more than ever reproduce a fantasy or myth of joyful female domesticity. So although more women are working outside the home and raising a family, the media continues to promote an ideal where women alone are emotionally invested in maintaining a clean house, cleaning the clothes of the family, and being the primary caretakers of children. In the media, it is only women who find meaning in the home. Indeed, the cult of domesticity is alive and well.

In order to get a better handle on our current cultural discourse around pregnancy, I, like Welter (1966) searched media: *The New York Times* online website (www.nytimes.com) and Lexus Nexus. The results from Lexus Nexus indicated that a number of popular weekly magazines had had substantial increases in the amount of stories published about pregnancy. Because most of the current magazines did not exist in 1996, I focused only on *People* magazine, which was one of the only magazines available throughout the time I was researching. Additionally, the magazine has one of the largest circulations of such magazines (3.73 million according to Goldsmith, 2006). I examined both results from Lexus Nexus and the archives on the *People* website (www.peoplemagazine.com). The search used the same date parameters: 1996–2000 and 2002–2006. Clearly terrorism existed before this date, global warming was a reality before this date, but, again, 9/11 and the ensuing invasions and attacks seemed to budge cultural denial.

THE NEW YORK TIMES

I began by searching *The New York Times* online database for the term *pregnancy* from 1996 to 2000 and from 2002 to 2006. To my surprise I did not find what I expected. There were no real differences in the numbers of articles referencing pregnancy (2,100 hits in the period between 1996 and 2000; 2,028 hits between 2002 and 2006). However, there was a change in distribution of coverage between sections. The U.S. section saw a large decline in articles on pregnancy whereas the Arts (including Art, Movies, Books, and Theater) and Health sections of the paper saw distinct increases. The U.S. section fell from publishing an average of 88.8 articles per year on pregnancy from 1996 to 2000 to 57.2 per year between 2002 and 2006. Looking at the titles of articles, it appeared that one potential cause of this drop was a change in coverage of teen pregnancy. In fact, coverage of teen pregnancy dropped in the entire paper. In the years 1996–2000, there were 436 articles on teen pregnancy in the total paper, 104 in the U.S. section. From 2002 to 2006, these articles numbered 64 in the total paper, 8 in the U.S. section. Before 2002 teen pregnancy comprised 23% of the articles on pregnancy in the U.S. section, 21% of those in the whole paper. After 2002, that percentage dropped to 3% in both. Although beyond the scope of this paper, the drop in articles on teen pregnancy might be related to the fact that rates of teen pregnancy have dropped since 1996 rendering it less of a cultural issue, although it only dropped for certain segments of the population, not all.[3] It might also be indicative of a shifting approach to pregnancy coverage qualitatively, which is discussed later.

As noted earlier, pregnancy coverage in the Health and all of the Arts sections (including Art, Books, Films, and Theater) increased. I collapsed the different art-related sections and found the average number of articles referring to pregnancy before 2001 to be 90 per year. After, it increased to 110 on average, with 2007 being a banner year with 187 references to it. (This year, being outside of my initial search range, was not included in my averages). The Health section averaged 90.8 articles per year before 2001 and 121 articles per year after. Given the previous discussion about the potential role of pregnancy for the culture, it follows that increases in coverage would be in the areas of projective representations (arts) and health, the latter of which can serve to monitor and provide specific guidelines for pregnancy.

I chose to focus in on the Health section because, as I noted previously, there had already been articles discussing this increase in the arts. Examining the different articles from the search, I found a large increase in the special section called ''Vital Signs,'' which reports on recent research in different sections of the paper. Here, coverage of research and advice about

[3]See Guttmacher Institute's 2006 report on *U.S. Teenage Pregnancy Statistics: National and State Trends and Trends by Race and Ethnicity*, available at www.guttmacher.org

pregnancy increased from 20 in the years leading up to 2001 (it began in 1998 so there were fewer years in this cluster) to 61 per year after. Taking averages, 1998, 1999, and 2000 averaged 6 articles in this column per year. From 2002 to 2006, the average was double at 12. There have been increases in medical research since 1996 in all areas and the frequency of this column in general also almost doubled since 2000, so numbers are not that compelling. Still one can see a shift from focusing on pregnancy as problematic and requiring preventative intervention (teens) to a focus on pregnancy as a deliberate, purposeful act that should be supported (medical research and advice on how to have a healthy baby). So although the numbers in general did not increase, searching by category and by newspaper section suggests that *The New York Times* has become more pronatalist since 2001.

Looking more in depth at the research articles about pregnancy and health, it seems the tenor of these also changed through the years. Before 2001, research primarily focused on the impact of antidepressants on babies, the effects of premature birth, and the development of various drugs for infections for mothers or infants. The titles are matter-of-fact and content driven, descriptive and seemingly objective or nonsensational. The reader knows what the articles are about from the titles:

- Vaccine developed to protect babies (December 3, 1996).
- More women report alcohol use in pregnancy (April 25, 1997).
- VITAL SIGNS: PRO & CON: Should women pace during labor? (October 13, 1998).
- VITAL SIGNS: PREVENTION: Taking folic acid in time to help the baby (December 15, 1998).
- VITAL SIGNS: A healthy space between the babies (March 2, 1999).
- VITAL SIGNS: THERAPIES: Cancer regimen found safe in pregnancy (March 16, 1999).
- VITAL SIGNS: CHILDBIRTH: Long-lasting scars of unwanted births (August 24, 1999).
- VITAL SIGNS: Light regimen for pregnancy depression (November 28, 2000).

Beginning in 2002, the titles shift to become more sensational. Some even require an explanation of the story, as I provide here:

- VITAL SIGNS: AT RISK: Early signs of problems with weight (February 12, 2002). The weight of the mother might influence obesity in the baby's first year of life.
- VITAL SIGNS: HAZARDS: Dangers from lead, in the womb (July 2, 2002). Women may have high levels of lead in their bones even before they conceive.
- VITAL SIGNS: AT RISK: Health clues during pregnancy (July 30, 2002). Mothers need to be monitored for disease and counseling on potential changes during pregnancy.
- VITAL SIGNS: AT RISK: Multiple births and older women (September 24, 2002).
- VITAL SIGNS: PREVENTION: When coffee puts fetus at risk (March 3, 2003).
- VITAL SIGNS: MENTAL SKILLS: Staying sharp in pregnancy (March 25, 2003).
- U.S. urged to educate women about food linked to dioxin (July 2, 2003). Dioxins are linked to birth defects.
- VITAL SIGNS: AT RISK: Putting time between newborns (August 19, 2003).
- Dealing with depression and the perils of pregnancy (January 13, 2004).
- U.S. infant mortality rate rises slightly (February 12, 2004).
- Two drinks can kill brain cells in a fetus, studies suggest (February 15, 2004).

- House confers legal protection on fetuses (February 27, 2004).
- VITAL SIGNS: NUTRITION: Fish dinners and birth weight (May 18, 2004). You should only eat fish at certain points during pregnancy.
- For mother and child, a lurking danger (November 23, 2004). This is actually a positive essay about ways to prevent preeclampsia or toxemia, although you would never know from the title.
- VITAL SIGNS: HAVING A BABY: Risk seen in weight gain between pregnancies (October 17, 2006).
- That prenatal visit may be months too late (November 28, 2006).

The tenor of the coverage seemed to shift dramatically. Notice that the Vital Signs column began to incorporate alarming subheadings of "At risk," "Hazards," and "Perils," heightening attention and vigilance in the reader, especially as they appear in capital letters. For instance, observe the difference in reporting the same advice to space children:

- VITAL SIGNS: A healthy space between the babies (March 2, 1999).
- VITAL SIGNS: AT RISK: Putting time between newborns (August 19, 2003).

These articles report the same conclusion, that having babies back-to-back can result in lower birth weights; however, in 1999 it is put in the positive as "a healthy space" urging people to space births. In 2003 the same message is reported with fear and warning, "At risk." Looking briefly at the reporting of medical research in general there has been a shift toward alarm as all news has become sensational. In fact, "Vital Signs" began using "At risk" as a subheading to report general medical research in 1999, on the precipice of the millennium, potentially another factor. However, these general medical columns were reporting on ways of controlling diseases and life-threatening illnesses. Here I am talking about pregnancy—a "naturally" occurring event in many women's lives. It is not a disease to be prevented. Yet, in the recent coverage, it is as if every detail of pregnancy is being scrutinized and picked apart, written in the paper as risks, hazards, and perils.

Although "At risk" and similar subheadings were used in general medical reporting in 1999, in the years before 2001, "Vital Signs" columns that reported on pregnancy typically used either no subheadings or those of "Patterns" or sometimes "Prevention." It was not until the end of 2002 that "At risk" and "Hazards" began being used for pregnancy reports. In these articles there is a language of warning and fear resulting in an increasing responsibility placed on women as future or current childbearers. Pregnancy is a "peril" with "lurking dangers." And watching your food and diet, your weight, your drinking, and what medications you take while pregnant is not enough. You need to worry about the levels of lead in your bones before you conceive. You need to make sure throughout your life your diet is balanced because cleaning up your diet when you conceive is too late to save your baby. Taking prenatal vitamins and getting relatively healthy to become pregnant is not enough: women must live a spotless life lest they be responsible for damaging their baby or for their own infertility. The temporal line of pregnancy is stretched to extend months if not years before conception. Not adequately preparing in advance for potential pregnancy places your child at risk for the rest of his or her life. The consequences are dire and only women are to blame for their poor planning and lack of self-restraint (i.e., lack of purity and piousness). The articles on pregnancy stretch time to focus on even nonpregnant women who might become pregnant in the future.

Since doing this more organized search, 2007 served up even more warnings for women as potential mothers. Cesareans were tied to breathing problems in babies (''Vital Signs,'' December 25, 2007). Women were warned that weight gain during pregnancy and gestational diabetes can lead to fat toddlers who will have a life struggle with weight (''Vital Signs'', September 4, 2007) and that even what have been considered ''normal'' pregnancy weight gains can be dangerous for babies and may result in obese children (''Vital Signs,'' April 10, 2007). Consequently, ''aggressive'' efforts are necessary to curb maternal obesity (Jaina, Denka, & Druse, 2007), such that women must diet AND exercise after childbirth to lose the baby weight (Jaina, Denka, & Druse, 2007), but dieting and yo-yo weight losses between pregnancies can negatively effect the health of the next baby (Gurevich, 2010). Indeed, according to some reports, dieting any time in your life may put your future baby at risk (www.baby-health.net). Pregnancy is imperiling and the risks of misbehavior are great. The headlines are anxiety provoking as it is unclear what (if anything) healthy behavior is, but there are dire consequences if one does not figure it out.

Certainly many of the articles are attempting to help women and men produce healthy babies. Given accurate or inaccurate interpretations of decreasing fertility, it makes sense to create the best circumstances within which to foster reproduction. However, the story these articles create about pregnancy is one where women are to be constantly monitoring their desires, bodies, and controlling their environment (avoiding toxins, smoke, and lead) and being engaged in self-denial and restraint. The articles instill fear and vigilance as one must stay on top of all of the potential dangers that are uncovered each day. The articles are also almost exclusively focused on women. Yes, women carry the baby, but given that the majority of reproducing women are still in relationships with men, and that men (whether partners or anonymous donors) contribute half of the genetic material to the baby, these articles, like those noted earlier about domesticity, paint pregnancy as an activity women embark on alone, the success of which is their sole responsibility.

PEOPLE MAGAZINE

As noted, *The New York Times* represents one form of media. In *People,* coverage of pregnant celebrities has multiplied exponentially. From 1996 to 2000, the magazine averaged only 23 stories or photos of pregnancy or babies per year. Although the web archive for 1996, 1997, 1998, and 1999 seemed less complete than the other years, even in 2001, where the archive was fuller, only 18 stories or photos appeared representing pregnancy. From 1996 to 2000, pregnancy and births were confined to the section about milestones, where they were reported on alongside of and with equal importance to deaths, marriages, and divorces. This entire section is typically one page and may or may not include photos. Coverage of births did not garner more type or photos than the other milestones. It seemed to be merely one of a number of one to 3 line notices in the section.

By 2002 the coverage on pregnancy jumped to 48. In 2005 it was 197 and in 2006 the magazine ran 372 photos or stories related to pregnancy. Celebrity coverage in general has increased in *People*, but coverage of pregnancy has taken over the structure of the magazine, resulting in regular photo columns titled ''Mom's Best Moves'' of children with their famous mothers and ''Mommy and Me Style,'' highlighting the impeccable fashions of celebrity mothers and their infants and children.

Part of this expanse in coverage was the addition of feature stories about celebrities who might be pregnant. These stories are based on photos that meticulously track a celebrity's body weight and shape in order to highlight any slight change in weight or stomach size. This is called the ''bump patrol'' in the magazine. This creates a new level of scrutiny of celebrity women where pictures of stomachs and sometimes breasts are enhanced and isolated for effect. Photos zoom in on all bellies as potential bumps. Celebrities carrying grocery bags or their purses or totes in front of their stomachs are captioned to be ''strategically covering a bump.'' If women wear lose clothes they are hiding a bump; if they wear tight clothes (and are not concave) they are advertising a bump. Basically, if women celebrities are seen in public, they may be identified as potentially pregnant if the story is needed.

Speculating on the motives of celebrities is yet another article category that can increase pregnancy coverage in each magazine. ''More children on the horizon for Meg Ryan?'' and ''Nicole Kidman: 'I would love to have a baby'' are two examples. Here celebrities with children are represented as pining away for more children. Similarly, stories about younger celebrities can focus on pregnancy by speculating where they see children fitting in their future (''Beyoncé says she wants kids in 10 years''). Here, comments from Beyoncé about her various jobs (acting, singing, and modeling) are not the pull quote or the selling title. Instead, what interests the magazine, and in relation, its readers, is when she will reproduce. Fame and fortune are great, but babies sell magazines.

Theme stories about pregnancy have also been created, such as ''New Mothers,'' ''Midlife Moms,'' and ''Mothers Over the Age of 40.'' There are also series of photos featuring celebrity mothers doing everyday activities with their children. Pictures of Kate Winslet and Reese Witherspoon picking up their respective children from school garnered special attention as the captions pointed out that they are ''Hands-on Moms.'' Here we readers are to be impressed that with all the high-paying acting gigs they are juggling, they always make time to pick up their children. There are also the individual stories where regular behaviors of women are covered with the add-on of the baby. For instance, ''Katie Goes Shoe Shopping,'' featuring a very pregnant Katie Holmes looking at shoes. These catch-all categories guarantee numerous weekly articles on pregnancy.

As with the 19th-century cult of domesticity where the upper class women were models to teach the middle-class women how best to behave, in *People,* these celebrity moms are models for all moms. *People* announces how ''Liv Tyler names her newborn baby'' and there are numerous pictures of celebrity moms with kids at grocery stores, picking them up from school, and playing in parks. But pictures of moms and their infants are cropped in *People,* so attending nannies and childcare workers are almost always absent from the photos (one exception was of Angelina Jolie and Brad Pitt boarding a plane and two of their four children were being carried by other women). This absence perpetuates the myth of parenting perfection. If busy celebrities can make time for their children (and do so smiling as most photos demonstrate), why can't every mother? Although fathers are shown with their children too, by far the majority of the photos and coverage is of women and their children.

The bulk of the celebrity-as-model-mom articles revolve around regaining control over your body after pregnancy. In fact, few articles about pregnancy fail to mention the amount of weight that has been gained or/and how it is proposed to be lost. These activities are inextricably linked. Gwyneth Paltrow and Jennifer Garner share postbaby workout secrets. Both lament their postbaby bodies as ''a horror,'' Garner for expanding to a size 6 or 8. (Need I point out the average

American woman is a size 12 or 14?) As she is quoted, "I am in the worst shape ever . . . my trainer just shakes her head and says, 'This is a disaster.' " In another article, "Liv Tyler reveals her baby-weight struggle" that involved a strict protein diet, a raw foods diet, colonics, and fasting in addition to daily workouts with a trainer. Paltrow engages in 3-hour daily exercise sessions to lose the baby weight. Regardless of the accuracy of these stories, they create models of behavior few women with babies can emulate. Although the experience of pregnancy and childbirth can feel colonizing and getting one's old/own body back can feel empowering and extremely important, these stories create a narrative where getting one's body back is the only acceptable outcome. Lingering in the postpartum body is not celebrated. Again, I attempt to analyze the media story about pregnancy, not the phenomenological experience of it, knowing that this is a complicated distinction.

Losing weight is a clear necessity that must happen in less than 3 months, the time Gwyneth and Jennifer lamented. And the rewards are worth it, as you can show off your "postbaby body," as Katie Holmes did, or Maggie Gyllenhaal, who was "psyched about showing off her svelte postbaby body." Although outside the range of my search, a cover story for a November issue of *Star* magazine was the "Best and Worst Post-Baby Bodies," where the average time from delivery was 2–3 months. That seems to be the time allotted to women celebrities to lose the "baby weight." A recent cover of *US Magazine* featured pictures of three celebrities who were back to their prebaby weights 3 weeks after giving birth. Calling it baby weight is also an interesting use of language. It is as if the weight belongs to the baby and not to the mother. As discussed later, this displacement causes a temporal slippage or distortion where the cause and effect of childbearing on the body is rendered fuzzy.

Lest anyone shudder at the fear of losing their svelte, pure, piously in-control body to pregnancy, it is also drummed into the reader that having a baby is the best and most important thing a woman can do. Whereas stories of men revolve around how they contribute to social change (i.e., "Bono, Elton John Fight Hunger, Hurricanes"), women celebrities can do no better than to have a baby. Mariska Hargitay, an Emmy Award-winning actress, says, "I feel like I've been waiting my whole life to do it." Jennifer Garner is "intoxicated" with her love for her daughter. Gwyneth says, "Being a housewife is 'amazing!' " and as noted in the beginning, has brought purpose and meaning to her life. If award-winning, multimillion-dollar celebrities are not complete until they have a baby, what hope do average women have? "No matter whether there was fame, achievement or wealth, all was ashes" if one did not meet the ideals (Welter, 1966, p. 152). Bringing a higher cultural status and respect to childbearing and parenting would be positively revolutionary, but the current cult of domesticity appears to be glamorizing and romanticizing it as well as writing it as women's work, erasing men's participation. This sets up women (who still do the majority of the parenting) for self-destructive failure. It also denigrates women who choose not to or who cannot have children and belittles the vast contributions of women's nonreproductive labor.

MANUFACTURING CULTURAL FAITH THROUGH TEMPORALLY DISTORTING WOMEN'S BODIES

According to the current cultural narrative about pregnancy, a woman's *past* eating, drinking, and drug taking behaviors are always present in her body's capacity for reproduction. Women who have *histories* of yo-yo dieting, obesity, or underweight might have unhealthy babies. In other words, women's bodies are not located in any one particular time; they are always potential vessels of babies, meaning that past, present, and future coexist within the female body. This form of temporal linking may function to patrol and limit women's behaviors. She is not situated in her own body but in the mythical future body of her baby. She is the embodiment of the future-oriented culture.

If the health of the baby were the sole motivation for this monitoring, successful reproduction would be celebrated. Period. However, as the magazine demonstrates over and over again, upon successful reproduction, women must immediately shed the evidence of having reproduced, which is not healthy for the mother or her baby, especially if she is breast-feeding. A postbaby, sagging, or full female body is more than just an affront to cultural ideals of fat-phobic, misogynous aesthetics. The glorification and reification of women who quickly lose weight, coupled with the mocking and censuring of those who do not, creates an atmosphere where the postdelivery body is not only denigrated and shameful but also abject—beyond cultural signification. Situating the postpregnant body in this way functions to erase it, which plays with time in a number of dangerous ways.

First, weight gain during pregnancy is *expected* and *anticipated* as a component of the reproductive process. It is an embodied signifier of the temporal links between the past (nonpregnant body), present (gestating body), and the future (postpartum body and the baby's body). To erase it is to erase the evidence of reproduction. The erasure of signs of reproduction indicates a disruption in established modernist temporal linking, cause and effect. The past recent pregnancy is erased and no longer a source of meaning-making for the future (or present). As noted earlier in the description of "emergency time" (Hesford and Diedrich, 2008), the past is reordered so that "action, myth and amnesia" can create a false sense of certainty (p. 181).

Second, if, as Hartman (2004) contends, women alone are identified primarily by reproduction, and reproduction is *a* foundation for our future temporal orientation, then women become associative signifiers of the future. If we live in a world where the future has become uncanny and unknowable, then women embody the contradictory cultural positions of being dependent upon reproduction for survival while experiencing intense fright and ambivalence about it as it represents the tenuous and unknowable future. Women and their potential reproductive processes become "vehicles" and "targets" (Brown, 2005) for cultural anxiety. So as noted earlier, with the psychological effects of trauma, the terror of uncertainty/abuse is contained within the identified (female) body of the culture, here, within the very process they alone embody (gestation). This dual function as both a target of projected anxiety and a vehicle of it is enacted in what appears to be the deeply troubled and ambivalent relationship to pregnancy in the media. One can see the culture as a whole struggling with each story, simultaneously celebrating a pregnant celebrity while anxiously tracking her weight gain, detailing how she is controlling her weight or how she will lose it in the future. There is a kind of natal-philia within the media concurrent with a denigration of postpartum bodies such that pregnancy in these magazines is a wonderful, delicious hot potato to be admired and tracked but not to be held or embodied. For even when pregnant, one must be thinking of the future postpartum body, which needs to be identical to the past prepregnancy one.

Third, as is apparent at this point, splitting pregnancy from the process of reproduction is complicated and demands distortions in temporal linking. Here nonpregnant women are linked to babies through warnings to remain pious and pure in order to create a better future (baby).

Through such warnings a nonpregnant body is projected into the future to become a pregnant one, thus taking it out of the present. A present, pregnant body is simultaneously projected into the past to embody the transgressions of the nonpregnant body and into the future in terms of making sure appetites are controlled to limit weight gain. And upon delivery, the past prepregnant body becomes the future goal. The present body that is so evidently a recent producer of a baby is shamed until it is reduced in stature. It must be evacuated of its recent creation of the future. The temporal links between women, pregnancy, and babies are anxiety provoking. They are simultaneously imperative to the cultural meaning-making project and intolerably threatening to it, as meaning can no longer rest in the future. These links are at once a constant embodied reminder of the lost faith in a future orientation and the limits to our existence that are now impossible to deny while being a representation of our only chance at literally going on being as a species. They are a vehicle for cultural anxiety and a target of it, and they can be disavowed if necessary for regulating anxieties.

The intense focus on pregnancy may also function as an attempt at mastery to reestablish and reembody a modernist future-oriented temporality even as it is also the embodiment of our uncanny sense of what is next. But with the changes in fertility, or just the ''natural'' unpredictability of it, pregnancy becomes the perfect vehicle for projected and legitimate anxieties about annihilation. So cultural splitting off of anxiety into the body of the culture (women) and having that body potentially fail to reproduce in a controllable and predictable fashion or choose not to reproduce at all compounds anxieties, resulting in further need to monitor and control women's bodies as future or current reproducers. So it is not surprising that as these links between women, pregnancy, reproduction, and babies are severed or made tenuous, bumps are manufactured and celebrated on pregnant and nonpregnant celebrities and tracked with meticulous attention.

In a Marxist sense, this setup is the ultimate experience of alienation and commodification; however, women are not being disconnected from the product of their labor, their babies, so much as being disconnected from their bodies as the producers of these babies. They are being separated from their labor itself. As babies take center stage in the culture, the media celebrates women who erase the proof that they produced these valued commodities.[4] This is a powerful pedagogical trick, for if we render invisible women's reproductive labor, then women's bodies are left as merely objects in a patriarchal world with no unique biological function. The reprofuturity (see Dinshaw et al., 2007) upon which our future-oriented culture relies is rendered devoid of female bodies. Future time (male) is physically liberated from the (female) past. Here the future does become what Brown (2005) described as a disembodied idea.

Erasing the gestational process of reproduction that only bodies that are culturally identified as female can enact (although of course, not all of these bodies can, will, or wish to reproduce) means the one process that many ''female'' bodies do that ''male'' bodies cannot do is forced into the cultural unconscious once the baby arrives with the erasure of the evidence of ever having been pregnant. This erasure creates a public suspicion—did she really have a baby? Was she really pregnant? Did that body reproduce? How could it have happened? It creates a magical spin on the primal scene by taking the female body out of the process of reproduction itself.

[4]It is important to acknowledge the market forces also driving these shifts. Babies are commodities and consumers. Pregnancy changes the body such that one needs to purchase new, larger clothes. The market potential for pregnancy and babies seems practically infinite. These consumer roles are extremely important, especially in a time of economic instability. A more in-depth analysis of this aspect, however, is beyond the scope of this paper.

The female body becomes a collapsed space of absence, literally collapsed, concave stomachs, toned thighs, and perky (not collapsed) breasts. We could actually believe the baby dropped from the stork, from the sky, from anywhere but that toned, buff body. It brings us culturally to a preoedipal state of mind where babies just appear, the primal scene has not reared its exclusionary head, and a "Third" (Ogden, 2004) has not been introduced to force us to deal with our ambivalence and the limits inherent in existence, especially those inescapable environmental limits we are being forced to contend with now. Given that pregnancy and the capacity to make babies remains an activity that temporally locates women and enables them to be culturally valuable (see Hartman, 2004), its erasure renders the embodiment of these bodies identified as female, uncanny, shadowy, insecure. It forces the primary productive processes granted to women out of the symbolic realm. By promoting the absolute importance of babies, then disavowing the production of them, the culture creates a form of temporal linking that symbolically erases women as productive beings, liberating babies from the female body, making them more than ever commodities of a patriarchy. Thus, the stories about pregnancy may also function to reestablish a more ideologically buttressed patriarchal organization.

So, our cultural focus on reproduction is not simply about creating babies in a time of war or a time of economic instability. It can be seen as a flight from anxiety and the unknown that plays with time by altering constructions of pregnancy, therefore manipulating women's bodies. It enacts a distinct flight from a present filled with annihilation anxiety into a controllable future based on a new fantasy of past gender arrangements that are similar to a preoedipal fantasy of omnipotence where men can be "committed to a brazen and unyielding refusal of maturity... nudged toward responsibility,... by a woman who represents an ideal amalgam of supermodel and mom" (Scott, 2008, p. 33). Dissociation is enacted spatially by containing cultural anxiety within the pregnant female body. To include men in the cultural narrative of reproduction would require embodying them, which would threaten the culture's separation of mind/body, male/female, and myth of male invulnerability.

As noted earlier of power and resistance, however, this neo cult of domesticity may also be a statement by women about cultural arrangements and the terror of the future. As Hartman (2004), Brown (2005), and others have noted, women's equality has been conceptualized as occurring only through access to the public sphere, having women act as men or have access to what men have access to. This makes "retreatism" to the private sphere and the neo cult of domesticity dangerously regressive. But what appears as complicity may also be an expression of distress or/and rebellion (Gentile, 2007). Women have not reached the parity of men in terms of status in the public world, promotions in the workplace, or wages. Additionally, they continue to have the bulk of the responsibilities in the private sphere (see Ehrenreich and Hochschild, 2004). As Tietjens Meyers (2001) notes, children can represent a way to "infuse value and significance" into women's lives (Tietjens Meyers, 2001, p. 750). With men maintaining access to power and success in the public sphere, the outside world getting more and more frightening and destructive, who would not want to "retreat" into or be surrounded by representations of a more controllable world of personal interaction and creation? On the other hand, in the face of the terrors of the future, the potential end of the planet as we know it, who would want to reproduce and leave the horrors of the future to their children? This anxiety and ambivalence can be embodied and organized through the neo cult of domesticity, where past gender arrangements can create a veil of safety to obscure the unknown dangers of the future.

Embracing the ideals of this neo cult could also be seen as a refusal to do it all or to play the masculine game, although as noted, class impacts one's ability to refuse. By having more children, there is a way in which some women may also be demanding cultural importance be placed back on the home and the invaluable work that is done there. Unfortunately, as Hartman (2004) noted, given the current isolation of house, childcare, and family care, it is unclear what cultural fruit will be generated in the homes of current mothers or whether households are a site of consciousness-raising and collective action. Emphasizing mothering also reinscribes the notion of biology as destiny. It fails to challenge our current notions of gender equality as being defined by women's access to the public sphere. The hierarchy of private to public is actually reinforced by this notion as is the understanding that the public sphere is the purview of (White) men. As the split between these spheres is reinforced, the enormous amount of unpaid labor that is confined to the private sphere is not only devalued but also rendered invisible. Given the potential lack of meaning available to women in the public sphere, the continuing "double shift" of home and childcare and family-care work for women (Hochschild, 1989), and the cultural attitudes that "valorize" and "romanticize" motherhood as being "rapturous" (Tietjens Meyers, 2001, p. 747), motherhood is a loaded "choice" for women.

At a time when women have more access than ever to the public sphere (even with its barriers) and the first ever viable female U.S. presidential candidate, having media messages implying that there is no higher purpose than to reproduce is particularly troubling. This complicated discourse implies that access to the public sphere pales in comparison to the riches of motherhood. It communicates a message that the achievements of the women's rights movements can be erased because they were not important in the first place. In the end, feminism was barking up the wrong tree. It was not freedom of movement between the public/private spheres or breaking down the artificial distinctions between these spheres that women needed. They just needed to understand that motherhood was the ultimate satisfaction and be happy with what they had. So the current discursive strategy simultaneously denigrates the goals of feminism while reinforcing a traditional notion of gender for both men and women, again, upholding the vulnerable notion of patriarchy.

This playing with time is dangerous also because it enables a new, more extreme level of cultural dissociation. Dissociation, as we know, renders one less prepared to deal with emergencies and less and less able to see what is really going on. Here the capacities to experience, identify, and react to the cause and effects of war and the devastation of natural disasters are also compromised. This form of distorted temporal linking results in displaced attempts to control and resolve anxiety and because it is always misplaced, it can never quell anxiety so it creates increased need for defensive reaction even as that reaction itself creates more anxiety. It is the embodiment of "emergency time" (Hesford and Diedrich, 2008).

Thus, the new cult of domesticity abides by the same tenets as its namesakes but in a new and more dangerous way. Instead of creating gendered female bodies by containing them within gender spaces of domestic labor, this new version of the cult manipulates the process of pregnancy itself, and in relation, of course, the female body. Pregnancy is the perfect vehicle and target for cultural anxiety because it can embody an ambivalent relationship to an unknown future. It does so by simultaneously embodying the safe and known past (childhood is the ultimate reminiscence) and a more knowable future, a promise of human life. But fears and anxieties about the future cannot be outrun, so pregnancy is increasingly monitored and postpartum bodies that signify the process of reproduction are erased. Using pregnancy in this way means women's bodies also become both the signifier and the embodiment of the uncanny future that must be controlled and monitored in the attempt at creating a form of meaning-making, temporal linking that will enable us to go on being in the face of annihilation. The neo cult of domesticity may be a cultural attempt to going on being, but it does so by sacrificing all bodies, and it enacts a displacement of very real, very dangerous anxieties that need to be addressed.

REFERENCES

Amott, T., & Matthieu, J. (1996). *Race, Gender, and Work: A Multicultural Economic History of Women in the United States*. Boston, MA: South End Press.

Belkin, L. (2003, October 26). The opt-out revolution. *The New York Times Magazine*. Retrieved from www.nytimes.org.

Bourdieu, P. (1977). *Outline of a Theory of Practice*. Cambridge, UK: Cambridge University Press.

Brown, W. (2005). *Edgework: Critical Essays on Knowledge and Politics*. Princeton, NJ: Princeton University Press.

Coetzee, J. (1982). *Waiting for the Barbarians*. New York, NY: Penguin Books.

Coontz, S. (2006, March 30). Myth of the opt-out mom. *Christian Science Monitor*. Retrieved from http://www.csmonitor.com/2006/0330/p09s01-coop.html.

Dargis, M. (2008, May 3). Is there a real woman in this multiplex? *The New York Times*. Retrieved from http://www.nytimes.com/2008/05/04/movies/moviesspecial/04dargi.html.

Davies, J. M. & Frawley, M. G. (1992). Dissociative processes and transference countertransference paradigms in the psychoanalytically oriented treatment of adult survivors of childhood sexual abuse. *Psychoanalytic Dialogues*, 2, 5–36.

———. (1994). *Treating the Adult Survivor of Childhood Sexual Abuse: A Psychoanalytic Perspective*. New York, NY: Basic Books.

Dinshaw, C., Edelman, L., Ferguson, R. A., Freccero, C., Freeman, E., Halberstam, J., . . . Hoang, N. T. (2007). Theorizing queer temporalities: A roundtable discussion. *GLQ: Journal of Lesbian Gay Studies*, 13(2–3), 177–195.

Ehrenreich, B. (1995). The decline of patriarchy. In: *Constructing Masculinity*, eds. M. Berger, B. Wallis, & S. Watson, New York, NY: Routledge, pp. 284–290.

——— & Hochschild, A. R. (2004). *Global Woman: Nannies, Maids, and Sex Workers in the New Economy*. New York, NY: Henry Holt.

Enloe, C. (2004). *The Curious Feminist: Searching for Women in a New Age of Empire*. Berkeley: University of California Press.

Fonagy, P. & Target, M. (1998). Mentalization and the changing aims of child psychoanalysis. *Psychoanalytic Dialogues*, 8(1), 87–114.

Franklin, S. & Ragoné, H. eds. (1998). *Reproducing Reproduction: Kinship, Power and Technological Innovation*. Philadelphia: University of Pennsylvania Press.

Freeman, E. (2005). Time binds, or, erotohistoriography. *Social Text*, 84–85(3–4), 57–68.

———. (2007). Introduction. *GLQ: Journal of Lesbian Gay Studies*, 13(2–3), 159–176.

Gentile, K. (2007). *Creating Bodies: Eating Disorders as Self-Destructive Resistance*. Hillsdale, NJ: Analytic Press.

——— & Gutwill, S. (2005). How to create social activism, or, turning the passive to active without killing each other. *Psychotherapy and Politics International*, 3(2), 122–132.

Goldsmith, J. (2006, July 9). People who need people: Sucking up to celebs builds mag as TW money machine. *Variety*. Retrieved from http://www.variety.com/article/VR1117946434?refCatId-18.

Gurevich, R. (2010). Dieting and Fertility: Why you should avoid yo-yo and extreme dieting. Retrieved from www.about.com.

Hall, S. D., Hobson, A. Lowe & Willis, P., eds. (1992). *Culture, Media, Language*. London, UK: Routledge.

Hartman, M. S. (2004). *The Household and the Making of History: A Subversive View of the Western Past*. Cambridge, UK: Cambridge University Press.

Haughney, C. (2007, September 9). Mansions in the sky. *The New York Times*. Retrieved from http://www.nytimes.com/2007/09/09/realestate/09cover.html.

Hesford, V. (2008). Securing a future: Feminist futures in a time of war. In: *Feminist Time Against Nation Time: Gender, Politics, and the Nation-State in an Age of Permanent War*, eds. V. Hesford, & L. Diedrich, New York, NY: Lexington Books, pp. 169–184.

——— & Diedrich, L. (2008). Introduction: Thinking feminism in a time of war. In: *Feminist Time Against Nation Time: Gender, Politics, and the Nation-State in an Age of Permanent War*, eds. V. Hesford, & L. Diedrich, New York, NY: Lexington Books, pp. 1–22.

Hochschild, A. R. (1989). *The Second Shift: Working Families and the Revolution at Home*. New York, NY: Anchor Books, 2003.

Jaina, N. J., Denka, C. E., & Druse, L. K. (2007). Maternal obesity: Can pregnancy weight gain modify risk of selected adverse pregnancy outcomes? *American Journal of Perinatology*, 24(5), 291–298.

James, P. D. (1992). *The Children of Men*. New York, NY: Vintage Books.

Kargman, J. (2007). *Momzillas*. New York, NY: Broadway Books.

Kristeva, J. (1981). Women's time. In: *Feminisms: An Anthology of Literary Theory and Criticism*, eds. R. R. Warhol, & D. P. Herndl, New Brunswick, NJ: Rutgers University Press, 1997, pp. 860–879.

Lifton, R. (2003). *The Superpower Syndrome*. New York, NY: Nation Books.

Loewald, H. W. (1980). *Papers on Psychoanalysis*. New Haven, CT: Yale University Press.

Mohanty, C. T. (2004). *Feminism Without Borders: Decolonizing Theory, Practicing Solidarity*. Durham, NC: Duke University Press.

Narayan, U. (1997). Contesting cultures: "Westernization," respect for cultures, and third-world feminists. In: *Second Wave: A Reader in Feminist Theory*, ed. L. Nicholson, New York, NY: Routledge, pp. 396–414.

Negra, D. (2008). Structural integrity, historical reversion, and the post-9/11 chick flick. *Feminist Media Studies*, 8(1), 51–68.

Ogden, T. (2004). The analytic *Third*: Implications for psychoanalytic theory and technique. *Psychoanalytic Quarterly*, 73(1), 167–194.

Scott, A. O. (2008, May 3). Here comes everyboy, again. *The New York Times*. Retrieved from http://www.nytimes.com/2008/05/04/movies/moviesspecial/04scot.html.

Shorto, R. (2008, June 28). No babies? *The New York Times Magazine*. Retrieved from http://www.nytimes.com/2008/06/29/magazine/29Birth-t.html.

Smith, T. (2007, August 5). Weekend Edition, WNYC radio.

Strozier, C. & Gentile, K. (2005). The mental health response to 9/11. In: *Living With Terror, Working With Trauma: A Clinician's Handbook*, ed. D. Knafo. Northvale, NJ: Aronson, 415–428.

Tietjens Meyers, D. (2001). The rush to motherhood: Pronatalist discourse and women's autonomy. *Signs: Journal of Women in Culture and Society*, 26, 735–774.

Welter, B. (1966). The cult of true womanhood: 1820–1860. *American Quarterly*, 18(2), 151–174.

AUTHOR BIO

Katie Gentile, Ph.D., is Associate Professor of Counseling and Gender Studies and Director of the Women's Center at John Jay College of Criminal Justice. She is the author of *Creating Bodies: Eating Disorders as Self-Destructive Survival* (2007, Mahwah, NJ: The Analytic Press).

What About the Episiotomy? A Response to Katie Gentile's Article, ''What About the Baby?''

Lynne Zeavin, Psy.D.
New York University Psychoanalytic Institute

This discussion of Katie Gentile's paper (this issue) raises questions about the underlying unconscious dynamics at work in the cultural icon of the supermodel mom. The ''supermodel mom'' offers a kind of seamless, bloodless, stretch-mark-less version of pregnancy and childbirth. In so doing, it provides us with a fantasied escape from those worrying dimensions of the female body in childbirth. On a deeper level this fantasied construction offers a means by which time is stalled, both future and past being eradicated and manically fended off. Using a clinical example of a woman pregnant with her second child, the article explores in detail some of the meanings kept alive by the idea of triumphing over pregnancy. The terror of the pregnancy and baby taking over one's body and one's mind is part of what is staved off with the fantasy of the supermodel mom. In addition, this fantasy protects against loss of all kinds—ultimately the losses associated with our own vulnerabilities.

I commend Katie Gentile's ambitious paper, ''What About the Baby?'' (this issue), for its foray into the sociocultural landscape—a landscape too often eschewed by psychoanalysts. In this provocative paper she investigates what she sees as a return to the cult of domesticity since 9/11. Signaling this return is the celebration of pregnancy and the rise of a new icon: the supermodel mom. The paper touches on many of the issues that concern us—global warming, the destruction of the planet, war, the economy, not to mention the redefinitions of gendered roles and gendered relations. Against this dark backdrop, Gentile alerts us to what she sees as the sinuous appearance of a regressive, worrisome elevation of pregnancy and motherhood.

Gentile's contention involves temporality, in particular how culture orients itself toward the future and how this future orientation of culture is embodied and reinforced by an emphasis on reproduction, This notion, what she calls reprofuturity, suggests that the interest in reproduction is organized in part to secure the culture's need for the future. Though I agree that a vision of the future is fundamental to the vision of the culture's survival, I am not sure that I would say that it is the future that is being assured in this onslaught of media images about pregnancy. I do think, with Gentile, that the assault on meaning, and with it, an assault on time—both the past and the future—is marked in these images. Gentile says, '' It is not the promise of a future itself that is being lost but the capacity to make meaning of the present by linking anticipation and expectation, using the past and future to create the experience of going on being in the moment. What is lost is the capacity to generate faith in a particular pattern of temporal linking'' (p. 43). I think the images she means to examine provide an extraordinary example of how our relationships to time and to meaning are simultaneously altered. It is a timeless present. Unlike Gentile, who sees much of the return to a cult of domesticity as a way to embrace the future, I think we are in a universe where time is meant to vanish. Even as we are in the present, we don't feel the effects of the present; we don't feel the impact of time; time's anxieties are staved off, just as time itself is held at bay. The supermodel mom is the perfect icon by which to represent this predicament.

More precisely, the supermodel mom is an image that freezes time, dispensing thereby with past, present, and future altogether. We can see this in the sort of pregnancy Gentile focuses on, which is not [is not focusing on] what might be called "ordinary" pregnancy. Instead, she is alert to what she sees as a heightened attention being paid to widely distributed images of the extraordinary pregnancies of extraordinary women—celebrities. These images convey a particular attribute of these extraordinary pregnancies: these are pregnancies in which it seems that we who are witnessing them and they who are experiencing them are able to freeze time. Time is of course frozen in the glitzy pictures we pore over. In addition, though, time is frozen over in a less obvious, more profound way, both psychically and socioculturally. Soldered onto the body of a celebrity (for this is how it seems—something external added, pregnancy becomes static, a thing, an accessory—a highly valued commodity at that—sentimental, yes, and coveted). This accessory, like, say, a diamond, plays into our deepest yearnings for seamlessness and perfection, our yearning that time stand still. Though pregnancy always is about the future, this pregnancy with its emphasis on NOW seems to hold the future at bay.

Gentile is noticing what we all notice at every visit to the grocery store. Pick nearly any magazine from the shelf as you wait in line and be up-to-date on the latest news of a four-star (mega karat) pregnancy. You can read who is newly pregnant; you can glimpse the fabulous nursery, the fabulous clothes. Look inside and you will see the postpregnant body returned to its fabulous shape. In addition to the straightforward norms that are tacitly prescribed for women here, what is it about these images that actually captures and holds our attention? What does the shopper revere? What is being celebrated, modeled, implicitly offered?

The celebrity pregnancy marks the arrival of a new cultural family romance, one where the woman is all-capable. A brief scan of recent films confirms Gentile's point that there is an upsurge of interest in pregnancy. The films have an interesting twist. Not only do they salute the celebrity mom, they also—and perhaps more important—salute the mom able to carry, deliver, and care for baby on her own. In *Baby Mama, Juno,* and *The Switch*, the wish for a baby trumps the wish to be in a relationship: what matters most is the woman's ability to conceive and bear a child.

Ostensibly a celebration of the female body, such tales implicitly derogate it. The bodies, the "people" we see in these magazines and films, bear little resemblance to the lived experiences of pregnancies in the bodies and people we might actually know. This postfeminist construction of this self-sufficient, unmarked mom presents the image of a "woman" simultaneously all-giving and all-desirable—one there for the seeing but never for the having. The classic triangle of the oedipal situation has collapsed into a single dense all-in-one point. For this lucky "woman" and her equally lucky "baby," then, there will be no oedipal couple to struggle against, no NO to be bothered by. Consumers of this image are lulled into a world with no limit—where not only the NO is eliminated but also the reality of time. This is a world constructed on an antioedipal illusion. Illusion always requires idealization of an imaginary relation.

Idealization like this refashions its object, stripping it of all that is fraught, difficult, and negative. Idealization helps us through nightmares—personal or societal. Think of the celebrated war hero whose return is meant to signal the triumph of war and thereby dampen down our awareness of its destructiveness. The hero there is offering reassurance instead of insisting that we remember. The same holds here. The object of Gentile's paper is meant to be seen as a new woman embodying the triumph of both the present and the future. Her imagined triumph aims to erase any problems that the notion of future contains. What Gentile spots in the new cult of domesticity has to do with the celebration of the future; what I believe is more insidious is the promise of a triumph over time, over maternity, and over the troubled domain of domestic relations; a turn away from terrifying images of future and past, and most important, a turn toward complacency. Complacency resists knowledge of the world outside of our own private making. Complacency is facilitated in a world where there are no oedipal restrictions.

As I consider these images against the backdrop of what I've come to see as the quotidian realities of pregnancy and childbirth, I have a different take on them than Gentile does. I don't think the future, or reprofuturity, is crucial to the new cult of domesticity or supermodel moms. After all, the child itself, who signifies the promise of the future, seems incidental in these images. The images focus not on children but on ''women's'' capacity to seamlessly conceive them. The pregnancies being pictured suggest neither a past nor future. They are placed firmly in the present, and though in the present, experience of the present has been eradicated. Meaning of the pregnancy, that is, the usual psychic consequences, is happily gone.

''Actual'' pregnancy—the kind not pictured in the supermarket—transforms a woman's body and identity. The transformations are both terrifying and rewarding. The supermarket images conceal terror, maternal hatred, and doubt. They portray a transformation that has occurred bloodlessly, a transformation that lacks the status of an actual event. There are no marks on the pregnant bodies of celebrities—none of the loose skin and all the rest that signify the reordering and restoration of the body back to its prepregnant shape. It is as if nothing has happened. And this, I think, is exactly the point.

In the images Gentile focuses on there is only now. Now is all that matters; not history, not future, and certainly none of the temporal disorder of actual experience. Consideration of the actual future is likely to be frightening if only because such consideration inevitably demands attention to the passing of time and to our helplessness in the face of that passing. The supermodel pregnancy offers an antidote to that helplessness. In identifying with the supermodel mom, our visions of perfection can be realized and helplessness foregone. We can live in a timeless world safe from all that time inevitably brings—aging, decline, death—she is heaven incarnate.

A clinical example comes to mind. My patient T. was in her 5th month of pregnancy. Prior to getting pregnant, T. prioritized the feeling of being in control of everything—her time, her work life, her body. Pregnancy was one of those things she had yet to have achieved. Because other friends were doing it, she felt inclined to do it as well. She didn't seem to so much want a baby as she wanted the accomplishment of having a baby. She did not want to be outdone. Getting pregnant was easy, and this confirmed a sense of ''being able to defy biology.''

Being able ''to defy biology'' in T.'s case is significant: the daughter of a Malaysian man and a German mother, T. has always struggled with an underlying feeling of being different; different was bad. Poor, the child of divorce, looking unlike any of her mother's relatives, she was embarrassed to have kids over. You would never know it now: as an adult, T. oozes complacency. Painful aspects of her past are pushed away and retold. Despite the difficult story that has slowly emerged in her analysis, T. resolutely maintains a self-representation of competence and impenetrability. Complacency demarcates a kind of split in T.'s world and in her functioning: it guards against momentary experiences of vulnerability, which themselves are linked with an underlying sense of loss. This loss, which has the potential to shatter T.'s story about herself, has to be fended off at all costs. In this way, T. lives a kind of timelessness—where the meaning of her upbringing and development is kept at bay.

In her life, T. has aimed at more than countering a feeling of being different; she has aimed at excising it. A graduate of the best schools and a professor at an elite university, T. must be better at everything that the average person (or think she is). Otherwise she sinks into despair. For T., complacency is a guard against despair. A version of this happened with T.'s achievement of pregnancy. It marked her as being like other women—she needed to do it not only well but better. Launched into this project, several anxieties began to crop up and to frighten her.

T. was worried about being taken over by the baby—if that even was in fact what it was, she quipped. Sometimes it felt more like a monster growing inside of her. T. is not psychotic, but the terror was very real. She worried about the health of the baby, whether it would be normal—or would there be something wrong? These were fears that she dealt with largely by putting them out of mind, "tying them up with a bow," is how she referred to them.

As the pregnancy proceeded, her body expanded and she felt "huge," unwieldy, and at times filled with self-loathing and panic about her changing shape. She couldn't adjust to the image of herself in the mirror; it didn't hold still long enough for her to adapt to it. T., who prided herself on running longer than any other woman she knew, or being able to get her body into the most taxing yoga position, now felt reduced. In addition, she, like most pregnant women, could not get a firm grasp on her rapidly changing body, and it left her feeling alien in her own skin. Bodily changes are difficult for many pregnant women—they are an enunciation of a changing self-representation that is at times frighteningly in flux. For T., I think the changes in her body were also a frightening reminder of time. It was as though time were refusing to stand still, and the development of the pregnancy was evidence of that.

Our own experience of pregnancy might well link us to the embodied memory of the first pregnant body about which we "knew." That pregnancy signaled not only the mother's sexuality and exclusive involvement with another parental figure but also the impending loss of the mother to another child. Our own pregnancies, then, link us to recollections of abundance, loss, sexuality, love, scarcity, now, then, and future—all simultaneously. But for T., and for those of us caught in the appeal of the supermodel mom, such associations have to be denied.

Of herself T. said, "I caught a glimpse of myself in the reflection today and I was so startled. It looked like me but like I had been taken over and possessed by something entirely alien." She had worries about the baby and the change it would mean in her life. For my patient, living imperviously was crucial. Admitting fear or vulnerability was tantamount to disaster. She strove to be the best, to be triumphant in all pursuits, to stave off an underlying idea of herself as "second class." In all things, T. proceeded with a manic ferocity to avoid the grip of this darker past. The same was true with pregnancy. She spoke of "mastering the newborn," which was T.'s fantasy of being able to get the thing under control and to eschew experience—particularly when the experience was likely to contain dimensions that were chaotic and potentially terrifying. This she could not tolerate—the mastery of the newborn was a way of encapsulating her need to master and be done with various frightening aspects of time and experience as well as the challenges pregnancy posed to her sense of self (which was as an active, dominant person).

Looking back now, nearly three years later, T. describes her labor as ‘freakish, disappointing, terrifying.'' Initially, she experienced a feeling of grandeur—like ''an endurance race, and I was ahead. I can do this, I am on top of this.'' She experienced little thought of the baby or the baby's health. ''It was just about me.'' Then, when the nurse said the baby would be born soon, she stalled. She was gripped by terror. How would the baby get out? Would it get ''stuck'' inside of her? Would she have to have an episiotomy and would she endlessly tear, would she come apart? This terror gripped her, and she stopped contracting and eventually needed ptosin and then a cesarean to deliver the baby. It was as though the specter of time, marching forward, was actually terrifying.

No matter how thrilling the birth of a baby, no matter how much wanted, it is always in a sense traumatic. Giving birth inevitably evokes our most primitive fears and fantasies: many women describe the fear of coming undone, of violence to the inside of their bodies, a fear of being unseemly and even grotesque. Pain itself is a source of fear as is the feeling of being out of control. The idea of a baby inside of one's own body, though easily romanticized and managed with an effusion of care, is scary to contemplate. The metaphor of an endurance race, as a way to avoid thought about the process of birth and its impact on the body, is one person's way of depicting what Gentile describes as a culturally vivid, wishfully rife imperative.

The supermodel mom has won the race, though she is unlikely to sweat while running. The supermodel mom shows no signs of wear and tear either on body or mind. Hers is a birth that gets folded into an idea of superwoman, the woman who can be it all and do it all, an ubermother and a sexual object, in perfect unison. I am reminded of another patient—who liked to say she had it ''all sewn up.'' This referred to her sense of triumphing over her own sense of femaleness—the female genital for her being a site of frightening openness, spillage, and being less. Being all sewn up was a guard, in fantasy, against this frightening fantasied condition of femaleness. The supermodel mom has it all sewn up.

What do we see in the supermodel that might appease our wishes and address our most basic fears? The supermodel is, in a sense, a figure who has triumphed over biology—the way we mean our heroes to. She is a kind of James Bond, or A-Rod, the nearest thing we have to a living superhero. She is the perfect image for the age of terror when an indomitable mother might come in handy. She can be the mother without embodying the terrifying aspects of the mother; she will not envy or age or grow flabby. As a mother she is, implicitly, tacitly, available to you and to me. Most promisingly, she eludes time. She is the embodiment of stasis. When her time has past she will be gone, but her kind will not: she will merely be replaced by another of her kind.

Talk to any actual supermodel mom, and of course she will tell you different. Time, in reality, is her greatest enemy. But as consumers of the culture, we happily forget all that, just as we forget the bloat and mishap that come with pregnancy to begin with. Just as the supermodel mom is able to defy birth—to defy the process of giving birth in all its meanings—she suggests the potential for defying death as well. For she is the master of flux, the master of flaw—and in her we find the realization of sexual wishes, wishes for care—the tricky part is that although she seems to elude misogynist sentiment, she is in fact the embodiment of it.

The cult of domesticity that Gentile refers to should be expanded to include a cult of the superhero, the cult of the supersized and superrich, of which this new cult of domesticity is one part. Wall Street and multimillion-dollar sports heroes and rock stars fuel our penchant for glamour and our sense of having no limit. Excess is reassuring—it offers a counterphobic solution to the problem of limit. Time is a limit, rules imply limit, as does structure. No structure, no limit. It is interesting that the supermodel mom herself seems free of structure. She is celebrated for herself as though she is self-conceived. There is no oedipal structure to contend with, no sense of anything in her midst being off-limits. Limits suggest a break in what is conceivable, what is possible. Breaks might too easily crack the culture of complacency that insidiously came about in the Bush era. As a society there was the feeling (a horrific illusion, it turns out) of plenty; there was more and more money, the myth of having what was needed, all in the service of complacency. Complacency served to make us sleepy, to dull an inclination to resist. Mark Danner referred to the Bush era, and particularly the Iraq War, as a ''frozen scandal'' (Danner, 2008). The supermodel mom, an icon of timeless, limitless potential, is the perfect mother for such a world.

When T. was talking about her own labor she said, ''IF I could just do it, do it without drugs, do it without surgery it would be like having a Prada bag.'' Likening her triumph to possessing this material status symbol was not lost on her. Here my patient seems to be voicing something like the feeling expressed by the image of the supermodel mom. Her physical feat is a cultural/material success, a triumph that would have rid her of vulnerability, pain, fear, and need. Her wish for an ecstatic (narcissistic) triumph would seem to guarantee the absence of any perceptible limit. T. is not a supermodel mom, but she helps us understand the appeal of one.

REFERENCE

Danner, M. (2008, December 4). The frozen scandal. *The New York Review of Books*. Retrieved from http://www.nybooks.com/articles/archives/2008/dec/04/frozen-scandal/?page-1

AUTHOR BIO

Lynne Zeavin, Psy.D., is a psychoanalyst in private practice in New York City. She is on the faculty of the New York University Psychoanalytic Institute and New York University Medical School.

Social Trauma and Models of Ideological Analysis: Commentary on Article by Katie Gentile

Lynne Layton, Ph.D.
Massachusetts Institute for Psychoanalysis

Although the author appreciates and agrees with Katie Gentile's (this issue) thesis, the author's commentary proposes some different models besides the model of ideological domination to think about both the social trauma she eloquently describes and the media discourses that seem only to exacerbate the trauma, obfuscate its origins, and oppress women. The models the author discusses question ideologies of progress, understood as central in creating our catastrophic circumstances, and they propose other ways of understanding media discourse; modernity; and subjective relations to past, present, and future.

Katie Gentile's (this issue) essay is rich both in ideas and methodology, and I am delighted to be able to comment on it. Although I offer some differing perspectives, I offer them in the spirit of sharing her concerns both about our current cultural traumas and how they affect women. The way Dr. Gentile ties the pregnancy boom in the upper middle class to anxieties about the future—anxieties caused by the human destruction of nature and, potentially, of mankind itself—is brilliant and utterly persuasive. Where I offer comment is in connection with some of the assumptions that support that argument. Although I am in complete agreement with the thesis (''Regulating pregnancy can function as a defense against anxiety and as an attempt to reestablish anticipation and expectation as the organizational structure of cultural meaning making''), my sense is that the pregnancy boom itself may be a useless way, but far from the worst way, to manage the anxieties about the future that currently plague us.

The thesis of Dr. Gentile's essay in its entirety is quite complex, and I thus begin by restating it as best as I can. Dr. Gentile argues that women have become, as she puts it, the vehicles and targets of contemporary cultural anxieties about a future that has become unknown, uncanny, and possibly nonexistent. Pregnancy, she writes, ''becomes the perfect vehicle for projected and legitimate anxieties about annihilation'' (p. 54). She convincingly demonstrates that cultural contradictions and the anxieties they produce are lived in the body. The thesis is demonstrated by examining media discourses that construct pregnancy in particular ways. In these discourses, women are asked to guarantee the future via pregnancy, and yet their pregnant bodies, and thus their role in reproduction itself, are erased.

The post-2002 articles Dr. Gentile examines reveal the ways that pregnancy has become a site for expressing social trauma. As we know, the sequelae of trauma always appear in split and polarized fragments. In the case at hand, the fragments are expressed in such contradictory injunctions as ''you need to lose your 'baby weight' immediately,'' but, ''beware, dieting can, at any time, be hazardous to your baby.'' The contradictions reveal that ''fears and anxieties about the future cannot be outrun.'' The ''deeply troubled and ambivalent relationship to pregnancy in the media,'' an expression of our vexed relationship to the future (the trauma), is a pedagogical trick that hides the trauma—that we are destroying our world and thus our future (p. 53). As such, it is not only an expression that is oppressive to women but also one that substitutes for the attempt to find the kind of solutions that would truly confront and grapple with the sources of our anxiety. The pregnancy mania in upper middle-class culture cannot allay those anxieties because it does not address their source.

Dr. Gentile argues that the media discourses reprise an old strategy for controlling women and their bodies: the 19th-century discourse of the cult of domesticity. Indeed, her argument indicts the influence of patriarchy in contemporary media discourses: the more that women are needed to guarantee futurity, the more anxiety is stirred up in men who, it is assumed, control or at least have the most to gain from dominant discourses about reproduction. Embedded within this thesis is an argument about temporal linking, the fact that becoming a self in the West (or perhaps anywhere) requires a capacity to link past, present, and an anticipated future. My comments on this paper begin with noting some of the difficulties I had with this particular argument. I suggest that if we play with models of ideology that are different from the model of ideological domination that Dr. Gentile adopts, we might find additional interpretations of the rich material presented here. I thus introduce two other models, one that comes out of Christopher Lasch's (1991) examination of the progress narrative in U.S. history and another proposed by sociologists Ulrich Beck and Elisabeth Beck-Gernsheim (Beck, 1999; Beck and Beck-Gernsheim, 2002).

Dr. Gentile's argument on temporal linking begins with a critique of Brown's (2005) notion that, as a culture, we need to mourn the progress narrative that has defined modernity. I do not know Brown's full argument, but I find that I am in agreement with the part of the argument presented here. In my reading, the weakness of the temporal linking argument is that it suggests that the need to anticipate the future (a need that I agree may be essential to subjectivity) is equivalent to a need to anticipate a future marked by progress and the promise of modernity.

As Lasch (1991) has noted, through most of U.S. history the belief in progress, a belief held by those on both the left and the right, has largely been expressed in the ideology that moral improvement goes hand in hand with technological development, unlimited economic growth, and acquisitive individualism. This fantasy, he argues, is bankrupt: ''It is the assumption that our future is predetermined by the continuing development of large-scale production, colossal technologies, and political centralization that inhibits creative thought and makes it so difficult to avoid the choice between fatuous optimism and debilitating nostalgia'' (p. 170). Fatuous optimism and debilitating nostalgia are each orientations toward past, present, and future. Neither one values the past as informing the present and the future: fatuous optimism idealizes and reifies the future; debilitating nostalgia does the same with the past. Each freezes the past in a way that makes the past useless for understanding the present and for anticipating a democratic future. Lasch's (1991) review of history and of the few movements that have countered the version of ''progress'' under discussion (e.g., agrarian movements, syndicalist movements—I add the various student movements of the '60 s) well demonstrates his thesis that ''development,'' that is, what is commonly understood as modernization, does not in fact make it possible for all to share in the wealth. If we have learned anything in the past 30 years, it should be that wealth does *not* trickle down. On the contrary, a society of consumers has little to do with a democratic society, and, as our recent history shows, development has actually widened the gap between rich and poor. If we think about the class implications of the upper middle-class pregnancy boom, then, we could conjecture that one of its functions might be to express unconscious guilt about all the poor Black and White U.S. children we have lost in Iraq, in prisons, and on the streets of the inner city.

As in his earlier writings (Lasch, 1977, 1979), Lasch (1991) decries the way experts, such as the ones from the pregnancy industry cited in Dr. Gentile's media analysis, attempt to dictate the terms in which life is lived. What is lost, he feels, is a version of autonomy that would rest on the practice of civic responsibility and direct democracy. I would guess that, in the main if not in the particulars, Dr. Gentile would agree with Lasch's (1991) critique, and yet here and there in the paper we find sentences that almost seem to lament the loss of the progress narrative (e.g., ''To lose the promise of modernity is to lose our reliance on the pattern of temporal movement through which we create subjectivity'' or ''The pattern of an automatic progress in the future is no more'' [p. 42].) My sense is that if the critique of the progress narrative is integrated into Dr. Gentile's reprofuturity argument we will have a better understanding of what the trauma is—for both men and women—and thus a better understanding of how to address it. For the trauma has everything to do not only with 9/11 but also with the free market fundamentalism of the past 30 years, which includes the abandonment of individuals by public bodies responsible for the welfare of their citizenry as well as the cooptation of feminist struggle into patriarchal structures of everyday life (see Peltz, 2006; Layton, 2009, 2010).

Now I switch gears for a moment in order to introduce something quite different into the discussion of social trauma and futurity. In Ulrich Beck's book *World Risk Society* (1999), he argues that we are living in a ''second modernity.'' First modernity was

> based on nation-state societies, where social relations, networks and communities are essentially understood in a territorial sense. The collective patterns of life, progress and controllability, full employment and employment and exploitation of nature that were typical of this first modernity have now been undermined by five interlinked processes: globalization, individualization, gender revolution, underemployment and global risks [pp. 1–2].

In second modernity, we have to respond to all of these processes simultaneously, and all five are unforeseen consequences of the victory of first modernity, which, as Lasch (1991) argues as well, was marked by the belief in technological and scientific progress. First modernity, Beck (1999) writes, spawned many dangers and disasters that were never taken into account as part of the calculus of progress, for example, the destruction of the environment, genetic engineering, nuclear threat, and the collapse of financial markets. For Beck, second modernity is risk society, a society in which individuals are forced to take account of ''manufactured uncertainties'' (p. 5). Unlike Lasch (1991), Beck does not question the goodness or badness of the belief in technological progress. Nor does he seem to care about the kind of communal traditions Lasch looked to as guides for the present and future. What he focuses on are the effects of risk society on subjectivity and politics.

Although much of my own work has used the model of ideological domination that Dr. Gentile uses (e.g., Layton, 2004, 2009, 2010, where I write about impoverished forms of neoliberal subjectivity that are the effect of free market individualism), I also find compelling models such as Beck's (1999) that look at new possibilities for agency brought about by the precariousness of second modernity. Beck and Beck-Gernsheim (2002), for example, focus on how the continued loosening of subjectivity from traditional stabilizers of identity (such as nation-state and extended family) has led to what they call "institutionalized individualization." In their view, individualization (not to be confused with free market individualism) emerges from the fact that everything in second modernity, even the entitlements of the welfare state, are geared to the individual and not the group (Beck and Beck-Gernsheim, 2002, p. xxii). This has both negative and positive consequences. But individualization is a decidedly future-oriented form of subjectivity even as it is a form that is fully aware of the precariousness of the future. Beck and Beck-Gernsheim posit a nonlinear subject (not unlike the multiple selves posited by much of contemporary relational theory) who reflects on knowledge that is probabilistic, possibilistic, uncertain, precarious. This "reflexive" subject has choices that no former subject has had, but she or he must choose quickly, often without proper time to reflect. Reflexive, for Beck and Beck-Gernsheim, means more than "reflecting upon." It also involves "reflex": contemporary individuals have to deal reflexively with unexpected and risky consequences of "progress," and they continuously confront themselves and are confronted with new kinds of life decisions. Although the downside of not having proper time to reflect is clear, the upside of individualization is that subjects in the West, they argue, increasingly demand the right to "a life of one's own": "each has a right to a life of his or her own and . . . the terms of living together have to be renegotiated in each case" (Beck and Beck-Gernsheim, 2002, p. xxiii); "anyone who wants to live a life of their own must also be socially sensitive to a very high degree" (p. xxii). They see signs in contemporary culture of "altruistic individualism" (p. xxii); they look for, and find, new and unexpected forms of the social. They suggest that in making our own life rules, our own decisions on how we want to live our lives, we become political subjects—within, of course, certain constraints.

Although the argument is that the right to a life of one's own has become part of everyone's consciousness in Western culture, obviously those who have the greatest possibility of exercising choice are the privileged, the subjects of Dr. Gentile's paper, and not the poor. This fact is not lost on Beck and Beck-Gernsheim (2002), but it is perhaps understated in their work, which is why I think that a good model for understanding ideology, and the relation between the individual and the cultural, needs to combine the dominant culture model with the insights gained from Lasch (1991) and from Beck and Beck-Gernsheim (2002). Like Lasch, Beck and Beck-Gernsheim believe that we need a different relation to the future besides the belief in continued progress. But, unlike Lasch, Beck and Beck-Gernsheim believe a different relation to the future already exists as a product of second modernity, a relation in which we can no longer ignore the dangers that first modernity created and disavowed. They do not lament a decline in values: for them, second modernity includes "the dynamics of political freedom, citizenship and civil society" . . . "a legally sanctioned individualism for all" (Beck, 1999, p. 10).

The risk society model, it seems to me, accounts for many of the traumas of contemporary life that Dr. Gentile addresses (including free market individualism), but I introduce it because I think in certain ways it accounts also for something different from what Dr. Gentile has found using her own model of ideological domination (a model I locate in such comments as "A culture's stability is dependent on controlling women's bodies"). For example, her findings about the post-2002 media emphasis on dangers in connection with pregnancy resonated for me with the risk society hypothesis, which not only reckons with the effects of dominant ideology but, like the Birmingham School's appropriation of Gramsci's (1971) work (see, e.g., Hall, 1982), also considers forms of possible and actual resistance to dominant ideology. Dr. Gentile is careful to say that her analysis is of the media and not of the subjects that media discourse targets. But she also says, and is right to say, that media messages not only reflect but also shape consciousness. What feels missing to me is (a) the link between media messages and how we are living our everyday lives, and (b) an awareness that even the media messages reveal signs of resistance to dominant ideology.

For example, the risk society model suggests that the media's emphasis on dangers not only reflects the kind of regulatory mechanism that Dr. Gentile so cogently critiques but also has the potential to alert its audience to dangers in the contemporary lifeworld. Let us take as an example the warning that pregnant women should not eat too much fish because of the mercury or PCBs. In Beck's (1999) model, such bulletins could, at any time, suddenly galvanize the public to organize and do something about our future-threatening man-made dangers. This model presupposes that corporate and governmental leaders are increasingly dependent on the consent of the people to rule (Beck, 1999, p. 98; note that this is also a precondition of any politics that draws on Gramsci's 1971 notion of hegemony, e.g., Laclau and Mouffe, 1985). Thus, a dominant form of contemporary politics is what Beck (1999) calls "subpolitics," examples of which include consumer boycotts of all kinds as well as the coalition of varied groups that, for varied reasons, came together to protest the World Trade Organization in Seattle. Yes, Beck and Beck-Gernsheim would say, we *are* AT RISK, and we'd better do something about it.

Like Dr. Gentile, I feel that we are a traumatized population, but I also feel that the link she makes between present media discourses and the cult of domesticity discourse doesn't quite do justice either to the data or to the particularities of the trauma we have undergone in second modernity. The trauma, I think, is the product of both the neoconservative foreign policy response to 9/11 and of capitalism's most recent form: free market fundamentalism. The dominant forms of neoliberal subjectivity on offer in the past 30 years (Layton, 2009, 2010) are intimately connected to the dark side of dominant progress narratives. These forms are marked not by individualization but by a heightened and anxious individualism that I understand to be one response to the population's abandonment by our public sources of containment (I speak of both government and corporate structures and I date this from the mid-1970s, when free market fundamentalism began its ascent, to the present, where this model has proven to be a disaster; at this writing, 2010, it looks as though President Obama will make some regulatory changes to address neoliberal excesses but that he will likely leave the rotten core of the system intact).

I spoke earlier of how the pregnancy boom might express the disastrous consequences of our recent foreign policy and our domestic policies toward the poor. An important effect of neoliberalism on women has been the triumph of a form of feminism that, unlike the socialist feminism of the '60s and early '70s, did not challenge the way family and work life had been traditionally organized. The result is that women of privilege have been given the opportunity to lead as harried and impossible a life as men lead. In "Working Nine to Nine: The New Women of Prime Time" (2004), I suggested that certain prime time television shows normalized women's repudiation of dependency while heightening the allure of a career that demands all your time—in fact, Jennifer Garner, now one of Dr. Gentile's exemplars of supermomism, in the not-too-distant past played the workaholic Sydney Bristow (*Alias*), a perfect example of the defensive autonomy subject position on offer to women of privilege. Although Dr. Gentile's focus is the opposite response—what she refers to as a retreat to home and domesticity—I think that the pedagogical trick accounting for both responses has something to do with hiding a particular neoliberal assault on subjectivity: a workplace that defines success as working 24/7 and a culture that is as family unfriendly as you can get (in terms of provision of childcare, the United States is certainly at the bottom of the pack of what Western industrialized countries offer their populations).

Given this contradiction, which is left to the population to solve on its own, I don't find it terribly troubling to see women who are able to do so opt out of the insanity of the workplace. And I don't think it's any crazier to want to have several babies than it is to want to work all the time and leave your babies with those nannies who, as Dr. Gentile tells us, are always cropped out of the celebrity pictures (again suggesting that it can all be done without any acknowledgment of dependency needs). Beyond the brilliant argument that women are made to carry, in their bodies, everyone's anxieties about a precarious future, what Dr. Gentile's data suggest to me is that the popular media is doing something quite different from what it was doing in the 19th century and post-World War II. I see it as normalizing the fantasy that women can do it all and thus contributing to the distress I very frequently hear from patients and friends about how impossible it is to balance family and work. Worse than that: I hear them beating themselves up about how weak and stupid and inefficient they are because they can't do it and others seem able to do it. Dr. Gentile argues that we have seen a return to rigidified traditional gender roles. I don't see that; what I see is women, and some men, manically trying to do everything (see Peltz, 2006). As Dr. Gentile says, the message is that women are supposed to be supermodel AND supermom. Perhaps the women who leave the workplace are registering the insanity. But it is also possible that the media's focus on downplaying career and on losing weight as fast as possible after pregnancy reflects a guilty penance for taking up too much space in the public sphere (maybe something like the guilt that Riviere (1929) spoke about in "Womanliness as a Masquerade"). Media discourses could normalize new subject positions for men and women, and some TV shows and films do just that. But the news media, as an industry, also thrives on the threat of danger (which keeps the audience anxiously tuned in) and on the promotion of expert advice. For me, the dark side of the media discourses Dr. Gentile analyzes is that they support oppressive fantasies that nothing really has to change to continue to have access to the version of progress Lasch (1991) decries. In this way, the media conspire with their corporate sponsors and with government to give women too much responsibility for the disasters of second modernity, the responsibility that business and government shirk.

The very morning I began writing this commentary, two women were on TV talking about their new book, *Womenomics: Write Your Own Rules for Success* (Shipman and Kay, 2009). They were arguing for a new model for the workplace, not exactly the old socialist feminist model, to be sure, but at least a model that recognized that current conditions make having a family difficult and are thus bad for the health of men, women, and children. In conclusion, I suppose that what I want to say is that, in periods of upheaval (which seem to be a continuous state in the West), what you find are progressive and regressive responses to oppressive conditions (e.g., socialist feminism—mainstream feminism—backlash against feminism), and this is true of popular discourses as well. In discourses that try to manage traumatic anxieties, my guess is that you will often be able to find material that could give rise to a resistant response and, at the same time, material that pulls for a submissive stance to domination. Dr. Gentile tries to make a clean separation between media discourse and what people are actually doing in their lives. But as media analysts influenced by the Birmingham School's Center for Cultural Studies have argued (see, e.g., Brunsdon and Morley, 1978; Hall, 1980; Ang, 1995; Morley, 1999), it is hard to draw conclusions about the influence of media without knowing what the messages mean to their projected audiences in their very varied social locations. An important next step, then, would be to draw out the relation between the media messages and how the targeted women are receiving them and living their lives. I hope that Dr. Gentile takes on that project.

REFERENCES

Ang, I. (1995). *Living Room Wars: Rethinking Media Audiences for a Postmodern World.* London, UK: Routledge.

Beck, U. (1999). *World Risk Society.* London, UK: Polity.

———. & Beck-Gernsheim, E. (2002). *Individualization: Institutionalized Individualism and its Social and Political Consequences.* London, UK: Sage.

Brown, W. (2005). *Edgework: Critical Essays on Knowledge and Politics.* Princeton, NJ: Princeton University Press.

Brunsdon, C. & Morley, D. (1978). *Everyday Television: Nationwide.* London, UK: British Film Institute.

Gramsci, A. (1971). *Selections from the Prison Notebooks.* New York, NY: International.

Hall, S. (1980). Encoding/decoding. In: *Culture, Media, Language: Working Papers in Cultural Studies*, 1972–79, eds. S. Hall, D. Hobson, A. Lowe, & P. Willis, London, UK: Hutchinson, pp. 128–138.

———. (1982). The rediscovery of ''ideology'': Return of the repressed in media studies. In: *Culture, Society and the Media*, eds. M. Gurevitch, T. Bennett, J. Curran, & J. Woollacott, London, UK: Methuen, pp. 56–90.

Laclau, E. & Mouffe, C. (1985). *Hegemony and Socialist Strategy. Towards a Radical Democratic Politics.* London, UK: Verso.

Lasch, C. (1977). *Haven in a Heartless World: The Family Besieged.* New York, NY: Basic Books.

———. (1979). *The Culture of Narcissism.* New York, NY: Norton.

———. (1991). *The True and Only Heaven: Progress and its Critics.* New York, NY: Norton.

Layton, L. (2004). Working nine to nine: The new women of prime time. *Studies in Gender and Sexuality*, 5, 351–369.

———. (2009). Who's responsible? Our mutual implication in each other's suffering. *Psychoanalytic Dialogues*, 19, 105–120.

———. (2010). Irrational exuberance: Neoliberal subjectivity and the perversion of truth. *Subjectivity*, 3, 303–322.

Morley, D. (1999). *The Nationwide Television Studies.* London, UK: Routledge.

Peltz, R. (2006). The manic society. In: *Psychoanalysis, Class and Politics: Encounters in the Clinical Setting*, eds. L. Layton, N. C. Hollander, & S. Gutwill, New York, NY: Routledge, pp. 65–80.

Riviere, J. (1929). Womanliness as a masquerade. *International Journal of Psycho-Analysis*, 10, 303–313.

Shipman, C. & Kay, K. (2009). *Womenomics: Write Your Own Rules for Success.* New York, NY: Harper Collins.

AUTHOR BIO

Lynne Layton, Ph.D., is Assistant Clinical Professor of Psychology, Harvard Medical School, and is a supervisor and on the faculty of the Massachusetts Institute for Psychoanalysis. She is the author of *Who's That Girl? Who's That Boy? Clinical Practice Meets Postmodern Gender Theory* (2004, The Analytic Press) and is the coeditor of *Psychoanalysis, Culture & Society.*

Reply to Commentaries: ''What About the Baby? The New Cult of Domesticity and Media Images of Pregnancy''

Katie Gentile, Ph.D.
John Jay College of Criminal Justice

It is exciting to have the intellectual attention of two such thoughtful scholars. As all three of us seem to concur, there is a startling cultural trend ''celebrating'' pregnancy. Inevitably, we come to three differing conclusions about the emergence and potential functions of this trend and to what extent it signals something worrisome or is just part of a larger problem of a limitless free market mentality. This opportunity to respond to them allows me to use Lynne Zeavin's and Lynne Layton's (this issue) points to further expand and deepen my own ideas about the evolution of the cultural narrative of pregnancy and postpartum embodiment.

My paper was an analysis of media images and stories, and Zeavin and Layton each responded to it in a different way. Zeavin used an apt clinical example to further her own thoughts about the media obsession with pregnancy, whereas Layton responded from her own use of cultural theory. Here I focus first on some of the questions raised by Zeavin and then respond to Layton's alternative take on my observations about the media.

In her response Zeavin writes that she sees this neo cult of domesticity not as a way to deal with an uncertain future but as an attempt to avoid the present and to erase time itself. Certainly when I describe the culture's seeming obsession with pregnant celebrities, the constant blaring of terrorizing research studies about the risks of pregnancy, and the microscopic lens taken to women's bodies 2 weeks after delivery, I am highlighting what I see as a dangerous and quite ambivalent relationship to time but not an attempt to erase it. I think what is happening is that there is an attempt to control time's duration, the ways in which it unfolds.

Duration is a concept described by French philosopher Henri Bergson, who is a subject of Grosz's (2004) recent work on time. According to Grosz, ''It is only the movement of time that ensures that not everything is given at once, that the universe is not over the moment it is born, that it occupies a duration, whose rhythms and speed, if they changed, would alter everything'' (p. 246). Duration is not about succession, causation, or space, but it can be illuminated through images. It is the unfolding of becoming by accumulating pasts, while this becoming is also simultaneously an approach to the inevitable end—death. Rewriting the past (i.e., romanticizing domesticity) while wringing the life out of the present (i.e., erasing the evidence of having given birth) in favor of a plan for the future (i.e., the promise of the baby) functions to compress the past, present, and future in an attempt at planning for and controlling the future, what Grosz would describe as attempting to eliminate duration. Here I think not that the future is embraced, as Zeavin interpreted from my paper, but instead that a fantasy of eliminating possible futures is enacted.

Zeavin and Layton both identify the fantasy of transcending limits and vulnerability that is reflected in this media story about pregnancy. Indeed. As I noted, it is like an oedipal fantasyland where ''no'' has not reared its frustrating head. Here there are no limits to what women can do: get pregnant at 20, 35, 48, or 62! have a great career and still clean the toilet. Zeavin suggests this ideal woman may serve as a superhero for girls and women. If so, I say it is dangerous one, for even Superman had his limits and vulnerabilities: Lois Lane and kryptonite. This superwoman, on the other hand, must do it all.

Zeavin suggests that the cult of domesticity be expanded to include opulence. Perhaps she missed it in my original description of the cult, but opulence was and continues to be central to it. The cult is shaped by rich, upper class women advising others as to how to spend time and money. Our current advice books are not limited to pamphlets and magazines but also include blogs like Gwyneth Paltrow's ''Goop,'' (www.goop.org) about ''healthy'' living and making the ''right'' choices for your family. Her advice is easy to follow as long as you can buy only organic foods and have the time, energy, or just the cook to prepare them. These media sites function like the original cult of domesticity to place responsibility for the family's well-being on women's shoulders. I discuss this idea of individual responsibility later.

I appreciate Layton's critique and her attempts to question my reliance on the model of ideological domination. Her disagreement with my use of temporal linking is well taken but I want to make clear I was in no way myself mourning the loss of modernity's assumptions about the progressive future, nor was I assuming progress is the only potential future. (If I could, I might get out of bed with less anxiety.) When I described losing the ''promise'' of modernity and stated that the ''automatic progress of the future is no more.'' I was attempting to emphasize that this loss is of monumental importance to our culture because it shapes our subjectivities. I was in no way casting a judgment on the loss. In fact, I think we must lose this seeming optimism in the future in order for any ''real'' sane future to unfold, understanding that it can never be guaranteed to happen. I was emphasizing that the loss of this assumed progression is an epistemological earthquake, the response to which may be the manipulation of time, which I think could be seen clearly in the narrative of pregnancy written in the media. As Grosz (2004) noted about Bergson's notion of duration, it cannot be consciously experienced but it appears in images. Similarly, the images and stories in the media about pregnancy, I believe, illustrate our attempts to control time's duration and erase our limits and vulnerabilities.

Psychological theories of temporality cannot rely on a cause-and-effect shape for anticipation. Instead time, as I theorize it, is much less about cause and effect than about becoming as a process based on accumulation (Grosz, 2004; Gentile, 2007). As Grosz writes, ''The future is that over which the past and present have no control'' (p. 184). This is not linear nor is it progressive. The future will always be new because the past is a ''condition for infinite futures'' (p. 184). The past as an accumulated collection of experiences creates the conditions for new interactions with the world. No experience can be experienced twice because even if the circumstances were exactly the same (which they never are because the world is always in motion) our memory of the first experience will necessarily impact the second. But here newness is not the same as progression. There are no guarantees a new experience will be qualitatively better in any way.

Duration is the ''flow'' (Grosz, 2004) connecting the past, present, and future, but it is not available for consciousness or symbolization even though it impacts what we do experience and symbolize. Instead Western culture manufactures a spatial form of duration where the past is located behind us whereas the future is in front (see Levine, 1997; Lakoff and Johnson, 1999; Zimbardo and Boy, 2008) and they are linearly linked by our constructions of cause and effect. So I agree with her analysis using Lasch (1991) to support that we ''freeze'' the past, present, and future and that doing so keeps us from learning and seeing how the past influences the present and future. That is what I stated in my article and it is quite dangerous. Why Layton did not see me conceptually carrying this critique of a progressive future throughout the article is unclear, for as noted earlier this critique was the basis of my article.

Layton's focus on the participation of the free market fundamentalism to this cultural story is a valid and important observation. After all, the cult of domesticity evolves in the 1800s as the industrialized components of manufacturing are changing our culture and landscape. And without question what she calls the ''patriarchal structures of everyday life'' have indeed co-opted feminism. This particular point is another way of thinking about this neo cult of domesticity and could be the focus of an additional article about feminist ideas of choice. It is described as a choice to stay home and mother, a choice to have more or just a baby. Co-opting the language of the feminist reproductive rights movement has been quite effective (McRobbie, 2004). How can any self-respecting feminist critique the ''choice'' to have a baby when that ''choice'' has been so hard won? By co-opting choice in this way, ''women are being cast as the ''privileged subjects of social change'' (McRobbie, 2004, p. 258) who have so many choices, but this casting just functions to invoke ''the specter of feminism'' (p. 259) in order to undo it. Thus, although I have sympathies with socialist feminism and agree that free market unfettered capitalism is central to our undoing, I think it too rests upon other cultural structures like White/Western supremist patriarchy and the corresponding ideal of selves existing and functioning as autonomous agents.

Which brings me to Layton's next point about the potential benefits to what she, using Beck and Beck-Gernsheim (2002), terms a second modernity, where subjectivity is individual and oriented to a future that is not presumed to be progressive. For Layton, these authors create a more useful analysis of subjectivity and resistance. I think here is another spot where our differences are just differences. The Western patriarchal construction of agency and resistance continually casts these as individual actions. I see agency and resistance as inevitable wherever power operates (see Foucault, 1972, 1980; Hoy, 2004) and like power, these actions are inextricably social (Collins, 1990; Petchesky, 1995; Hoy, 2004). Yes, as Layton and others (see hooks, 1984; Collins, 1990; Narayan, 1997; McRobbie, 2004; Mohanty, 2004, to list a few) have noted, access to individual self-determinism is dependent on one's gender, race, class, nationality, and so forth, but it is also a fantasy of limitless omnipotence.

Tronto (1994) articulates a philosophy of care to underline subjectivity that creates a more fluid and relational sense of agency and resistance based in responsibility. Black feminists describe a ''bodily integrity'' from which to base resistant action and responsibility that is ''communal and extended rather than individualized and privatized'' (Petchesky, 1995, p. 398). As Petchesky contends, our Western notion of individuality is based on that of private property (owning one's self), which emerges with industrialization and capitalism. Part of what is reified in the images of pregnant women is that of individual achievement. No woman can get pregnant on her own without the participation of either a male partner or sperm donor yet the males are absent from this pregnancy narrative. Scientific research focuses primarily on women and when the babies are born, as I noted, nannies and fathers are usually absent from the photos.

A fantasy of autonomy is central here. As noted earlier, it is tough to critique individual choice when supposedly exercised by populations that have had so little opportunity for it (see Petchesky, 1995; McRobbie, 2004; Pitts, 2005; Jeffreys, 2008), but part of the patriarchal and free market ruse is conceptualizing choice as individualized and free when it is always constrained and exercised within dense social and cultural networks. Thus, any model that takes individuality as a given cannot adequately articulate ''choice,'' responsibility, or resistance.

Layton points to the risk society model as providing a better way of analyzing this cultural narrative because, according to her, it provides a space for two things she sees as missing from my article: how the media images impact how we live our lives and the awareness of potential spaces of resistances to the dominant ideology. Here she points to the positive potential for media pointing out risks so that we might have healthier babies. Certainly learning about potential dangers for pregnant women can be very important. I was not critiquing the content but the form of these articles, which has changed since 9/11. Having headlines, research, stories, and images that clearly place the responsibility for having a healthy baby exclusively on the mother is exceedingly dangerous. It reinscribes the fetish of individuality and enables the free market machine and government to shift responsibility for producing healthy babies exclusively onto women, as Layton too notes. If fish is so dangerous to eat we need to clean up the rivers, stop unfettered industrial growth, and CARE in a collective sense (Tronto, 1994) about sustaining all life. Flying my ecofeminism flag here, I think the other danger in individualism is the fantasy that we are separate from, in opposition to, and in a position to dominate nature. Spar (2006) reviews research with pregnant women that points to a cycle of dependence created by these scare tactics whereby the medical research fans the flames of pregnancy anxieties, telling women they are exclusively responsible for what can only be a dangerous endeavor. Anxious women then turn helplessly to their doctors for unquestioned guidance reinforcing the medical establishment's hegemonic hold on prenatal knowledge and authority.

I also agree with Layton that the cult of domesticity is only one way of understanding what is going on. I stated as much in my article. And although I, too, note that 9/11 was a tipping point beyond which it was rendered more difficult to keep our collective heads in the sand about global warming, economic disparities, and many other dangerous conditions, because it does function as a line in the sand, it is an important marker. Of course the time after 9/11 is linked to the past (pre 9/11) but the events of 9/11 shaped future policies that continue to impact us, giving it even more importance as a dividing line. Changes in cultural organizations of pregnancy often signal significant shifts in the culture (see Ginsburg and Rapp, 1995). This article was an attempt to explore potential meanings for a shift I have observed since 9/11 and clearly this task requires more than just an article.

In my article I tried to make it clear that I was not saying women actually are retreating into the home but that the ideals are increasingly emphasizing women's domesticity. There, again, I agree with Layton and Zeavin. The neo cult of domesticity functions to provide women with the opportunity to do it all, as I said earlier. In which case, I would say women now have the opportunities to be more harried than men—being in charge of the perfect house, being perfect mothers, taking care of the family (including male partners), dieting, exercising, *while* having successful careers. These ideals for women may not be exactly traditional, but they certainly are rigid. Here the fetish of neoliberal individuality and the fantasy of individual agency works its magic (dominant ideology again), for as Layton notes, women often respond with self-blame when they can't meet these standards instead of perhaps expecting equal participation from male partners or organizing to promote family leave policies. This functions to uphold a particular *patriarchal* not just *free* market system of labor. As Layton exclaims, who could blame a woman for refusing to participate in this crazy system? And as I noted in my article, perhaps some women who opt out are ''resisting'' the pressures to be superwomen. However, as I have written elsewhere in reference to eating disorders (Gentile, 2007) and as Pitts (2005) writes about body projects, this individualized form of protest does little to change the labor market that relies on women doing an estimated 80% of the world's work for free (unifem.org). It also does not confront in any public or collective way the split between the workplace and its policies and care work (prenatal care, childcare, family care, self-care). In writing this I am not trying to place yet more responsibility on individual women; I am attempting to make this continuing problem more public. As Layton also notes, our work and family policies are some of the worst in the industrialized world, which I think points out clearly how these practices uphold not a free market but a patriarchal one. So I agree with where Layton is going but I disagree that the risk society model and a focus on the free market without a critique of the foundational Western patriarchal system is the way to get there.

In a culture that so vehemently splits public and private, free market values and caring and responsibility, reifying the domestic sphere and ''mothering'' could definitely be seen as transgressive. It could also be seen as an attempt to elevate care work, which is so needed in this narcissistic, limitless culture. It may also serve to create a space of safety and comfort in a world of uncertainty and danger, as I noted in my article. But the ways in which this revaluing may be occurring functions to reinforce not challenge the hierarchal social arrangements that promote limitless markets, fetishized autonomy, and a pattern of conjuring a fantasy of a comfortable past (signified by shifting gender roles) in order to avoid facing up to our responsibilities to create the conditions for a new future to unfold (whatever that future brings).

I thank Layton and Zeavin for their stimulating discussions of my article.

REFERENCES

Beck, U. & Beck-Gernsheim, E. (2002). *Individualization: Institutionalized Individualism and Its Social and Political Consequences.* London, UK: Sage.

Collins, P. H. (1990). *Black Feminist Thought: Knowledge, Consciousness, and the Power of Empowerment.* London, UK: Routledge.

Foucault, M. (1972). *The Archaeology of Knowledge and the Discourse on Language.* New York: Pantheon Books.

———. (1980). *Power/Knowledge.* New York: Pantheon Books.

Gentile, K. (2007). *Creating Bodies: Eating Disorders as Self-Destructive Survival.* Hillsdale, NJ: Analytic Press.

Ginsburg, F. D. & Rapp, R., eds. (1995). *Conceiving the New World Order: The Global Politics of Reproduction.* Berkeley: University of California Press.

Grosz, E. (2004). *The Nick of Time: Politics, Evolution, and the Untimely.* Durham, NC: Duke University Press.

hooks, b. (1984). *Feminist Theory From Margin to Center.* Boston, MA: South End Press.

Hoy, D. C. (2004). *Critical Resistance: From Poststructuralism to Post-Critique.* Cambridge, MA: MIT Press.

Jeffreys, S. (2008). Keeping women down and out: The strip club boom and the reinforcement of male dominance. *Signs: Journal of Women in Culture and Society*, 34(1), 151–173.

Lakoff, G. & Johnson, M. (1999). *Philosophy in the Flesh: The Embodied Mind and Its Challenge to Western Thought.* New York, NY: Basic Books.

Levine, R. (1997). *A Geography of Time: The Temporal Misadvantures of a Social Psychologist.* New York, NY: Basic Books.

McRobbie, A. (2004). Post-feminism and popular culture. *Feminist Media Studies*, 4, 255–264.

Mohanty, C. T. (2004). *Feminism Without Borders: Decolonizing Theory, Practicing Solidarity*. Durham, NC: Duke University Press.

Narayan, U. (1997). Contesting cultures: ''Westernization,'' respect for cultures, and third-world feminists. In: *Second Wave: A Reader in Feminist Theory*, ed. L. Nicholson, New York, NY: Routledge, pp. 396–414.

Petchesky, R. P. (1995). The body as property: A feminist re-vision. In: *Conceiving the New World Order: The Global Politics of Reproduction*, eds. F. D. Ginsburg, & R. Rapp, Berkeley: University of California Press, pp. 387–406.

Pitts, V. (2005). Feminism, technology and body projects. *Women's Studies*, 34, 229–247.

Spar, D. L. (2006). *The Baby Business: How Money, Science, and Politics Drive the Commerce of Conception*. Boston, MA: Harvard Business School Press.

Tronto, J. C. (1994). *Moral Boundaries: A Political Argument for an Ethic of Care*. New York, NY: Routledge.

Zimbardo, P. & Boyd, J. (2008). *The Time Paradox: The New Psychology of Time That Will Change Your Life*. New York, NY: The Free Press.

AUTHOR BIO

Katie Gentile, Ph.D., is Associate Professor of Counseling and Gender Studies and Director of the Women's Center at John Jay College of Criminal Justice. She is the author of *Creating Bodies: Eating Disorders as Self-Destructive Survival* (2007, The Analytic Press).

Index

Note: Page numbers in **bold** type refer to figures
Page numbers followed by 'n' refer to notes